A REGIONAL HISTORY OF
THE RAILWAYS OF GREAT BRITAIN

General Editors:
DAVID ST JOHN THOMAS and J. ALLAN PATMORE

VOLUME V

THE EASTERN COUNTIES

Third Edition

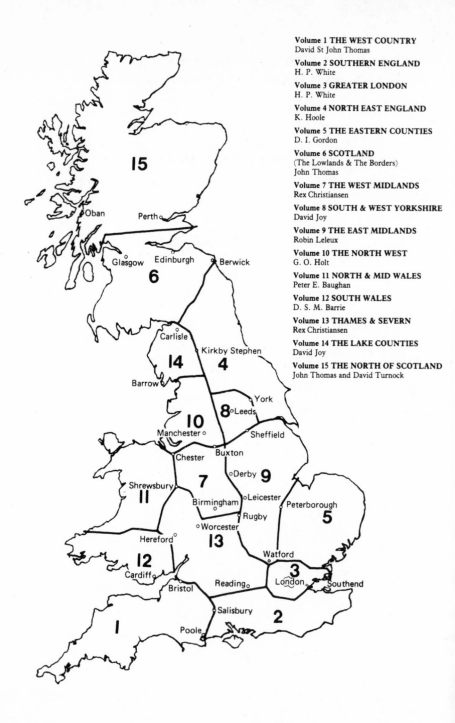

Volume 1 THE WEST COUNTRY
David St John Thomas

Volume 2 SOUTHERN ENGLAND
H. P. White

Volume 3 GREATER LONDON
H. P. White

Volume 4 NORTH EAST ENGLAND
K. Hoole

Volume 5 THE EASTERN COUNTIES
D. I. Gordon

Volume 6 SCOTLAND
(The Lowlands & The Borders)
John Thomas

Volume 7 THE WEST MIDLANDS
Rex Christiansen

Volume 8 SOUTH & WEST YORKSHIRE
David Joy

Volume 9 THE EAST MIDLANDS
Robin Leleux

Volume 10 THE NORTH WEST
G. O. Holt

Volume 11 NORTH & MID WALES
Peter E. Baughan

Volume 12 SOUTH WALES
D. S. M. Barrie

Volume 13 THAMES & SEVERN
Rex Christiansen

Volume 14 THE LAKE COUNTIES
David Joy

Volume 15 THE NORTH OF SCOTLAND
John Thomas and David Turnock

An Eastern Counties Railway porter of 1860. To thousands like this youth the railways meant security of employment and, whether in the railway service or not, opportunities beyond the reach of earlier generations in this predominantly rural region

A REGIONAL HISTORY OF
THE RAILWAYS OF GREAT BRITAIN

Volume V
THE EASTERN COUNTIES

D. I. Gordon

Third Edition

WITH 43 PLATES
8 ILLUSTRATIONS IN TEXT
8 MAPS AND FOLDING MAP

DAVID ST JOHN THOMAS
DAVID & CHARLES
NEWTON ABBOT NORTH POMFRET (VT)

British Library Cataloguing in Publication Data

Gordon, D. I. (Donald Ian)
    The eastern counties.—3rd. ed.—(A Regional history of the
    railways of Great Britain, v. 5).
    1. Railway services – East Anglia, to 1977
    I. Title   II. Series
    385.09426

    ISBN 0-946537-55-0

Printed in Great Britain
by Redwood Press Limited, Melksham
for David St John Thomas
and distributed by David & Charles plc
Brunel House   Newton Abbot   Devon

Published in the United States of America
by David & Charles Inc
North Pomfret   Vermont 05053   USA

Contents

I   BACKGROUND AND THEMES   11
    The railway companies

II   CENTRAL ESSEX   37
    The Eastern Counties main line to 1843 . Shenfield to Colchester since 1843 . the branches

III   COLCHESTER, CLACTON AND HARWICH   58
    Colchester . the Tendring Hundred . Colchester to Ipswich . Harwich

IV   IPSWICH AND EAST SUFFOLK   82
    Ipswich . the East Suffolk line . from Ipswich towards Norwich

V   TWO MAIN LINES   105
    Origins . Broxbourne to Cambridge . Cambridge line branches to the east . railways to Hertford . the GNR main line

VI   THE CAMBRIDGE REGION   139
    Cambridge . south and east of Cambridge . west and north of Cambridge

VII   THE CENTRAL DISTRICTS   158
    The Stour and Colne Valleys . railways to Bury St Edmunds . Ely to Norwich

VIII   NORWICH, YARMOUTH AND LOWESTOFT   176
    From Norwich to the coast . Lowestoft . Great Yarmouth . Norwich

IX   NORTH-EAST NORFOLK   194
    The East Norfolk lines . the Midland & Great Northern Joint Railway . junctions at Cromer and North Walsham

X   KING'S LYNN AND WEST NORFOLK   206
    King's Lynn . south and west of Lynn . east and
    north of Lynn

XI   PETERBOROUGH AND THE SOUTHERN FENS   222
     Lines to March . Wisbech, Sutton Bridge and
     Spalding . Peterborough

XII POSTSCRIPT: 1990   241

     BIBLIOGRAPHY AND ACKNOWLEDGMENTS   249

     INDEX   255

Note on the Second and Third Editions

Since this book was first written in 1968 decimal currency has
been adopted, the traditional weights and measures are being
abandoned and local government has been reorganised. In
regard to the first the original references to shillings and pence
have been left unchanged; in the second, recent freight figures
have been given in tonnes but the earlier references to tons left
unaltered. Local government reorganisation from 1 April 1974
in fact obliterated Huntingdonshire as a separate entity in that
it was absorbed by Cambridgeshire. As with the money and
weights the original forms of the first edition have been left as
they were. To do otherwise would have added little to clarity
but much to the expense of resetting.

Illustrations

PLATES

Frontispiece: An Eastern Counties Railway porter of
1860

                                   page

1 The Kelvedon, Tiptree & Tollesbury Pier Light
    Railway   17

2 Woodham Ferrers in 1911   17

3 Sible & Castle Hedingham station in 1947   17

4 The opening of the Eastern Union at Colchester in
    1846   18

5 Colchester main line station between 1875 and 1878   18

6 Marks Tey in 1956   18

7 The quays and hotel at Harwich in 1880   35

8 An aerial view of Parkeston Quay West under con-
    struction   35

9 The opening of the Eastern Union Railway at
    Ipswich, 1846   36

10 Ipswich station in 1881   36

11 Ipswich station from the south in 1901   36

12 Construction gang at Felixstowe, 1876 or 1877   53

13 A GER freight crossing the marshes near Snape   53

14 Aldeburgh station and yard in 1956   53

15 Stoke station, Suffolk, soon after its opening in 1865   54

16 A GER bus service in 1908   54

17 Laxfield, Mid-Suffolk Light Railway, in 1951   54

18   Railways and education; Newport station in 1959   71

19   Bishop's Stortford in 1960   71

20   Branch train at Saffron Walden in 1956   72

21   Thaxted terminal in 1951   72

22   Ware station, Hertford branch, in 1956   72

23   Six Mile Bottom, 1936   89

24   Soham station in Great Eastern days   89

25   Mildenhall branch train near Isleham   89

26   Up train approaching Ely, about 1850   90

27   An aerial view of Ely station   90

28   The original Norwich station, seen in 1851   107

29   Yarmouth Vauxhall to the quays through the streets 107

30   Cromer Beach before 1923   108

31   Aylsham Town in Eastern & Midland days   108

32   A royal occasion at Lynn, probably 1863   125

33   East Dereham in 1911   125

34   Mundesley station   126

35   The terminal of the Newmarket & Chesterford as in
     1966   126

36   The original Spalding station as seen about 1848   143

37   The Wisbech & Upwell Tramway at Outwell in 1929   143

38   An express on Welwyn Viaduct in 1962   144

39   Peterborough North station from the south   144

40   Hatfield Peverel station in 1989   163

41   Witham station, 1989   163

42   Newport station 1989   164

43   Woodham Ferrers station in 1989   164

IN TEXT

Great Eastern Railway; notice of special rates, 1880   22

Great Eastern Railway; holiday accommodation and fares   33

Early Colchester line timetable   43

An excursion to Walton, 1876   65

Notice of a typical GER excursion, 1868   122

Saffron Walden Railway; timetable of 1872   128

East Anglian Railways; the first timetable, 1846   212

Peterborough, Wisbeach & Sutton Bridge; 1866 timetable   230

MAPS

Principal navigable waterways in 1845   15

Numbers of licensed stage coaches running between principal centres in 1834   38

Cambridge (diagrammatic)   140

Yarmouth, Lowestoft and Haddiscoe   182

The Midland & Great Northern Joint Railway in relation to other lines   198

Cromer and North Walsham   204

King's Lynn   207

Peterborough (diagrammatic)   235

GENERAL MAP (the Region as in 1968) inside the back cover

Sources of Illustrations

Many firms and individuals have generously assisted me in the search for illustrations and I am indebted to the secretaries of the Norfolk Railway and the Midland & Great Northern Joint Railway societies for putting me in touch with their members. Mr R. G. Pratt of the Suffolk Photographic Survey (Suffolk Rural Community Council) has been of immense assistance and has provided plates 11, 12, 13, 15 and 16, number 12 being reproduced by kind permission

of Mr Mason of Mason's Photographic Service, Felixstowe. Plate 1
is by courtesy of Mr D. R. Leavett and number 34 of Mr J. Watling.
Mr H. C. Casserley has kindly supplied numbers 6, 14, 17, 20,
21, 22, 23, 25, 29 and 37. Plate 10 is by permission of the East
Suffolk County Librarian and plates 8 and 27 of Aerofilms Ltd.
Plates 35, 40, 41, 42 and 43 are by Barbara Gordon.

Above all I am indebted to Mr M. B. Thomas, the Public Relations and Publicity Officer of British Rail, Eastern Region, for all
the help he has given me and permission to use plates numbers 2, 3,
4, 5, 7, 9, 18, 19, 24, 26, 28, 30, 31, 32, 33, 36, 38 and 39. To these
and all others who have helped, my very warmest thanks.

In respect of the illustrations in the text my particular thanks are
due to Mr Thomas for the ECR, EAR and PW & SB timetable pages,
to the County Archivist of the Essex Record Office for the GER
holiday pamphlet and 1880 notice, and to the Curator of the Saffron
Walden Museum for the Saffron Walden Railway timetable and the
GER leaflets of 1868 and 1876. The page from Bradshaw is reproduced by permission of Henry Blacklock & Coy. Ltd. of Manchester.

CHAPTER I

Background and Themes

At Narborough, in Norfolk, there is a rotted barge so firmly em-
bedded in the bank of the Nar that trees grow in it. Within a
few hundred yards the river, last used for navigation in the early
1880s, is crossed by the now derelict branch railway from King's
Lynn to East Dereham and by the increasingly busy A47 trunk
road from Birmingham to Norwich and Great Yarmouth. On
the former the diesel multiple-unit service from Lynn to Norwich was finally withdrawn in 1968; nearby Narborough &
Pentney station, from 1846 to the 1930s central to the life of the
two villages and surrounding areas, survives only by virtue of
the station houses, the goods yard is closed and the siding
beyond the barge to the maltings and the road has rusted into
decay. An old coaching inn stands alongside the maltings, a
continuing witness to these three overlapping ages of transport
history. Once near the terminals of both the navigation and the
turnpike road from Lynn it has in the motor age regained the
prosperity lost when the railway came to displace them.

The village of Narborough typifies much else of the social and
economic evolution of the eastern counties over the last 140
years. Church and hall remain as symbols of centuries of relatively self-contained rural isolation within a clearly defined
social order. They are reminders too of how their respective
occupants strenuously resisted the railway, forming with the
Marriott brothers, owners of the maltings and navigation, an
association of affected landed interests (indemnified by the Marriotts against all costs), claiming that the line was an un-
warranted attack on private property, 'unnecessary and without
any promise of return'. The movement failed, as well it might,
for it cost 5s to bring a ton of coal the 8½ miles from Lynn to the
village and a wide area laboured under the 'intolerable incubus'
of the Nar, but pacification cost the railway company dearly in

compensation; the handsome Hall Lodge of 1846 (now enlarged) exemplifies how some of the money was spent. Other remnants of the old village are the bakery, now a cafe and shop, the disused mill and the Foresters' Hall, combined with a garage, but the older cottages and the houses built by the Marriotts for their employees are almost completely gone, two bungalows occupying the site of the latter. After 1945 local government rehousing moved the village centre a quarter of a mile to the east, where now two extensive private housing estates dominate the scene and reflect the remarkable growth in prosperity that has occurred in the eastern counties since the early 1970s.

Before 1918 the people of the old village knew much poverty although the maltings, flourishing with the railway, prevented this from being as crushing as in many outlying communities. Today, however, consequent upon the effects of two world wars, the emergence of organised labour, the development of mass communication media, the establishment of light industries in the local towns (frequently because electricity has overcome the traditional regional handicap of lack of coal), the use of road transport and, latterly (see Postscript), a new social and economic emphasis on the eastern counties, the village enjoys affluence and full integration in national life. A new primary school replacing the old all-age school (at nine, children go to Swaffham) is another factor explaining why the present generation is almost totally divorced from the outlook, customs and even dialect of sixty years ago. A village cricket team and the successful effort to provide a village hall are survivals of corporate self dependence, but livelihoods, recreation and necessities are found far beyond the village, in King's Lynn, Swaffham and even in Norwich, 42 miles distant. To these, buses and cars were the normal means of access well before 1968 for although the new village adjoined the line it was a full fifteen minutes' walk from the station. Motor transport had also permitted employment in places far from the line and the towns, as at RAF Marham, a World War I foundation 3 miles away that for many years made use of Narborough & Pentney station.

Although change has appeared most obvious in the last fifty years, and particularly so in the last twenty, it began in fact in the earliest days of railways when, for reasons discussed below, the influence of towns received a new emphasis, breaking down isolation and creating the beginnings of a more democratic and enterprising spirit in the countryside. Movement into the towns, so prominent a feature of the period, took from the villages many of the more adventurous (Narborough's 1981 population was 1187 but at 423 in 1961 had barely grown in a century) and to a certain extent inhibited these new attitudes, concealing them from the unobservant. This explains how a prominent local landowner could unwittingly expose himself to a humiliating lesson that the days of socially-based personal authority were already numbered when, one day in 1890, disregarding the warnings of the East Winch stationmaster he persisted in descending to the track and flagging down a non-stop train to return him to Narborough; for thus obstructing the train he was fined £25 and bound over for six months in recognisances of £100 at the subsequent Quarter Sessions.

Railway influence remained dominant until the 1920s when road competition first displaced it as the arbiter and then, after 1945, as the principal prop of the regional economy, but still left it as a major element in regional life. The economic basis on which the railway originally depended was totally unpromising. Lack of coal and reluctance to adopt new methods had precluded participation in contemporary industrial advances elsewhere, and even by 1800 internal weaknesses had virtually destroyed the once-prosperous textile industries. In the 1840s industrial activities were invariably small and localised. Most, such as milling, malting, brewing, agricultural implement making and the like, were dependent on the soil; cottage industries provided footwear, clothing and many other requirements, but inefficiently so. Commercial fishing was undeveloped for lack of suitable inland transport and the holiday trade was as yet barely conceived. Norwich, with 62,344 inhabitants in 1841, was the largest town, followed by Ipswich with a mere 25,264. Agriculture, central to the economy, was progressive but in the doldrums since the post-1815 slump in corn prices and the reduction in demand for local wool. In 1831 it gave 31,491 of Suffolk's 61,533 families their livelihood (18,116 were in trade, manufacturing and handicrafts) and in 1841 employed 12·2 per cent of Norfolk's population of 412,664, but, with depression and over-population, wages averaged only 7s to 9s a week, cottage rentals could be £5 a year or more, and everywhere insecurity and wretched hardship were prevalent.

This state was perpetuated by the inadequacy of the existing transport system. For the movement of freight much of the region depended on coastal shipping and the river traffic, although both were slow and the latter not only charged monopolistic rates but was unreliable and irregular and exposed goods to all weathers and a 5 per cent pilferage rate. They also served to confirm ports such as King's Lynn in comfortable commercial monopolies that, in the latter's case at least, were costly and stagnant. Greater use of the existing roads was no solution. Apart from the turnpikes (only 7 per cent of Norfolk's road mileage) their condition was poor, and because of low speeds and the limited carrying capacity of individual units, just as expensive. A van took 24 hours from Lynn to London (99 miles), a four-horse wagon with a maximum twenty-four sacks of grain nearly two days over the 50 miles from the former to Norwich. Carriers' carts abounded but nowhere covered more than 24 miles in a day. After a journey along the River Nar to Narborough (8½ miles from Lynn by land but 12 by water) and then by road, coal, sold on landing in Lynn at 16s to 18s a ton, cost 27s or 28s at Swaffham (14½ miles) and 30s or more at East Dereham (26½ miles), but under the prevailing conditions small market towns such as these had no possible alternative source of supply.

Offering cheap bulk transport at speed, the railways released the region from this type of restriction. As will be seen the rivers experienced a variety of fortunes, although movement on all seriously declined, but the roads were almost immediately deserted by through traffic. Norwich and London were first connected by rail on 30 July 1845: on 6 January 1846 the last regular coach between the two came off, 700 horses having by then been displaced. In the 1846–7 winter Norwich merchants committed heavy goods for Ipswich to a 196 miles rail journey via London rather than one of 40 miles by roads 'half a yard deep in mud'. On the other hand local traffic, centred on the new stations, greatly increased, many formerly employed on the coaches were enabled to turn to omnibus services and, overall, horse prices actually rose. The worst sufferers were undoubtedly the inns, many depreciating as much as 70 per cent in value and

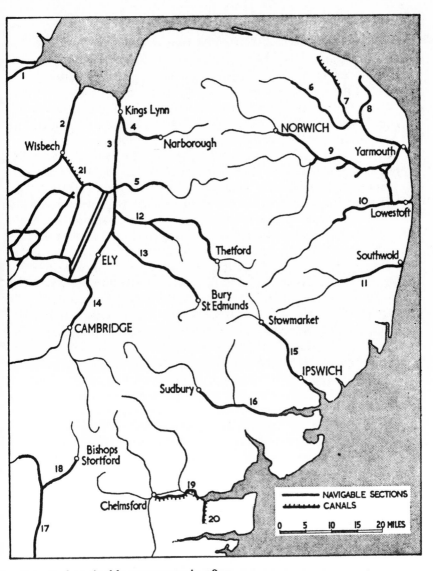

Principal navigable waterways in 1845
1 R. Welland 2 R. Nene 3 Great Ouse 4 R. Nar 5 R. Wissey 6 R. Bure
7 R. Ant and North Walsham & Dilham Canal 8 R. Thurne 9 R. Yare
10 R. Waveney 11 R. Blyth 12 Little Ouse 13 R. Lark 14 R. Cam
15 R. Gipping 16 R. Stour 17 R. Lee 18 R. Stort 19 Chelmer & Blackwater Navigation 20 Mundon Wash Canal 21 Wisbech Canal

others being forced to close. The Bird-in-Hand at Tasburgh accommodated 9,300 beasts, consuming 50 tons of hay, in its stables during the 1845 droving season, but by the half-way stage of the next there had been only twelve eating 8½ cwt.

Not even the benefits of rail communication could quite overcome the lack of coal. Between 1841 and 1931, the combined populations of Norfolk, Suffolk and Cambridgeshire grew from 830,563 to 1,043,028 but fell from 5·2 to 2·6 per cent as a proportion of the totals for England and Wales. The latter percentage still held in 1961, when their population was 1,223,429, but road transport and the use of electricity in industry were more important than railways in arresting the decline. Since 1961, however, the situation has radically altered in that the region now has the highest expansion rate in the kingdom, rising from the 1,469,600 of 1961 (adjusted to include the former Huntingdonshire) to 1,865,021 in 1981; by 1987 a further 6.3 per cent increase had occurred. Although the railway system was not a basic cause, its response, primarily through electrification, has reinstated it as a highly significant factor.

At the same time the region is sharing substantially in the new technological age and already has a wide diversity of light industries, ranging from electronic equipment to plastics. Most have appeared since 1945, but others, particularly various kinds of food processing, extend back into the period when railways helped to make engineering, in its many branches, the principal industry of the eastern counties. Before 1918 this, together with clothing, footwear, fertilisers, printing, horsehair and coconut fibre working and brush making, were amongst many activities

ESSEX BRANCHES
1 (top)   The Kelvedon, Tiptree & Tollesbury Pier Light Railway in early years. On one occasion 110,000 oysters left this station in a single day; heavy goods and cattle were loaded from the ramp on the right
2 (centre)   Woodham Ferrers in 1911; the 'New Essex' line to Maldon is straight ahead, that to Southminster curves off to the right just beyond the station. Note the cattle pens and the numerous milk churns
3 (bottom)   Sible & Castle Hedingham station in 1947, a focal point for varied activities. This was the former Colne Valley Railway line that remained independent to 1923

that owed something of their success to railways. Internal technical improvements—themselves facilitated by the concentration produced by the railways—sometimes coastal shipping, and an individual's enterprise were other contributory factors. Milling, malting and brewing all expanded with the railways, gravitating at first towards the new lines and then, from the 1890s, tending to concentrate in fewer but larger units in the coastal ports where both water and rail facilities could be exploited. The development of Lowestoft as the fifth most important fishing centre of the kingdom epitomised the growth of an activity dependent for success on speedy inland transport, and the massive holiday industry of the coast and Broads (in 1955 it was estimated that Norfolk alone would accommodate one million visitors during the summer months) the breakdown of regional isolation through good transport.

Despite such developments, agriculture remained predominant into the post-war era, and still in 1990 contributes some five per cent (about £600m) to the Gross Domestic Product of Norfolk, Suffolk and Cambridgeshire. In 1961, even with intensive mechanisation, it still employed 84,910 in these three counties (the old Cambridgeshire and excluding the Isle of Ely), while occupying 95, 94 and 96 per cent respectively of their areas. Changes in county boundaries and statistical bases preclude exact comparisons, but in broad terms the labour force in agriculture, fisheries and forestry had fallen to 37,500 in 1981 and to 32,000 in 1987 (when, overall, there were 850,000 in employment). The three counties produce some 20 per cent of the nation's wheat and 12 per cent of its barley. Grain,

---

COLCHESTER MAIN LINE

4 (top)   The formal opening of the Eastern Union at Colchester to join the Eastern Counties on 11 June 1846. Peto's 1843 hotel is central to the drawing and a good impression is given of local contours and the distance of the station from the town

5 (centre)   A view of Colchester station at some time between 1875 and 1878 from the tower of the former hotel, by then an asylum. Little development had yet occurred west of the line although some of the houses appear to be relatively new

6 (bottom)   Marks Tey, junction for the Stour Valley line, in 1956

handled via a network of central depots, has, in fact, become the principal bulk freight of the region's railways. Large tracts of land are given over to sugar beet and potatoes (in 1965 Cambridgeshire and the Isle of Ely had 48,700 acres of the first and 41,000 of the second). Vegetables, orchards and soft fruit (the two latter especially so in the rich Cambridgeshire Fenlands), pigs, cattle for both meat and milk, poultry and sheep are all important. On the thin Breckland soils of Norfolk and Suffolk, many thousands of acres are devoted to Forestry Commission plantations, while Essex, with 600,000 acres of good farming land, despite intensive urban development, remains significant in terms of cereals, live-stock fattening, fruit growing and market gardening.

Science having reduced the importance of regional differences in soil, and road transport giving direct access to markets from all parts, proximity to a railway is no longer a major farming asset. In earlier days, however, the presence of a railway station meant the advantages of closer ties with London, a wider choice of markets (with greater price stability in consequence) and readier availability at lower cost of coals, fertilisers, animal foods and other supplies. In addition, the reduced overheads allowed profitable cultivation of hitherto marginal or inferior land. Equally important was the elimination of costly droves to London, resulting not only in direct savings in weight formerly lost en route—this was worth £600 a year to Hudson of Castleacre, near Narborough, as early as 1850—but also increased turnover in that livestock, no longer to be subjected to severe physical strain, could be despatched to market at an earlier age. Again, poorer land could be made profitable permanent pasture.

Other factors were involved but it was no coincidence that the advent of railways was closely followed by the prosperous era of 'High Farming' (about 1850 to the mid-1870s) when loss of protection against foreign corn (1846) was countered by rationalisation and the application of science to the industry. The trend from arable to mixed farming was hastened; the movement of stock from Scotland into Norfolk for fattening, shared by the Eastern Counties and London & North Western railways, nearly doubled each year between 1848 and 1851, and the former company directly encouraged small men, unable to afford the risk of losing costly equipment, by providing hampers (peds) at a small rental for the conveyance of meat to London. The metropolis, sustained in its growth, and the region's farmers benefited alike; in 1859, for example, the ECR carried in 165,156 quarters of wheat, 451,931 of malt, 30,352 of barley and 16,028 of oats as well as 563,295 sacks of flour, thousands of livestock and substantial quantities of meat, poultry, milk and other commodities.

Then, from the later 1870s, improvements in marine engineering, canning techniques and refrigeration were amongst the factors that allowed the onslaught of massive competition in corn, meat and dairy produce from America, Australia and New Zealand. Farm values fell 40 per cent or more, good land was taken out of cultivation and many faced ruin; there was some recovery about 1900, substantially so from 1914 to 1918, but farming was never to be quite the same again.

Worst affected were areas like West Suffolk where railways were fewest, for it was only a few pence cheaper (9d to 1s as opposed to 1s 4d) to bring a bushel of corn from, for example, Clare to London than it was from New York, and transport costs from an outlying farm to a station could be enough to price a man out of the market; the farther from London the more serious the problem. Inland farmers complained bitterly of railway rates and envied those who could use coastal shipping, but this was manifestly unjust. The Great Eastern reduced its charges to an absolute minimum (in the 1880s a 112 lb hamper of vegetables could be sent from Norwich to London for 8d), and built or encouraged a number of lines such as the Wisbech & Upwell specially to help the farmers. Moreover, railway facilities were crucial in the specialisation, particularly in perishable produce, that saved so many; Fenland fruit and flower growing is a major example. The GER's 'Egg & Poultry' demonstration train of October and November 1916, visited by 46,000, typified that company's constant encouragement of the farmer and smallholder.

After 1918, farming, still depressed, turned increasingly to road transport, although for a time after 1925 the extension of sugar-beet growing under subsidy (in Norfolk the acreage rose from 1,087 in 1920 to 74,627 by 1930) actually increased agricultural traffic on former GER lines over pre-1914 levels. By 1939, however, the railways were losing ground, and after a

Great Eastern Railway.

Goods Manager's Office,
Liverpool Street Station,
London, E.C., 1st October, 1880.

Brewers' and Distillers' Grains.

Scale of Rates for the conveyance of the above traffic, in truck loads of 5 tons and upwards, at the Owner's Risk, Station to Station, and exclusive of loading and unloading between Country Stations (with a few exceptions), distant 50 miles or more apart, on the Great Eastern Railway :—

	Per ton.	
	s.	d.
Up to 50 miles	4	2
51 to 60 „	4	7
61 to 70 „	5	0
71 to 85 „	5	5
86 to 100 „	5	10
101 to 120 „	6	3
121 and above	6	8

W. GARDNER,
Goods Manager.

The Great Eastern Railway rates shown here, in many instances well under 1d per ton mile, could hardly be described as adding to the problems of farming in depression

temporary wartime revival, severely so; the railway's share of raw beet delivered to the Ely refinery dropped from 66 to 6 per cent between 1926 and 1960. Beet traffic then became confined to transfer of pulp and surpluses between factories, but even here, by 1983, only Cantley and South Lynn retained rail links, used for receiving bulk loads of limestone from Wirksworth (Derbyshire). Milk traffic ceased with that at Halesworth on 19 April 1965, soft fruit and livestock were diverted to the roads, so that in 1990 only bulk grain remains of a once massive traffic.

Depression kept the region's labouring majority in poverty, only in part relieved by the cheaper transport of coal and goods into the region. Continuous hardship and lack of opportunities had long produced a drift from the rural areas into London and other towns, but with the railways this assumed increasingly large proportions. As early as 1853 the *Essex Standard* was lamenting the loss of the county's best workmen to London where wages were generally 'double the amount' paid locally, and between 1851 and 1861 the inhabitants of Norwich and Yarmouth increased by 6,684 and 3,458 respectively although Norfolk's total population actually fell by 7,916 to 434,798; in that county and Suffolk generally the proportion living in rural areas fell from 70 to 49 per cent between 1831 and 1931, Cambridgeshire grew by 25 per cent between 1841 and 1911 (102,826 to 128,322) but Cambridge itself by over 100 per cent (24,453 to 51,161). In Essex 201 parishes had smaller populations in 1901 than in 1851 and 83 smaller than in 1801, while in West Suffolk, disregarding slight boundary alterations, there was an overall fall from 117,568 inhabitants in 1841 to 106,137 in 1931 (128,918 in 1961).

In various ways the railways encouraged and furthered this trend. The greater accessibility of towns caused concentration of specialist services in them, thus compelling greater urban awareness in rural areas. Direct dealing with towns was not only possible but desirable as what had formerly been localised village crafts (clothing, basketry, woodwork etc) now became progressive and organised industries in competitive fields. Travel at even the cheapest rates remained a luxury for most but the occasional visit to a town, the even rare excursion to the sea or even London, (perhaps with a Sunday School and more commonly after Bank Holidays began in 1871), the first-hand news

entering the villages, and the very sight of the trains were all
disturbing influences on the restless, the ambitious and the
bored. With the train a new life was only a few hours away and
as the same was true of home, to leave a village need no longer
be total severance. As employment and marriage partners were
found over a wider field and families became dispersed pressures
increased on those who remained.

The essential complement to the exodus from the countryside
was the demand for cheap labour in the expanding industries of
certain regional towns. Initially the momentum of growth had
stemmed from the release of capital resources hitherto bound up
in the uneconomic deployment of labour, reserve stocks and
warehouse premises necessitated by the inadequacies of existing
transport and inefficient methods. Railways overcame the first
and, to the detriment of cottage industries, promoted the concentration that made possible the conquest of the second, thereby creating further opportunities for expansion—milling and
the manufacture of clothing and footwear are amongst several
examples of this. In the long run, of course, their most important
contribution was to afford wide choice of markets and cheap
availability of raw materials, which besides the obvious benefits,
destroyed the former inhibitive dependence on the locality and
permitted continued growth even in times of deepest agricultural depression.

It must be stressed that such expansion only affected a limited
number of towns. The pattern, largely perpetuated today, crys-
tallised in the 1860s out of the flux which followed the dissolution of traditional river-based spheres of commercial influence.
Amongst the principal beneficiaries were Norwich, increasing
from 62,344 to 122,270 between 1841 and 1981 (121,236 in
1951, 120,096 in 1961), Ipswich (25,264 to 120,447), Colchester (17,790 to 81,945), Lowestoft (4,837 to 55,231) and Yarmouth (24,086 to 48,273); in each of these, coastal shipping was
an important factor supplementing the railways, and in the last
two cases vast sums were spent by railway companies in developing fishing and harbour facilities. Elsewhere, Cambridge
(24,453 to 90,440) Peterborough (6,959 to 114,108) and
Chelmsford (6,789 to 58,159) have become thriving centres.
This pattern arose partly through the accident of unforeseen
consequences, but it was also in part the result of the deliberate

promotions of the 1840s when the mercantile communities of Ipswich, Norwich and King's Lynn, fearful of continued dependence on water while a rival gained rail communication, busily promoted railways as weapons of both offence and defence within a developing framework of main lines. William Everard of Lynn, one so engaged, illuminated the situation when remarking in 1844 how two years earlier he had thought his town would neither need nor ever have a railway but now that one was coming to Ely (thereby threatening its southern markets) it could not afford to be without. King's Lynn was in fact the heaviest loser. It retained reduced significance as a port but markets in central Norfolk were lost to Norwich and those of the Bury St Edmunds area to Ipswich, while the rise of Cambridge, released from former dependence on river traffic from Lynn, and of Peterborough, another emancipated river port, pressed severely on it from the south and west respectively. Its population increased from 16,039 to only 27,536 between 1841 and 1961 although in 1981 it had jumped to 33,340.

East Dereham, a junction, and Stowmarket, with main line facilities, are examples of several smaller towns that acquired considerable and lasting prosperity in the new situation, Swaffham and Dunmow, both midway along secondary lines, of those eclipsed by a larger neighbour after a temporary boost. Hadleigh is one of a number of branch terminals that enjoyed a longer period of relative prosperity before the competition of better-placed rivals bore them down. Lavenham exemplifies the towns which achieved no significant place in the changed order and Saffron Walden, one of several forced to change its traditional market day to avoid direct competition with centres hitherto at a safe commercial distance, those where a railway came too late to gain one.

Wells, Aldeburgh and Southwold were amongst minor ports squeezed out by better-placed rivals with fewer of the problems such as silting that tended to become insupportable as railways brought an overall reduction in coastal shipping and concentrated trade on a few well-equipped centres. As indicated, Lowestoft and Yarmouth received particular favour from the railways, as also did Harwich which was developed into a leading port for continental traffic; by 1917 Great Eastern Railway accounts showed an expenditure of £1,066,534 on dock and harbour facilities (with £549,813 on ships); during the 1970s a further £8 million project was completed at Harwich. Resorts such as Clacton (also a commuter centre), Felixstowe (also with docks) and Hunstanton are examples of villages turned into thriving towns by the excellence of railway service backed by sound advertising and imaginative rates, while Cromer, Sheringham and Walton were similarly built up from only small beginnings. Finally, March (with Whitemoor Yards) and Melton Constable (locomotive and rolling-stock works) were two small junction towns where the railway became the principal industry, although the latter is now entirely without rail communication since the closure of most of the Midland & Great Northern Joint Railway.

In assessing railway achievement in the eastern counties regard must be paid to the constant difficulties under which the system laboured. For long periods agriculture was depressed and the working-class majority beset by acute poverty. Even so agricultural and holiday traffic constituted the main strands of revenue; both, however, were essentially seasonal in character and liable to severe fluctuations, so exacerbating a situation in which at the best of times extensive and uneconomic provision of stock and plant had to be made. Coal traffic was ever small and even with the opening in 1882 of a joint line towards Doncaster by the Great Northern and the Great Eastern the latter's share in the through movement to London remained only marginal. Nor, contrary to popular misconception, were the railways in the region easy to work. The Fens of the north-west section are flat but ease of working has always been offset by the costly maintenance involved in the shrinkage of the inland peat, competition (although not very successful) from the numerous waterways, and by the sparsity of population. To the east and south of the Fenlands the East Anglian Heights are nowhere more than 420 ft high, but like the undulations of the East Anglian Plateau (boulder clay on chalk and the region's principal natural feature) flanking them often proved too much for the strained budgets of the local companies. To avoid expensive earthworks lines were often made to follow the contours, so producing a legacy of curves, sharp gradients and numerous level crossings (provision of and accommodation for staff at these have become major problems of expenditure particularly in the last thirty years); by the same token weak bridges were common, restricting axle loads and thereby increasing operational difficulties and limiting speeds as traffic grew to require heavier trains without full scope for appropriate increases in locomotive power.

In the east and south of the region early settlement was from the coast and along the river valleys, towns growing either at the lowest fording points (as at Colchester and Ipswich) or the limits of navigation (for example, Norwich and Sudbury); in the east the fertility of the soil and the prosperity of the woollen trade caused proliferation of villages and small market towns. Settlement of the plateau area was later and selective of good ground, hence the countless scattered hamlets and small villages of northern Essex and West Suffolk and the absence of large centres. The overall effect of this pattern was to preclude the direct rail approach from London to Norwich, the economic heart of the region, because the intermediate areas would never be able to supply sufficient originating revenue to make such viable. Rather, the main routes had to be via Cambridge, which afforded possible access to the north but to Norwich was circuitous, or via Ipswich, which brought in the main towns but involved direct competition with coastal shipping throughout as well as the necessity to cross a series of rivers and their watersheds. To ease the difficulty of the latter and to combine some service to the central districts with their principal purpose the main lines tended to follow an inland course so increasing the number of branches needed to serve the small ports and centrally-placed market towns; the irony was that as the railways caused greater concentration of activity on the larger centres many of these branches, which contributed directly to this, were progressively reduced in value.

THE RAILWAY COMPANIES

With so many problems of construction and operation much depended on the quality of the companies involved, and for many years the region was very badly served. Initially, the general economic depression and inertia of the eastern counties discouraged investment if not schemes until in 1836 the Eastern Counties was authorised to construct a line from London to

Norwich and Yarmouth via Ipswich, and the Northern & Eastern from London to Cambridge. However, by 1843, after colossal expenditure, the one had reached no farther than Colchester (Chapter II), the other only to Bishop's Stortford (Chapter V). Their obvious failure and general economic depression in the nation had effectively precluded further enterprise, and at the outset of 1845 the region's share in the national total of 2,235 route miles actually open barely exceeded 100; Norfolk had a mere 20½ (the Yarmouth & Norwich), Suffolk none at all.

Then, in 1843, as depression was giving way to recovery, the newly projected Norwich & Brandon invited both the ECR and the N&E to build to meet it. The outcome of negotiations was that from 1 January 1844 the former took the latter (already compelled to share the ECR's Shoreditch terminal) on lease and thereby secured control of both routes from the region into London. The same year it obtained powers to extend from the N&E line to Brandon and, by a branch from Ely, to the London & Birmingham at Peterborough, and also committed itself to a line towards Lincoln. The Norwich route via Cambridge opened to public traffic on 30 July 1845.

It was largely in anticipation of these developments that the 'Mania' period produced a whole mass of schemes, the way being opened for them first by the failure of the ECR to provide a comprehensive regional network as had been intended, and secondly by the new willingness of a gullible public, finding the unoccupied spaces of the eastern counties an irresistible attraction, to view projects in the general rather than the particular context. In April 1845 the *Norfolk Chronicle* reported:

> Norwich is to be the nucleus of eight railways, Lynn of four, Ely of seven, Thetford of nine, Bury St Edmunds of thirteen, Diss of eight, Dereham of five, Newmarket of seven, Wisbeach [sic] of seven, Cambridge of eight, Beccles of three and the small village of Royston of six.

Scrip was being eagerly taken in each although only Norwich and Cambridge of the places named could boast a population of even 20,000. Investment in the regional towns, frequently motivated by purely commercial considerations, was commonly limited and short term being designed primarily to 'salt the mine' for outside investors; the landed interests, preferring the benefits without the risk, generally took little part. Inevitably the majority of the projects failed even to reach Parliament but by 1850 the region possessed a fairly substantial network of completed lines.

In 1845–6, however, the principal concern was for a second route to the north to improve on that existing since 1840 via Rugby and Derby. Two Parliamentary sessions were occupied before the ECR and its allies were worsted and the Great Northern Railway (initially the London & York) emerged as the victor. Ruin of ECR hopes in 1845 after it had given preference to a Midland Railway bill brought George Hudson to the chair at the invitation of 1,240 proprietors; a bait of £1,000 in shares was rumoured but probably the whole matter had been engineered by Hudson himself. Hudson insisted on complete control and 'whenever thwarted in his views' threatened to leave the direction. He immediately refurbished the ECR's tarnished public credit by payment of unearned dividends—3 per cent, equivalent to 6 per cent for the whole year, was declared for the six months ending December 1845 before the books were even made up and, overall, 6¼ per cent was paid for 1846 by improperly charging revenue expenses to the capital account and refusing a badly needed depreciation fund. His primary concern was to defeat the London & York in protection of his Midland Railway interests and to this end an ECR northern extension bill was entered unsuccessfully in 1846 when the former's bill, deferred from 1845, reappeared in the new session.

Although beaten Hudson continued his fight to cripple the GNR but at the same time drove the ECR on to dominate its smaller neighbours, themselves riven as they feuded one against the other and sought to resolve internal conflicts between parochial commercial interests and those of the investors per se, the latter invariably proving successful when heavy expenditure was rewarded by poor returns. Amidst the tangle of suspicion and recriminations the ECR pursued a ruthless policy of blackmail, obstructionism, rate wars and sheer dishonesty, and it succeeded, although public benefit was frequently only incidental.

In February 1849 Wylie and the Liverpool group in the ECR expelled Hudson, but from 1851 his former deputy and traffic manager Waddington came to the chair and continued along the same paths until himself driven out in 1856. By then, in 1852, an unusually virulent clash over the railways of King's Lynn had led to a fourteen years' truce of mutual exhaustion between the GNR and the ECR and a *modus vivendi* which left the latter a free hand east of the King's Cross to Peterborough line. By 1854 it had acquired a virtual hegemony over its discordant neighbours, the last and most obdurate, the Eastern Union, coming to it on lease from 1 January of that year. By 1856 the ECR controlled 617½ miles, by 1860 700¾.

Preoccupation with railway politics rather than sound operation and some ill-conceived economies in such matters as staffing (in 1851 2,933 employed on 103 stations and 332 miles appears to be roughly the national average of nine to the mile, but obscures the disproportionate number in the London area) deservedly earned the ECR a poor reputation for service. Major accidents were few, the worst being near Brentwood on 19 August 1840 and a derailment at Tottenham on 20 February 1860, with four and seven deaths respectively, but minor mishaps were numerous. A correspondent to the *Railway Record* in August 1845 described 'scandalous negligence' and an incident in which only a 'special interference of providence' prevented fatal results:

> It appears that two miles below Romford a spare engine is kept in readiness for the purpose of propelling such trains as, owing to the wretched inefficiency of the plant, may appear to be in need of assistance up the incline to Brentwood. And further it seems that the driver is allowed to run his assistant engine on to the train while it is in motion. On Friday last the collision was sufficiently violent to floor the passengers in the whole train and snap the coupling irons attaching the last carriage to the other three, leaving this single carriage jumping by itself on the top of a high embankment, and us, who were in it, in the certain conviction that we were going over. Many passengers were injured. . . . Having lost my ticket in the melee I was required at Chelmsford to pay a second fare from London; thus I rode twenty-six miles [sic] and paid for sixty; I suppose the luxury of the concussion was reckoned equal to the other thirty-four.

With standards like this it can only occasion surprise that in the first half of 1850 1,537,868 passengers were carried without a single fatality, and indeed an 1851 ECR guide could still claim that there had not been one since July 1846.

Some attempt at reform was made from 1856 but was hampered by lack of funds; in the first half of that year the 13,000 trains run by the ECR earned an average profit of only 5½d and lack of public confidence made fund raising difficult. Jobbery, fraud in the stores' department and inadequate supervision had brought the ECR to a very low ebb. The worst immediate problem was the appalling state of the permanent way. For a time annual maintenance expenditure had averaged only £45 a mile, raised to £97 in the latter part of 1855 but still less than on other lines. In December 1855 it was estimated that £150,000 would be needed to set matters to rights, but by September 1856 £175,000 had gone on one small section and the necessity for further vast sums had to be faced. Rolling stock remained grossly deficient in quantity and quality. Between 1856 and the start of 1860 mileage rose by 83¼ to 700¾ but the number of locomotives only from 271 to 292, and of these 207 had required 'thorough repairs' in 1859. In the same period wagon totals increased from 6,103 to 6,305 and that of carriages from 1,105 to 1,178, although of the latter 1,650 had been through the shops in 1859, meaning that a substantial number had needed two 'thorough repairs' if not more in one year. In the first half of 1859 there was not a single piece of new stock, a fact probably connected with the £2 16s 3d per cent dividend paid for 1858, the highest genuine level attained by the ECR. All in all an 1860 pamphleteer could still truthfully write:

> Notoriously there is no railway system in the Empire so badly worked as the Eastern Counties. There is no system on which the Passenger Trains are so few or so irregular; none on which the rates for Passengers and Goods are so excessive; and few, in any, where accidents are more plentiful.

It was then, for example, impossible for a passenger from London to spend more than 2¼ hours in Norwich and return the same day, and the services via Cambridge and via Ipswich were so timed as to neutralise each other.

In 1854 Parliament had ratified the ECR's supremacy but for the sake of financial stability and the public benefit had insisted that the company should, by the close of 1861, prepare a bill for

total amalgamation. The companies continued their endless
intrigues, now in order to raise the values of their respective
stocks before fusion, but on 7 August 1862 the Great Eastern
Railway was incorporated and the region could at last antici-
pate the full benefits of rail communication, although Norwich,
Ipswich and several other towns expressed serious apprehen-
sions of the 'giant monopoly' that the new company would
enjoy.

Such fears were needless. Although in its first years mismanagement of an already difficult inherited situation brought
the company to a very low ebb, and even into Chancery and the
hands of a Receiver in 1867, the corner was turned in 1868 with
the coming of Lord Cranbourne to the chair. Thereafter the GER
was rapidly on its way to becoming a model of enlightened
self-interest, ever concerned to help itself by helping its region,
the limitations of which it well understood; it was with the GER
that the region made the great progress indicated in previous
pages. As the years passed, it built or operated lines wherever
traffic offered, provided comprehensive services at imaginative
rates designed to help the small man and foster any potential
traffic, and supplemented its efforts with extensive mercantile
interests, hotels, bus services (from 1904) and other kindred
activities. Its trains were not fast but from the early 1880s
average speeds compared favourably with those of other companies and its best holiday expresses were of the top rank;
punctuality was justifiably its especial pride. Relations with
interlopers in its territory were sometimes strained but rarely
bitter, and in several notable ways involved direct co-operation
as in the formation of the Norfolk & Suffolk Joint Committee
with the Midland & Great Northern Joint Railway in 1898 and
the establishment in 1879 of a joint line with the Great Northern
to the northern coalfields, completed in 1882. Strident opposition from anti-monopolists and other companies caused withdrawal of a 1909 bill for amalgamation with the Great Northern
and the Great Central.

The GER spent generously but wisely in unremitting efforts to
build and sustain traffic. In 1862 the combined stocks of the
constituent companies amounted to £13,396,884, but by 1923
the GER's capital debt stood at £55,073,850. By 1913 the company owned 1,107¼ route miles, partly owned 150 and leased or

County.	Name.	Address.	Description of House.	Sitting Rooms.	Bed Rooms.	Nearest Station on Great Eastern Railway.	Distance from Station.	Return Fares from London. 1st Class	2nd Class	3rd Class	Period for which Return Tickets are available.	Remarks.
Cambridge-shire continued	Mrs. Inker	Ickleton	Draper & Grocer' shop	1	2	Gt. Chesterford	47	13/0	10/5	7/5	1 Week	With use of kitchen.
	Mr. Joshua Unwin	Impington	Farm House	1	2	Histon	61	17/0	13/0	9/6	1 Month	Horse and Trap if required.
	" W. Crags	Main Street, Littleport	Butcher's Shop	1	1	Littleport						Good Fishing.
	" S. Blows	High Street, Littleport	Private House	1	1		77	21/4	17/1	12/10	"	
	" E. Thoday	Willingham	Farm	1	1	Long Stanton		17/0	13/6	9/9	"	Fishing and Boating. Pony and Trap.
	R. Norman		Private	2	1							
	A. S. Wright	Norwood House, Station Road, March	"	3	3	March	86	22/0	17/2	12/6	"	
	" Smith	Westfield House, Little Shelford	"	2	4	Shelford	14					Large Grounds, Garden, Tennis Lawn, Good Stabling, &c. Stabling and Large Garden.
	Mrs. Greaves	The Lynes, Shelford	"	2	3			13/0	11/10	8/11	"	Board with family if required.
	" Shreeve	The Poplars, Stapleford, Cambs	Farm	3	3		54					Recommend to ... Waterville ... with fond interesting occupation in the District.
	Miss Livermore	Little Shelford	Private	1	1							
	Mr. R. Aspland	Wicken	Grocer's Shop	1	1	Soham	71	20/7	16/0	12/0	"	
	Mrs. Myrton	The Row, Sutton	Private House	1	2	Sutton	76	20/7	12/11	11/4	"	Good Fishing.
	Mr. Jas. Scott	Reach	Farm House	1	1	Swaffhamprior	1	66	18/1	14/5	10/7	"	Good Fishing, 2 miles from Newmarket. Heath.
	" Norman	Over St. Ives	Private	1	1	Swavesey						Near River Ouse. Good fishing.
	" J. Rogers	Post Office, Swavesey	"	1	1		66	17/6	13/6	9/9	"	
	Mr. J. Sizer	Swavesey	Farm	1	1							Good Fishing. River Ouse.
	Mrs. F. Reade	Elm Road, Wisbech	Private	1	1	Waterbeach	61	17/9	13/9	10/0	"	Near the River Ouse.
	" Kilford	Peampford	"	2	2	Wisbech	94	24/10	18/6	14/0	"	Fishing in neighbourhood.
	" Aitkin	Alm House Street, Whittlesea	"	1	1	Whittlesford	1	80	13/10	11/1	8/4	"	
						Whittlesea	2	94	26/3	19/9	12/6	"	
Hunting-donshire	Mr. S. Holdich	Orton, Waterville	"	2	2	Peterborough	3					Close to Park and Woods.
	" J. Orton	" "	"	2	1	"	2					Good Fishing.
	" J. Wagstaff	Longueville	"	1	1	"	1	50	14/2	10/0	12/6		
	" W. Clarke	Sidney House, Woodstone	"	1	1	"	1					
	" S. Wood	Woodstone	"	1	1	"	1					
Suffolk	" S. Meadows	Wyndham House, Aldeburgh	Private House in its own Grounds	6	16	Aldeburgh						Whole House from July 29 to September 15; at other times Apartments.
	" R. Watson	Rushmere Lodge, Friston	Farm House	2	6	"	3	100	27/9	22/1	14/0	15 Days	Attendance. Pony and Phaeton if required.
	" C. Mitchell	Anlaby House, Aldborough	Private "	3	6	"			25/0	11/9	9/6	Fridy to Tuesy	June, July, and after middle of September.
	Mrs. W. Smith	Grafton Arms Farm, Barnham	Farm	1	3	Barnham		88	26/7	20/11	14/3	1 Month	

County.	Name.	Address.	Description of House.	Sitting Rooms.	Bed Rooms.	Nearest Station on Great Eastern Railway.	Distance from Station.	Return Fares from London. 1st Class	2nd Class	3rd Class	Period for which Return Tickets are available.	Remarks.
Suffolk continued	Mrs. P. J. Allen	Ferndale, Station Rd., Beccles	Private House	3	4	Beccles	close					Good Fishing and Yachting.
	Rev. J. Howsell	Rectory, Beccles	" "	3	8	" "						Whole House from Aug. 1st for Six weeks. Overlooking River. Fishing, Boating, and Tennis Court.
	Mrs. Read Crisp	Blyburgate Street, Beccles	" "	1	4	" "						Whole House, lawn & garden.
	Mr. Wm. Garrard	London Road, Beccles	" "	2	4	" "		30/0	24/5	18/4	1 Month	To be let from last week in July to middle of September.
	" S. S. Jones, jun.	Newmarket Place, Beccles	" "	4	8	" "		10/0	27/0	20/9	15/0	15 Days	Boating and Fishing.
	Miss Cowles	Northgate Street, Beccles	" "	2	5	" "	1	20/0	15/0	10/6	Fridy to Tuesy	
	" Eccleston	London Road	" "	2	5	" "						Garden in August.
	" Nicoll	Hillside	" "	3	4	" "						
	Mrs. Hayward	Watermoor House	" "	2	4	" "	1½					Boating and Fishing.
	Captn. Martin	Yoxford Villa	" "	3	5	" "	1½					Large Garden; near River; Tennis Court, &c.
	Mr. T. P. Angel	St. Peter's House, Beccles	" "	3	5	" "	1½					

To encourage holiday traffic the Great Eastern published unusually detailed lists of available accommodation (a portion is shown above)

worked 13, the whole being operated at a high level of efficiency with 1,274 locomotives, 5,817 carriages and 27,092 goods vehicles. But despite its quality and determination the restrictions imposed by the region were such that it could never be a wealthy concern. Only from 1865 to 1868 and in 1874 did it fail to pay any ordinary dividend, but the £3 17s 6d per cent of 1899 was the highest level attained.

Under the London & North Eastern Railway, in 1923 a worthy successor to the GER, the fundamental weaknesses in the region's lines were made increasingly apparent as road competition mounted. From the 1920s even holiday traffic tended to decline and by the later 1930s agricultural patronage was falling steadily away. Rural passenger levels and overall seasonal fluctuations remained as disheartening as ever—in 1939 the estimated number of tickets collected in the whole of Suffolk reached only 21,000 in January and 97,000 in August. The LNER achieved many economies, notably the closure of some routes and reduction of service on others after acquiring substantial holdings in local bus companies from 1929 as authorised in 1928. During World War II the presence in the area of numerous army camps and over eighty airfields and the emphasis on domestic food production ensured that the region's system was used to capacity, but after 1945 the decline continued seemingly unabated.

Selective closures were effected in the 1950s, and wholesale axing followed the 1963 Beeching Report. Rationalisation of the remainder (particularly freight) was continued but in the mid-1970s closure of all lines north of Cambridge and the reduction of Norwich to terminal status for just the Ipswich line were still possibilities. The suburban electrification from King's Cross and Liverpool Street and to Clacton and Walton were the only bright spots. But with the ending of steam traction (September 1962 on GER lines) diesel power, improved operating methods and better services (although the region was the poor relation for rolling stock) the system was enabled to consolidate and even regain some ground. Thus, as the region's economic transformation dawned, the railways were in a position to grasp the new opportunities offered. Essentially with electrification, this they have done to secure themselves an assured and even expanding role for the future.

THE HARWICH SCENE

7 (top)   A water-colour impression of the quays and the Great Eastern Hotel at Harwich as in about 1880. 8 (bottom) Parkeston Quay West under construction. The features of the original development, the marshy nature of the Isle of Ray and the railway workers' houses are clearly visible. The cramped site of Harwich, beyond, is also evident. At the top right is Dovercourt and Felixstowe is seen at the extreme top left on the opposite side of the Orwell Haven

CHAPTER II

Central Essex

THE EASTERN COUNTIES MAIN LINE TO 1843

The Eastern Counties Railway was incorporated on 4 July 1836 with a share capital of £1,600,000 to provide a 126 miles line from Shoreditch to Norwich and Yarmouth via Colchester, Ipswich and Eye. As surveyed by Braithwaite and Vignoles in 1834 it would require neither tunnels nor major works, would follow existing traffic streams and be within 'available distance' of 739,697 persons, a number that would increase as branches were added to Harwich and elsewhere. Industry would be fostered, agriculture revived (although the three counties involved already supplied half London's needs), the 'overwhelming evil' of the Poor Rates (then nearly £1 million in Norfolk, Suffolk and Essex together) reduced by the additional employment the line would stimulate, fishing increased 'ten-fold', and Harwich and Yarmouth reinstated as leading ports for the continent and northern Britain. These last two places were losing trade to London since steam navigation had reduced passage time on the Thames, but the traveller from eastern Scotland to the capital would still save up to 24 hours on the water by disembarking at

IPSWICH
9 (*top*)   *The original Ipswich station shown at the formal opening of the Eastern Union Railway on 11 June 1846*
10 (*centre*)   *The 1860 station seen from the north in 1881 when there was still only one main through platform. The entrance to Stoke Hill Tunnel may be discerned beyond the signal*
11 (*bottom*)   *Looking north in 1901 from near the tunnel mouth. The down island platform had been added in 1883*

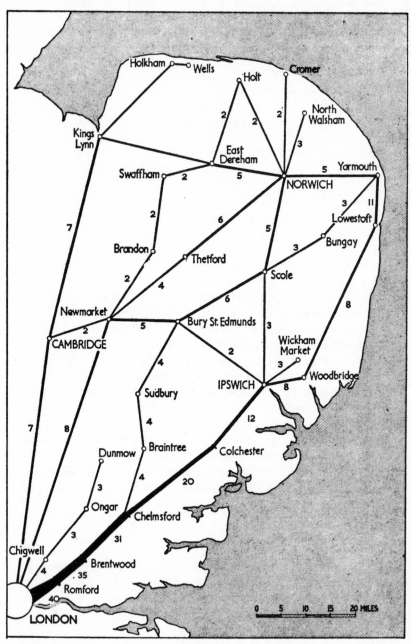

Numbers of licensed stage coaches running between principal centres
in 1834

Yarmouth for a 6¼ hour rail journey. As 'transmarine sources' would almost certainly cover working expenses and the line produce a general increase in traffic, a 22 per cent return on capital was probable; needless to say such calculations totally disregarded both the resilience of coastal shipping and the possibilities of north to south trunk railways.

Despite these impressive claims the company had a hard struggle. By September 1836 only 2,324 of the £25 shares remained unissued, but 'little more than one twelth' had been taken locally even after a regional 'progress' by the chairman, Bosanquet, and two directors in November 1835. Indeed, it was only a month earlier, with six weeks left for the final compilation of the bill, that a Provisional Committee had been formed of sufficient respectability and local connections to carry the project through. This had dispelled suspicion of the promoters, including the engineer John Braithwaite and the London firm of solicitors, Dimes & Boyman, who would gain from professional services without necessarily incurring the risk of investment and who had turned to the Norwich concept only when an Edinburgh line (proposed to them in 1834 by Henry Sayer) was judged too ambitious; but it achieved little else within the region. Many were rendered cautious by never having seen a railway, others were depleted in personal resources by depression in farming, and there was widespread fear, despite the company's repeated reassurances, that the line would increase the poor rates by displacing workers in road transport, and that this, coupled with reduced demand for horses and fodder, would lead to further depreciation of land values.

There was a more sympathetic reception in Liverpool where the merchants, successful pioneers in railway enterprise, subscribed 'upwards of one third' of the required capital, and in the northern industrial areas generally. Unhappily much of the balance came from 'men of straw' (vice-chairman Rigby in 1841) so making the ECR 'little better than a bubble company'. However, when the pressure of calls revealed this the solidarity of the 'Liverpool Leviathans', who at an early stage had displaced the local men and assumed control of the board, permitted transfer of forfeited shares to 'men of substance'.

In Parliament 'strenuous opposition', backed by 'a portion of

the press', was encountered from the Northern & Eastern and
Great Northern companies, both seeking a line to Cambridge
and the north with a branch to Norwich. 'A formidable array
of dissenting owners and occupiers' had to be pacified by secret
and extravagant promises of compensation. The seemingly
superior merits of the ECR bill carried the day against the rival
companies, although the Commons actually divided on the
second reading before giving it a majority of only 74. During
these anxious days the directors busied themselves in raising
petitions of support within the region, but as Gladstone in-
formed the Commons, that from Norwich at least was 'got up
by the foulest means', each signatory being rewarded with a
'good lunch'.

Success attained, the confidence of the ECR knew no bounds.
Characteristic of this was the curious 5 ft gauge adopted at
Braithwaite's behest. He argued that for adequate boiler room,
steadier motion and less wear on moving parts his locomotives
would require 4 ft 11¾ in, but in carrying his point failed to
convince entirely those directors who, perhaps a little less shortsightedly, had pressed for the 7 ft 0¼ in of the Great Western and
insisted on provision for future conversion to such if found
desirable. The outcome was an expensive road-bed 30 ft wide
bearing a 5 ft gauge track, and engines that in fact turned out
to be of smaller internal dimensions than many already at work
elsewhere on the 4 ft 8½ in gauge.

Late in March 1837 construction began, but at the London
end only, incomplete land negotiations preventing the concur-
rent start planned between Norwich and Yarmouth. Endless
troubles now beset the ECR. The marshes near Stratford, and
London Viaduct both presented unexpected problems and consumed vast quantities of time and capital. Further delays ensued
from the abnormally wet weather of 1838-9, and as time passed
iron and other prices were rising. Landowners, great and small,
set themselves to exact the uttermost penny in compensation for
real or imaginary damages, and amenities disturbed, while the
secret promises of 1836, made by the original local directors,
had to be honoured. Lord Petre of Ingatestone Hall received
£120,000 (with which he bought a new estate) and nearby
Labouchère £35,000 although their combined properties
affected only 6 miles of line. Like Sir Edward Kerrison, who

received £20,000, Labouchere was obliged to resort to the
courts when the ECR attempted evasion, but on his death, the
estate not having lost value as expected, his son did remit
£15,000. This was a unique occurrence, however, and by 1843
the 51·2 miles to Colchester had cost the ECR £600,000 in land
and compensation alone.

Forty per cent of the capital had been called by October
1838, but only 9 miles were under construction. Creditors
were pressing and each fresh call on the proprietors was serving
only to provoke resistance and further depress the value of company stock. Only decisive action could avert total ruin. Hence,
in April 1839, 'in accordance with the wishes of the Lancashire
proprietors who have so great a stake in the undertaking' (*Norfolk Chronicle*), the decision to terminate at Colchester was made.
To increase public confidence, efforts to commence operation
were redoubled and, after a formal opening two days earlier, the
first public trains ran between a temporary terminus at Mile
End and Romford on 20 June; extensions at each end, to Shoreditch and Brentwood respectively, followed on 1 July 1840.
Meanwhile, Robert Stephenson had been called in but could
only confirm the estimate of £520,000 needed to complete to
Colchester. By applying the brutal logic that everything spent
could still be lost the mutinous shareholders were persuaded to
meet their calls (one of £2 per share in January 1840 producing
£148,000), and in 1840 Parliament was successfully approached
for authorisation of a further £350,000 share capital; with these
assets and the additional borrowing powers sanctioned in 1840
the final section could be contemplated.

Wisely this was treated as one unit so that the heavier works
could be undertaken while means allowed. Prolonged rain in
1841 caused serious delay and damage to earthworks already
completed, and at different times there were various mishaps
such as the collapse of an underline bridge at Kelvedon and
the subsidence of a timber viaduct at Mountnessing, but
eventually goods services opened to Colchester on 7 March
1843, passenger trains commencing on 29 March. Altogether
seven years and nearly £2½ million had been consumed in
covering the 51·2 miles; works alone, at £1,631,330, had cost
rather more than the total construction estimate for reaching
Yarmouth.

SHENFIELD TO COLCHESTER SINCE 1843

In July 1843 the ECR gained the mail contract and from the withdrawal of the *Golden Path* coach in the November was left as the only.means of public conveyance between London and Colchester. Services suffered, however, from the usual defects of ECR operation and the only progressive step in early days was conversion to 4 ft 8½ in when the lease and authorised extension of the Northern & Eastern in 1844 brought the imminence of contact with other lines. A third rail between Shoreditch and Stratford, to accommodate what would become standard-gauge trains from the N&E and beyond, was considered, but, on the advice of Robert Stephenson, rejected because of cost, technical problems at junctions and the undesirability of maintaining two separate rolling-stock establishments. The work of conversion, conducted in sections along each running line in turn to avoid disruption of traffic, was effected between 5 September and 7 October 1844 at a cost of roughly £1,000 a mile, a heavy but essential burden as the necessity for manual transhipment between gauges would have crippled both the company and regional development.

In January 1846 one daily service was reaching Colchester in 90 minutes, eased to 95 minutes in the summer; by this time the principal services had been extended over the Eastern Union to Ipswich and Bury St Edmunds. But then, after a period of worsening relations, the Eastern Union completed its line to Norwich in December 1849 (Chapter IV), thus establishing a rival route to that via Cambridge, wholly controlled by the ECR since taking the Norfolk Railway on lease in 1848. It now became a matter of deliberate, albeit self-immolating policy to discourage through Norwich traffic via Colchester. Slow, dirty and unpunctual trains were run at inconvenient times and by the end of 1850 there was nothing faster than 130 minutes to Colchester.

In the end the EUR was forced to concede defeat (Chapter III). The assumption of its working by the ECR from 1 January 1854 brought some improvement, but only with the GER accelerations of 1863–4, by which the 10 am down was timed to Colchester in 70 minutes, did the line, its ill-repute at last dis-

EASTERN COUNTIES.—Colchester Line—50¼ Miles.

Down Trains.

Mls	Stations.	3rd cl. 1	2 a.m.	3 a.m.	4	5	6	7	8	9	mail. 10	Sundays. 1 a.m.	2 a.m.	3 p.m	4 p.m.	5 p.m.
	Trains leave	a.m.	a.m.	a.m.		p.m.	pm	p.m	p.m	p.m.	a.m.	a.m.		p.m.	p.m.
	Shoredtch	7 30	8 30	11 0	12 46	1 30	3 0	4 15	5 30	6 30	8 30	8 30	9 45	2 0	4 0	8 30
4	Mile End	7 35	8 34									8 33½	9 48	2 4	4 3	
7	Stratford	7 48	8 41	11 11	12 46	34		4 26	5 41	6 41	8 40	8 43	9 58	2 13	4 13	8 40
12	Ilford	8 0	8 49	11 18	50	45	3 16	4 33	5 48	6 48	8 46	8 51	10 6	2 21	4 21	8 46
18	Romford	8 20	9 1	11 30	1 22	2 23	3 28	4 45	6 0	7 0	8 56	9 20	10 19	2 34	4 34	8 56
23	Brentwood	8 42	9 15	11 45	1 46	2 17	3 43	5 0	6 15	7 15	9 11	9 20	10 35	2 50	4 50	9 11
30	Ingatestone	9 2	9 31	‡							9 35	9 37			5 7	9 35
	Chelmsford	9 45	9 41	12 12	2 34		4 12	5 16	6 42		9 49	9 52			5 22	9 49
35	Hatfield	10 3	9 57					6 55				10 16			5 36	
38¾	Witham	10 25	10 7	12 34	3 10		4 33		7 14		10 13	10 27			5 46	10 13
42	Kaelvedn	10 43	10 17	12 44	3 20		4 43		7 24		10 23	10 38			5 57	10 23
7	Mrks Tey	11 10		12 54					7 31			11 0			6 8	
4	**Colchestr**	11 25	10 45	1 13			5 11		7 45		10 49				5 30	10 49

Up Trains.

	Stations.	mail. 1 a.m.	2 a.m.	3 a.m.	4 a.m.	5 a.m.	6 p.m.	7 p.m.	3rd cl. 8 p.m.	9 p.m.	3rd cl. 10 p.m.	Sundays. 1 a.m.	2 a.m.	3 p.m.	4 p.m.	5 p.m.
		a.m.	a.m.	a.m.	a.m.	a.m.	p.m.	p.m.	p.m.	p.m	p.m.	a.m.	a.m.	p.m.	p.m.	p.m.
4	**Colchstr**	2 45			9 0	11 0		3 10	5 0	6 0	7 0	2 45	8 30		4 0	
9	Marks Tey				9 10		3 10		5 12		7 6	3 10	8 52		4 22	
13¼	Kelvedon	3 10			9 22	11 22	3 22		5 34	6 22	7 36	3 10	9 3		4 33	
16	Witham	3 20			9 32	11 32	3 32		5 49	6 32	7 52	3 20	9 14		4 44	
21	Hatfield				9 45				5 58	6 45			9 24		4 54	
	Chelmsford	3 45		8 45	9 59	11 54	3 54		6 24	6 54	8 28	3 45	9 38		5 8	
28	Ingatestone	4 3		8 54		12 8	‡		6 50	7 8		4 23	9 53		5 23	
33	Brentwood	4 23	8 40	9 10	10 25	12 23	4 22	5 30	6 57	7 23	9 14	4 23	10 10	0 5	5 40	8 0
39	Romford	4 38	8 56	9 26	10 41	12 39	4 37	5 45	7 15	7 39	9 33	4 38	10 26	1 15	5 56	8 16
44	Ilford	4 48	9 6	9 36	*	12 49	4 47	5 55	8 6	7 49	9 58	4 48	10 39	1 26	5 9	8 29
47	Stratford	4 54	9 14	9 46		12 58	4 55	6 3	8 47	8 4	10 14	4 54	10 47	1 33	5 17	8 37
50	Mile End			9 52					8				10 58	1 47	5 26	8 46
51	**Shordtch**	5 4	9 27	10 3	11 11	1 12	5 11	6 19	8 50	8 15	10 35	5 4	11 0	1 45	5 30	8 50

Fares.

Quick Trn. 1st cl 2d cl	Ordinary Trains. 1st cl. s. d.	2d cl. s. d.	3d cl. s. d.
	0 2	0 0	0 4
	1 4	0 9	0 7
	2 1	1 1	0 6
	3 6	2 6	1 6
	5 0	3 6	2 6
	6 0	4 6	2 11
	7 0	5 0	3 3
	8 0	6 6	3 11
	9 0	6 6	3 6
	10 0	6 7	3 10
	11 0	7 6	4 3

Fares.

Quick Trn. 1st cl. 2d cl	Ordinary Trains. 1st cl. s. d.	2d cl. s. d.	3d cl. s. d.
	1 0	0 7	0 4
	2 0	1 1	0 9
	2 6	1 6	0 9
	3 6	2 1	1 1
	4 6	3 2	1 7
	6 6	4 6	2 9
	7 6	5 0	3 3
	8 0	6 6	3 3
	9 0	6 6	3 6
	10 6	3 7	3 11
	11 0	7 6	4 3

On Wednesdays the Train marked thus * stops at Stratford, and the Train marked thus † at Mile End, to take up and set down Passenger.

‡ These Trains call at Ingatestone on Fridays.

§ This train starts from Colchester at 7 5 a.m. on Mondays, calling at all the intermediate Stations, except Ingatestone and Mile End.

Early days on the Colchester line; a page from Bradshaw

pelled, recognisably become part of a major trunk route. The 10 am, comprised of four-wheeled coaches without a continuous brake and hauled by Sinclair's 2-2-2 locomotives, was, however, an exceptional train even when, as happened within a year, an additional 5 minutes was allowed. Other services, although gradually improving from 1864, lagged a long way behind in terms of speed and more accurately reflected the limitations of rolling stock, locomotive power, track and signalling, the severe slacks necessary at Stratford (10 mph), Chelmsford (5 mph) and Witham (5 mph), sharp gradients as at Brentwood, the heavier trains that came with increasing traffic and the lack of funds that precluded any rapid overall improvement. It was not until 1879, after several fluctuations, that the superiority of this over the longer Cambridge route to Norwich was finally established. By then daily down services to Colchester had increased from eight as in 1864 and 1874 to fifteen; in 1884 the total had risen to sixteen, three of which were by slip portions at Colchester. In that last year the best time was again down to 70 minutes and average times had fallen to some 95 minutes as compared with the 119 of 1864 or the 101 of 1879.

The 1870s witnessed two particularly beneficial developments. One was the removal in September 1877, within a few days of its owner's death, of Sir John Tyssen Tyrell's private station at Boreham House (3½ miles north-east of Chelmsford): Sir John had not infrequently exercised his right, wrested from the ECR as part of his compensation, to stop any train at will. The other, increasing line capacity, was the extension of slip coach services. These had begun at Chelmsford in June 1872; in 1892, they were being employed on the Colchester line at Brentwood, Shenfield, Ingatestone, Mark's Tey and Colchester itself —at another period Witham was also so served. With over twenty daily examples in the early years of this century (twenty-five daily in 1904 was the peak but there were only fourteen by 1914), the GER for several years made more use of this practice than any company except the Great Western, and, although it was virtually discontinued after World War I, one survival, with a special bogie corridor coach, remained under the LNER at Marks Tey until 1939.

Thornton's 'Radical Alterations' timetable of October 1914 laid down an ambitious 65 minute standard timing for all ex-

presses to Colchester, equal to an individual schedule introduced
in 1895 and only one minute slower than the best so far, a 64
minute train that ran almost continuously between 1898 and
the summer of 1914. War conditions intervened, however, and
in fact the LNER was doing well by the spring of 1939 (when
eleven daily down services out of twenty-five took 76 minutes or
less) to have brought its best time down to 66; between the wars
this schedule had been beaten, but only by one 60 minute train
introduced in July 1936 and then withdrawn as an economy
measure in the December of 1938. These overall achievements
owed much to Gresley's B17 locomotives and his rebuilding of
the ex-GER B12s, to the extension of colour-light signalling from
Shenfield to Chelmsford in 1937 and the widening undertaken
west of Shenfield to alleviate the growing congestion of suburban
traffic (see Volume 3); further major relief came from 26 September 1949 when the Liverpool Street–Shenfield suburban
services were electrified.

From 2 July 1951 'Britannia' locomotives (by then bridge
restrictions on the main line had been overcome) on the non-
stop London to Ipswich runs of the new Regular Interval Norwich services were exceeding the best pre-war standards of the
line, and in 1952 one Norwich express calling at Colchester was
due there in only 58 minutes from Liverpool Street. On 11 June
1956 1,500 volts DC suburban electrification was extended to
Chelmsford under a £2½ million scheme (including the Shenfield to Southend line) begun in spring 1955. This further increased operational possibilities as did the introduction of diesel-
electric locomotives in 1958. In June 1958 the best non-stop
timing to Colchester was down to 56 minutes (the 'Britannia'-
hauled 'Essex Coast Express') and the average for the twenty-
five daily trains was only 73, with thirteen in 71 or less. From
5 January 1959 further accelerations were introduced, principal
expresses ceasing to call at Marks Tey (Stour Valley passengers
for the west were carried through to Colchester without extra
charge or were obliged to change into a local train for Chelmsford and change again) and subsequently at Shenfield.

During 1960–1 electrification to Colchester was pushed ahead,
while for four months a diesel multiple-unit service, running in
peak hours, replaced the Chelmsford electric trains to allow
conversion of stock and equipment to the 25 kV AC standard

adopted by British Railways in 1956 and on which the local
Colchester–Clacton–Walton lines had been working since 13
April 1959. After a start with the winter timetables of 1962–3
and the introduction of the first main line multiple-unit sets on
7 January 1963, the full electric service between Liverpool
Street and the Clacton area was implemented on 17 June 1963,
allowing further main line accelerations. By the summer of 1964
there were seventy daily examples of 60 mph or over running
over some part of the Shenfield–Colchester section, the fastest
stretch being between the latter and Witham where seven up
and five down, calling at both, averaged just over 68 mph. In
1977 ten daily services, diesel hauled and non-stop, reached
Colchester in 50 minutes, a timing cut to 45 (eight services) by
October 1989 under the overall improvement made possible
from May 1987 by extension of through electric services to
Norwich; the average for the seventy-three daily down trains on
the Colchester line from May 1990 was 58 minutes.

At first, poor quality services had minimised the line's useful-
ness. In 1850 'frequent cases of incendiarism' marked a cut in
local farm wages from 9s 6d to 8s 6d, and Caird noted one
instance of 400 acres of good land, four miles from a station and
only an hour from London, selling at £6,500 after being purchased for £9,000 only a few years before. Under the GER,
however, the line contributed fully and directly to the local
prosperity of the 'High Farming' era, but then in the ensuing
depression the area was at first badly hurt, an 1881 report on
the Chelmsford district describing the situation of farming as
'deplorable', some land being 'altogether derelict' and more
'full of weeds and natural rough grasses upon which a few cattle
were picking up a bare living'.

By 1900, however, relative stability had been attained, based
primarily on rapid rail transit of perishable produce to London.
More poultry and store cattle were kept, but in particular dairy
farming was developed, cows in milk or calf increasing 52 per
cent in the Chelmsford, Maldon, Braintree and Ongar districts
between 1882 and 1892, and further afterwards. Market gardening, with a particular reputation for green peas (11,582 tons
came to Bishopsgate in one year, and 1,000 tons on 7 July 1906
alone, mainly from Essex), spread down the main line and along
the Maldon and Braintree branches, and fruit growing, hitherto

confined to the London area, was firmly established around
Chelmsford, Witham, Maldon, Kelvedon and Colchester. In
Essex as a whole, orchards increased from 1,046 acres in 1873
to 2,598 by 1902 when there were also 2,065 of 'small fruit', a
fourfold increase since 1888. At Witham two large seed warehouses were built adjacent to the station, and at Marks Tey
increasing quantities of coriander, caraway and teazle were
grown for confectionery purposes, the heads of the latter also
being despatched by rail to Leeds for use in raising the nap of
certain types of cloth.

Chelmsford, the Essex county town, the north-western part of
which the ECR crossed on a long viaduct, lost most of the benefits
of the Chelmer Navigation (completed from Maldon in 1797 at
a cost of £50,000 and making £6,000 profit in 1845) with the
opening of the Witham to Maldon branch in 1848 but between
1841 and 1861 population grew from 6,789 to 8,407, the market
was confirmed as one of the busiest in Essex and the old town
was much improved. In 1856, when the Royal Agricultural
Show was held in the town, a £10,000 Corn Exchange was built
and, at a cost of £4,462, a new station was opened on the
present site, the original timber-framed structure on an island
platform 200 yd to the north-east being re-erected as a dwelling
half a mile away. Between the 1860s and 1901, when population
was 12,627, foundations for future industrial growth were laid
with the establishment of general and electrical engineering
firms. In the 1890s the town came to possess two of the five steel
roller mills in Essex, in 1898 a ball-bearings factory, and in 1902
a fertiliser plant; brushes, brick and tile making were amongst
several minor activities to follow the railway. The GER provided
an extensive system of sidings to serve these growing industries.
Meanwhile, market activity was flourishing and was further
boosted by the GER from 9 September 1905 when the company
inaugurated a bus service to Danbury; others were operated to
Writtle and Great Waltham until absorbed by the National
Steam Car Company in July 1913.

After 1901 printing and other industries were established and
since 1945 there has been further considerable growth and
diversification, but, from the railway viewpoint, the most significant development has been the increase of London commuters
in a population rising to 58,159 in 1981. Electrification doubled

the rail traffic of later steam days; in 1964 446,954 ordinary tickets were issued and 810,315 collected while within the period season-ticket sales had risen to 49,670 as compared with 13,602 in 1958. In 1975 season ticket sales reached 55,562 (including 2,528 annual and 19,083 monthly or quarterly) and those of ordinary tickets 542,996. The upward trend being sustained, from November 1986 a complete rebuilding of the station was begun, a new Travel Centre, Parcels Office, shops and lifts being included amongst the many facilities completed during 1989.

Electrification has also increased commuter settlement at Ingatestone where the Tudor-style station, replacing the original wooden building of 1846, was reputedly designed at Lord Petre's insistence to match the nearby Hall. This was a village 'much injured' by the railway through lost road traffic, population being only 926 in 1881; however, the 4,823 of 1971 and the 6,111 of 1981 (producing 560 daily commuters in 1980) indicate the trend. Hatfield Peverel, 1,244 in 1881, 3,179 in 1981, has evolved similarly since electrification in 1963; in 1980 there were some 400 daily London commuters. The station, now refurbished and with extended platforms, opened on 1 March 1878, the original Hatfield of 1844 having burnt down in February 1849; in the intervening years there had been no station at all. Goods facilities were lost on 27 June 1960. Mark's Tey, in 1990 with a rail served Tarmac depot despatching trainloads of builders' sand, and Kelvedon have only recently grown despite junction status. Their 1981 populations were 3,332 and 4,021 respectively, each in 1980 with just over 450 daily commuters. Witham, once a railway crossroads, the 1907 station replacing the original destroyed by fire, was badly hurt by agricultural depression, falling from 3,455 to 2,966 in population between 1861 and 1881 before local seed growing, a roller mill and maltings brought revival to 3,454 in 1901. In 1961 it was still only 9,459 but by 1981 25,373; in 1980 there were 2,600 daily commuters. Witham was the scene of the disastrous accident of 5 September 1905 when the fourteen coach 'Cromer Express' was derailed at 70 mph at a crossover where permanent-way men had rashly loosened a rail fastener; eleven lives were lost.

THE BRANCHES

Apart from the Stour Valley line at Marks Tey (Chapter VII) there were three branches between Shenfield and Colchester. The 10 mile long standard-gauge Kelvedon, Tiptree & Tollesbury Pier Light Railway, conceived in the Tiptree Rectory parlour in May 1895, was designed to help the farmers in depression, serve the local fruit growers and the Wilkin's jam factory (opened in 1885 and by 1907 producing 450 tons a year) and make the 1,770 ft Tollesbury Pier, the monument of an earlier scheme to develop the Blackwater estuary to rival Harwich, into a yachting centre; A. C. Wilkin was the secretary and guiding light of the scheme, and the firm gave the land for Tiptree station. Eventually a Light Railway Order was obtained in 1901; the Treasury contributed £16,000 (just over one-third of the estimated cost) and, after some hesitation, the GER agreed to work the line, which, from its own platform alongside Kelvedon main-line station, opened to Tollesbury on 1 October 1904, and, 1½ miles, to the desolate area of the pier on 15 May 1907. Apart from a few shrimp boats and weekend yachtsmen little activity developed at the pier and this latter section was closed on 17 July 1921, although in World War II it provided accommodation for four WD locomotives with mobile guns; the pier track was lifted in 1940 shortly before access to the pier from the shore was severed as a counter-invasion measure. Elsewhere, the line, worked except for the first months by J67s (for a time with shortened coupling rods to reduce wear on the many curves) served a valuable purpose, carrying fruit and its pickers in season, bringing manure and other requirements to the farmers, and encouraging some horticulture and milk production in the area.

In the early 1920s decline set in. A local garage commenced a bus service to Witham for which the line, with its 16 mph restriction, mixed trains making frequent stops for shunting and the opening and shutting of gates, antique central-gangway coaches (with conductor guards) and sparse station facilities (old coaches served as shelters on several and Inworth had none at all), was no match; in any case Witham was the natural local centre rather than Kelvedon. Improved stock was acquired from the Wisbech & Upwell line in 1928 but passenger traffic continued to fall. The same was true of freight. Pea traffic was heavy but seasonal, while the jam factory, well supplied with sidings and its own light railway, was requiring only seven or eight wagons a day even at the height of the season. The trends continued after the war, trains sinking to one bogie coach and wagons, until passenger services finally ceased on 7 May 1951. On 29 October goods facilities were withdrawn beyond Tudwick Road sidings, a fruit collection centre half a mile beyond Tiptree; the remainder retained its service until 1 October 1962, since when the line has been entirely demolished.

The Maldon, Witham & Braintree Railway was promoted in 1845 and authorised in 1846 to develop the former's harbour and preserve for it the flow of agricultural traffic, including 10,000 quarters of seed and corn per annum, from the latter, then 'the depot for the whole county'. Shrewdly, the ECR permitted the newcomer to cross its main line on the level, thus in effect creating two branches as through traffic required reversal at Witham, then in 1846, deceitfully promising dividends of 8 to 10 per cent and exploiting the financial over-commitment of some of the directors and local fears that the line would not pay, absorbed the whole, which opened for goods on 15 August 1848 and for passengers on 2 October. Having thus successfully blocked a possible drain of traffic from its own line, the ECR made no effort to deepen the Blackwater as the promoters had intended, nor did it pursue its own scheme for an extension to Saffron Walden.

Until recent times the Braintree branch, reputedly built as double track, but narrowed in the Crimean War when the military bought the rails, had a placid existence. A new Braintree station was provided in 1869 to give through running to the Bishop's Stortford line, the original site becoming the goods yard. With two lines Braintree developed footwear and brush making as well as engineering, but despite these and the survival of the silk industry, grew only from 3,670 to 5,330 between 1841 and 1901; Bocking meanwhile declined from 3,437 to 3,347. Daily services on the Witham branch were five in 1874, eight by 1892 but still only eight up and nine down in the early summer of 1939.

Predictably marked down for closure in the Beeching Report the branch survived by the designation of Braintree as a site for

London resettlement and through the vigorous efforts of a local Railway Campaign Committee. Diesel railbuses replaced steam on 7 July 1958 until themselves supplanted by multiple units from June 1963. In 1958 Braintree & Bocking station had issued 538 season tickets and 34,759 ordinary, but in 1964 1,462 and 61,405 respectively. Population in Braintree and Bocking combined was also climbing—to 20,600 in 1961, 24,856 in 1971 and 30,110 by 1981. By the latter year traffic potential had led to electrification of the branch as from 3 October 1977, although industrial dispute delayed implementation. Of twenty-one daily trains, eleven down and ten up (1990) are through London services. Even by 1980 daily commuters had increased from the 491 of 1972 to 760, most from Braintree but Cressing (remodelled in 1977) and White Notley (rebuilt) also contributing. In 1979 local councils subsidised the introduction of summer Sunday services, but by 1989 these were running throughout the year unaided. Although in 1965 5,000 tons of freight originated on the line (including 2,800 of window frames) outward traffic subsequently ceased. However, in 1969 Shellstar opened a private siding at its Braintree distribution depot to receive bagged fertiliser; this, in 1975 contributing 11,200 tonnes out of 12,030 inward freight, continues.

On the Maldon section services were increased from five daily in 1874 to nine by May 1883, but had reverted to seven by 1892. This fairly reflected the check on the growth of Maldon. Between 1841 and 1881 it had increased from 3,967 to 5,468, the nearby Heybridge to 1,565, as iron founding and agricultural-implement making, both partly based on water transport, had expanded alongside the granaries and maltings and it had become a favourite resort for day trippers. A steel roller mill followed and locally the branch had encouraged market gardening (with a particular reputation for green peas) and fruit growing, for which Wickham Bishops had become the station, but at an early date the railway had virtually destroyed the traffic of the Chelmer Navigation, failure to improve the harbour had restricted entry to vessels of 200 tons burthen so driving trade away, and, by 1890, the town was falling increasingly under the shadows of Clacton and Southend as an excursion centre.

By 1901 Maldon's population was still only 5,565 despite the opening of a second branch, that from Woodham Ferrers, on

1 October 1889. With the Shenfield–Southend (Volume 3) and Wickford–Southminster (via Woodham Ferrers) lines this was one of the GER's 'New Essex' promotions of 1883, designed to regain access to Southend, achieved over the Tilbury route until 1880, and open up a new area in the south of the county. As far as Maldon was concerned the new venture proved a grave disappointment, as did the intended Colchester–Southend traffic flow, to facilitate which triangular junctions were laid in at Wickford, Maldon and Witham. However, through passenger traffic was confined to a Saturdays only train each way between Colchester and Southend that ran from March 1890 to 1895, and with its withdrawal the spurs were closed on 1 March 1895.

Despite some recent industrial growth Maldon and Heybridge combined had a population of only 13,891 in 1971. For many years the Witham branch did no more than hold its own, despite a developing timber trade through the harbour, and although by 1939 there were nine daily trains activity was not appreciably greater than in the 1880s except that on summer Sundays (when tickets from Langford & Ulting and Wickham Bishops were issued on the train) there were seven services rather than three. British Railways made determined efforts to revive the branch. By the summer of 1958 eleven daily services, eight on Sundays, were offered, and sixteen from 15 September (though none on Sundays) when diesel railbuses, followed in June 1963 by diesel units, were introduced, but by 1964 under 400, sometimes 300, passengers a day were using the line which was in competition with three bus routes (it was 5s cheaper to

---

SUFFOLK COASTAL BRANCHES

12 (top)   A construction gang and its equipment in 1876 or 1877 at the building of Felixstowe station, subsequently known as Beach after the opening of Felixstowe Town. An impression may be gained of the extensive open spaces on which Tomline intended development to occur

13 (centre)   A GER freight crossing the marshes near Snape on the East Suffolk Railway's 1859 branch. The line never carried a passenger service

14 (bottom)   Aldeburgh station and yard as in 1956. Opened in 1860, goods facilities were withdrawn in 1959, passenger services in 1966

54

use the bus to Chelmsford on a day trip to London) and losing £10,000 a year; the need for expenditure of £9,900 on engineering works over five years was imminent. The passenger services were withdrawn on 7 September 1964, when the intermediate stations of Langford & Ulting and Wickham Bishops were closed entirely, freight, mainly sand, tinned fruit and a little agricultural machinery from Maldon continuing until 18 April 1966.

The 8¾ miles single track from Woodham Ferrers, with stations at Cold Norton and Maldon West, was opened on 1 October 1889; it ran through sparsely populated country and came at a time when Maldon was already experiencing serious obstacles to further growth. Thus the seven daily trains each way of the 1890 summer had become five in the 'Radical Alterations' timetable of 1914, and from 22 May 1916 to 1 August 1919 Maldon West was closed as a wartime economy. The post-war years brought growing road competition. Valiant efforts were made to make the line viable; on 10 July 1922 a halt was opened at Baron's Lane and on 24 September 1928 another at Stow St Mary. Conductor guard working was introduced from 2 October 1922, in the summer of 1923 the section between the two Maldon stations was singled, and by 1933 the whole line had been made one single staff section. All this was in vain, however, and on 10 September 1939 passenger services were finally withdrawn. Stow St Mary was closed entirely, but the rest of the line was served by a daily goods as required until 1 April 1953; a

---

INTO RURAL SUFFOLK

15 (top)   Stoke station between Haverhill and Long Melford probably just after its opening in 1865. The wheels on the platform appear to operate the signals. Note the mill in the background

16 (centre)   GER buses played an important role in reaching a number of isolated communities and linking them to the rail network and local market centres. This view of 1908 is of the service between 'The Cock' at Stanton and Bury St Edmunds

17 (bottom)   A train at Laxfield in 1951. The evident rural isolation clearly indicates the nature of the problems that faced the Mid-Suffolk Light Railway before its absorption by the LNER in 1924. Note the lorry and its load

freight link remained between Maldon East and Maldon West to 1 September 1954 and from 31 January 1957 to 31 January 1959, but the rest of the line had been demolished by the end of 1954 and at Cold Norton houses stand where the railway once ran.

The 16½ miles single-track 'New Essex' branch from Wickford to Southminster, the market centre of the Dengie Hundred and with 1,311 inhabitants in 1881, was opened to goods on 1 June 1889 and to passengers on 1 July, the GER expending £13,560 on coal bunkers, an iron reservoir, cottages and cattle pens at the terminal and planning an extension to the Bradwell maltings. Large crowds were attracted to the markets and to coursing events at Southminster; Burnham-on-Crouch, already noted for its oysters, became a minor resort and a centre for yachting, boat building and market gardening. Some excursions were run to the line and local services increased from six to ten daily between 1892 and 1914. Between the wars road competition was felt but settlement in the area still justified nine trains in each direction daily, with Saturday extras and five on Sundays in the summer of 1938.

Conversion to diesel multiple units in September 1956 and the electrification of the Southend line (December 1956) together gave the branch a new lease of life, raising it into the 5,000 to 10,000 passengers a week category, so escaping the Beeching axe. Sixteen up and fourteen down weekday services were offered in 1977 together with thirteen on Saturdays and, guaranteed by Essex County Council subsidy, nine on summer Sundays. By 1979 1,000 commuters were using the line daily, a total now to rise sharply as the County Council began development of the 'New Town' of South Woodham Ferrers—the 1981 population was 7,017 and rising steadily; meanwhile between 1961 and 1981 Burnham-on-Crouch and Southminster had grown from 4,167 to 6,308 and 1,897 to 3,206 respectively. Such trends led in January 1984 to approval of electrification plans. The use of steel pile mast bases (driven by compressed air and requiring only one line possession at each catenary) made the work speedy and at £3m relatively cheap. After partial implementation in preceding weeks, full electric operation began on 13 May 1986. By 1989 the weekday service had settled to twenty-two down, twenty-three up; Sunday services, nine each way and no longer subsidised, run throughout the year. Four up and three down each weekday are through London trains, the former filling before they leave the branch. Freight facilities were withdrawn in 1965 and sand traffic from Southminster (182,000 tonnes in 1975) has ceased, but on Thursdays a path is left for a nuclear waste train from Southminster (the material brought by road from Bradwell Power Station) to Temple Mills and on to Sellafield.

CHAPTER III

Colchester, Clacton and Harwich

COLCHESTER

The ECR's Colchester terminal, opened to passengers on 29 March 1843, lay a mile north of the town centre, convenience having been waived for the sake of cheaper land and avoidance of awkward gradients. Its position tempted Samuel Morton Peto to speculate in the nearby £15,000 Victoria Station Hotel (designed by Lewis Cubitt, later of King's Cross fame), but the line's small traffic, and the success of the established inns in sending omnibuses to meet each train, undermined the venture from the start, and by 1850 the building, now a hospital, had been converted into an asylum. Even the advent of the Eastern Union from Ipswich on 15 June 1846 (goods services began on 1 June and there was a formal opening on 11 June) to an end-on junction with the ECR and use of that company's station failed to save it.

Fortunately for Colchester and future railway operators the EUR had abandoned its original intention of an independent through station on the Nayland Road, even farther north of the town, and a junction with the ECR half a mile beyond the latter's terminal. Instead it had adopted an option under its 1844 Act whereby it could enter the town along the route selected by the ECR in 1836, from the point of intersection, 2½ miles out, with its own projected line. Compensation had to be paid as the ECR had purchased some land in preparation for an extension to Harwich. A legacy of the arrangement was the difficult curves through the station area which, until 1962, were to restrict through running to 40 mph.

In 1841, with a population of 17,790, Colchester was a quiet market and harbour town giving no indication of future prominence. Today, however, with 81,945 inhabitants in 1981, it holds its own between Ipswich and London as the commercial centre for extensive areas of Essex, has a professional football team and county cricket ground, and contains the University of Essex. It also has considerable industrial importance with engineering, milling, malting, brewing, clothing and printing dominant amongst many diverse activities; it was in fact a principal . contributor to the traffic flow of nearly 2,000,000 tons carried in the first twenty-one weeks of 1960 that led on 13 June 1960 to the inauguration of the 'East Essex Enterprise' express freight, starting daily at Chelmsford, calling at Witham, Colchester and Ipswich and giving next-day deliveries in the Midlands, North and Scotland. This ended in April 1966 with the inauguration of the National Freight Train Plan, but the town remains on the freight network. At the Hythe is a coal and scrap metal terminal and in July 1985 Speedlink began a service carrying DAF road-trucks to Scotland and Northern Ireland.

Coastal trade through the Hythe was always important, but Colchester's growth derived essentially from the railway network that grew round it in the forty years after 1843. In 1849 the Colchester, Stour Valley, Sudbury & Halstead (Chapter VII), operated by the EUR, opened from Marks Tey to Sudbury, reaching Colchester by running powers over the ECR and bringing into the town much of the traffic hitherto conducted along the Stour between Sudbury and Manningtree. Earlier, on 1 April 1847, the same company had opened a 1½ miles goods branch from near the station to the Hythe, already a busy centre for coal and corn. This harbour branch was to provide the nucleus for much industrial development, but it was also to preserve the navigation (immediate river improvements were stimulated between 1847 and 1854) and provide the basis for the lines into the Tendring Hundred where development, particularly at Clacton, gave Colchester an accession of strength at a time when agricultural depression might have imposed a severe check. On 8 May 1863 the Tendring Hundred Railway was built from the Hythe branch a further 2½ miles to Wivenhoe (see below), and on 1 March 1866 it completed a short line from junctions at the Hythe and East Gate to St Botolph's station near the centre of Colchester as authorised in 1862. The line to St Botolph's became particularly important for parcels and freight, but with the growth of Walton (reached by the THR in

1867) and Clacton (given its railway in 1882) it acquired substantial passenger traffic, being used both as a terminal and, with reversal, as an intermediate station. Meanwhile, the Colne Valley line (1860), and the Hadleigh (1847) and Harwich (1854) branches were serving Colchester and in 1865 the GER's extension of the Sudbury line to Shelford, just south of Cambridge, opened up further important outlets. A GER bus route to West Mersea in the years prior to 1914 completed this pattern of service.

Trade so grew that in 1844 the Corn Exchange of 1820 had to be replaced, a process necessary again in 1884 despite the current depression; similarly the cattle market, where from 1843 London dealers made extensive purchases each week, had to be moved to a larger site in 1861 and then replaced in 1898. From the early 1850s thousands of rose blooms were despatched daily in season by rail to London from the newly-established gardens; during the depression market gardening and fruit growing were developed locally and in the same period Colchester gained a steel roller mill. The town itself, with a population rising to 19,443 in 1851, 23,730 in 1861 and 38,373 by 1901, grew largely towards the main-line station (popularly known as North), but by 1860 the old part had been greatly improved under powers that had lain dormant until the railways arrived. In 1856 the new barracks marked the beginning of Colchester's rise as a permanent and leading military centre, the choice of site being much influenced by the excellence of rail communication and especially the opening of the Harwich branch in 1854. By the 1890s 1,600 to 2,000 troops were regularly stationed there (a valuable support of local commerce) and army traffic had become an important feature of railway operation, although the THR had never implemented powers to construct a tramway from St Botolph's to the camp area. Another valuable benefit to the railway was the development of the local oyster trade to a national level so that by 1891 the Colne beds were earning £5,000 to £10,000 a year. But it was in the industrial field that the principal gains were seen. Brewing, malting and milling had greatly expanded, and newcomers included brick making (1848), patent starch (1859), footwear and clothing (1860s), but most striking was the impetus given to engineering, epitomised in 1865 by the establishment of Paxman's, a firm soon to gain an international reputation; in recent years it made engines for the HST 125s.

The main-line station has evolved with the town. In 1854 refreshment facilities, extra sidings and a new telegraph office were provided for £1,012. Rebuilt in 1865 it was again remodelled in 1894 (by John Wilson). War prevented LNER plans for extension and resignalling, but in 1962, in connection with electrification the whole area was modernised at a cost of £1¼m. Two extra platform tracks were added (creating the longest platform in Great Britain), colour light signals installed, a diesel depot opened and a 1,200 yard dive-under for the down Clacton line provided. Over the weekend of 3–5 December 1983 a two storey electronic signal box was commisioned, initially controlling 35 route miles but later 95, the main line just east of Chelmsford to Diss, plus branches. In 1964 ticket sales were 401,874 ordinary and 7,137 season, but in 1975 502,526 of the former and 11,153 weekly, 8,456 monthly and quarterly and 1,070 annual season tickets. By 1980 2,280 commuters used the station daily.

THE TENDRING HUNDRED

Clacton-on-Sea (43,571 inhabitants in 1981), equipped with every amenity expected of a modern resort, accommodating 70,000 or more annual visitors and attracting thousands of day trippers from London and a wide area of the eastern counties, now developing a range of light industries (eg TV and radio components) and, with its suburb of Holland-on-Sea, containing a growing number of London commuters, has an air that belies its comparatively recent origins. As late as 1871, when a speculative land company first produced a development plan, it was still a rural village with a population of only 1,206, but by 1875 'handsome residences' had 'sprung up in all directions' and hotels, gas, public halls and other amenities, including a pier (1873), were complete or in hand. The 1881 population was still only 1,963, but in 1882, a branch railway was built from Thorpe-le-Soken: by 1901 the town had grown to 7,456 and spending at least one summer day there had become a habit for thousands of Londoners and residents of Essex.

Walton-on-the-Naze had begun to develop as a select resort after the opening of the ECR to Colchester in 1843, but had only

729 inhabitants in 1851. The railway from Colchester, a brave enterprise designed to develop Walton's popularity and boost local agriculture, arrived in 1867, and between 1871 and 1901 population grew from 1,070 to 2,014. By 1901 there were five large hotels and some 6,000 annual visitors, with Londoners having displaced Essex and Suffolk gentry as the principal clients; the making of pump machinery (1875), an iron foundry and a brick works had meanwhile broadened the base of the economy. At Frinton population grew from 55 in 1881 to 644 in 1901 although the principal growth, primarily residential, was to occur after 1903 through the efforts of Sir Richard Cooper. The 1981 population of Walton and Frinton combined was 11,413 and, as at Clacton, London commuters have long been settling there.

The Tendring Hundred Railway, incorporated in 1859, opened on 8 May 1863 and was operated by the GER for 70 per cent of the receipts. It originated as a 2½ mile long venture from the Hythe branch to Wivenhoe, the port of Colchester where vessels too large to reach the town were served by lighters. The inconvenience of double manual transhipment, main-line competition and the deepening of the Colne to the Hythe (1854) ruined Wivenhoe as a port but the branch helped its establishment as a principal packing station for oysters and a yachting centre that reached the peak of its fame in the 1870s.

In 1863 the THR was authorised to extend 14 miles to Walton from a point ¼ mile beyond its station at Wivenhoe, the intervening section having been appropriated in 1861 by the Wivenhoe & Brightlingsea, although construction had not yet commenced. In 1864, the THR was obliged to obtain further powers whereby it could build this short section itself if the W & B remained in default by the November; it did, and disputes over costs (all to be borne by the W & B), and subsequently over the division of receipts, were to last a full decade. Other delays ensued from the bankruptcy of Munro, the contractor, obliging Bruff, the THR engineer, to complete the work, and so it was 8 January 1866 before the line opened to Weeley, 28 July 1866 before Kirby Cross was reached and 17 May 1867 when the single-track line was finally completed through to Walton.

Meanwhile the Mistley, Thorpe & Walton, also incorporated in 1863, had run into serious difficulties. Designed to bring in traffic from Ipswich and areas to the north, it owed its success in

Parliament, as did the THR extension bill, to the favour of the GER which promised financial support to both, but the price had been further Acts of 1864 causing both lines to deviate to a junction at Thorpe-le-Soken and so avoid wasteful duplication of routes into Walton. Work had begun in April 1864 but Munro had made such slow progress that he was dismissed in 1865. Disagreement over accounts, however, made him refuse to hand over the works: the upshot was a pitched battle on 11 April between fifty of his own men and sixty Harwich longshoremen hired by the company to effect his removal. The new contractor proved little better and by the close of 1868, with the company owing him £12,000, all work had again ceased. Its credit gone, the company was dissolved in 1869, the few rails actually laid being sold. The East Essex revived the concept in 1873 but achieved nothing.

THR services at first comprised three or four trains daily between Colchester and Walton with Sunday services in the summer only. Good London connections were provided and in the summers of 1869 and 1870 a two-hour journey to Walton was possible each day. The GER offered reduced rates and ran excursions to the line from places such as Cambridge (for 6s in 1876), but progress was slow and it was only the acceptance of debenture stock by creditors in 1874 that saved the company from serious financial difficulties and gave it a breathing space. The real boost came in 1882 when on 4 July the independent Clacton-on-Sea Railway, authorised in 1877, opened its 4½ miles single track to Thorpe-le-Soken; a Walton-facing spur was authorised but never built. The new line was worked by the GER for 60 per cent of the receipts until purchased by it on 1 July 1883; the THR (from 1882 also worked at 60 per cent instead of 70) was absorbed on the same day on the very favourable terms of £70 ordinary GER stock for £100 of its own.

Under GER management traffic rose steadily, although as late as 1892 basic local services, normally dividing and reassembling at Thorpe-le-Soken, comprised only six each way daily. However, summer visitors continued to increase and the re-establishment of two-hour London connections was amongst factors encouraging the beginnings of commuter settlement in the area. The introduction of two daily through services in the 1890s was in direct recognition of this; already railway services and the fortunes of Clacton and Walton were involved in the spiral of mutual stimulation that continues still. Between 1884 and 1886 the Colchester to Wivenhoe section was doubled, that from Great Bentley (where there was a brick works) to Thorpe-le-Soken in 1890, and the intervening section in 1898; Frinton station had been opened on 1 July 1888 and in 1899 crossing loops were installed at Great Holland (on the Clacton line and for summer use only) and Kirby Cross station. In the years immediately prior to 1914 the principal developments were in the London services, the best down time falling to 102 minutes and then 95 in the 'Radical Alterations' tables. Restaurant facilities had appeared on the Monday morning up service in 1898 to balance the down working of the famous Saturday midnight supper train (in that year reaching Clacton in the then exceptional time of 97 minutes), but in October 1910 a specially-built set was provided for daily use on the 7.03 am up and the 5.06 pm down.

Between the wars these trends developed further. From November 1920 a daily Pullman car was tried on the Clacton service but proved unsuccessful and was withdrawn in July 1924. On the other hand the 90-minute summer-Sunday Pullman excursions begun on 16 July 1922 (until 1929 named the 'Clacton Pullman', and then to 1939 the 'Eastern Belle') became a very popular feature; the 'Eastern Belle', ranging widely over the LNER system each summer day, sometimes additionally included Clacton and Walton in its weekday itinerary from Liverpool Street. By 1939 there were basically five down and six up through workings between London and Clacton daily, the best down time being 93 minutes; one Walton and two Clacton trains each way, specially designed for business men, offered restaurant facilities. On 30 November 1929 a rebuilt station was opened at Clacton, and in spring 1938 Frinton was made a crossing point: on 12 January 1941 double track and automatic and semi-automatic colour-light signals were brought into use between Thorpe-le-Soken and Clacton, completing work begun under the 1936 scheme of government loans at 2½ per cent. Unsought had been the necessity in 1929 to relay further inland nearly a mile of track between Frinton and Walton threatened by coastal erosion.

During the 1950s national trends encouraged both a boom in

GREAT EASTERN RAILWAY

A DAY AT THE SEA-SIDE.

On Wednesday, August 2nd, 1876,

A SPECIAL CHEAP

EXCURSION TRAIN

TO

WALTON-ON-THE-NAZE

AND BACK,

Will run as under :—

From	Train at	Fares to Walton & back.	
		First Class.	Covered Cars.
	a.m.		
Cambridge........	6 20	6s.	3s.
Shelford..........	6 26		
Linton	6 40		
Saffron Walden....	6 25		
Bartlow	6 45		
Haverhill	7 0	5s.	2s. 6d.
Clare	7 20		
Melford	7 40		
Walton, arr. about	9 45		

Returning from Walton at 7.0 p.m. the same day.

No Luggage allowed.

London, July 1876.   S. SWARBRICK, General Manager.

PRINTED AT THE COMPANY'S WORKS, STRATFORD.

Encouraging the seaside habit

seaside towns and extension of commuter settlement. British Railways continued the long tradition of excursions from London and the eastern counties generally, and on summer Saturdays Clacton was widely connected by through services; in 1958, for example, these included trains to and from Leicester, Birmingham, Manchester, Bury St Edmunds and Cambridge as well as twenty-five from Liverpool Street; Walton had three London services to itself as well as portions on twelve of those to Clacton. Summer-Sunday workings in that year included eight up and four down London services and one each from Cambridge, Bury St Edmunds and Braintree. In the previous summer a further train had begun and terminated at Haverhill on the Cambridge line.

Weekday services were transformed from 5 June 1950 with the 'Clacton Interval Service', hourly from London in the summers, two- or three-hourly in the winters, mostly equipped with buffet cars and additional to the business expresses. Thus, even in winter there were seven or eight daily trains to London with numerous additional connections at Colchester. Late in 1957 'Britannias' first appeared on the line and from 9 June 1958 enabled the business trains to be accelerated, the best to 89 minutes up as compared with 104 in the previous summer. On 15 September 1958 winter expresses were increased to nine daily in times of 97 to 110 minutes up, and 98 to 108 down, except for one of 133 up and the star performances of the 'Essex Coast Express' (introduced 9 June 1958) of 89 up, 86 down. Further acceleration came from 5 January 1959 when 'Britannia' schedules were extended to the Interval Service, so that in that summer thirteen of the seventeen daily trains made the up journey from Clacton in 102 minutes or less, Walton portions requiring an additional 8 to 16 minutes. Thereafter electrification works on the main line between Colchester and Chelmsford caused some temporary retardation.

The decision to electrify the lines to Clacton had been made in the mid-1950s, as a means of further encouraging traffic and of alleviating the serious operational problems of peak Saturday congestion at Clacton (where perhaps 12,000 passengers would be handled), the single track into Walton and the seven-minute pause for marshalling at Thorpe-le-Soken. Continuation of the Chelmsford scheme at 1,500 volts DC was initially determined, but in 1958 the Colchester–Clacton–Walton lines, possessed of a self-contained local traffic as well as the through workings, were chosen as an ideal testing ground for the new British Railways standard of 25 kV 50 cycles AC (a short 6·25 kV section was to be inserted for test purposes at Great Bentley). Work included the alteration of twenty-two bridges and track at several stations, new sidings at Clacton, Walton and Stanway (near Colchester), continuous track circuiting to allow abolition of block working and closure of intermediate boxes, and searchlight signals (except between Thorpe-le-Soken and Walton where semaphores were retained). The scheme was complete by March 1959; on 16 March multiple electric units with four-car sets working in tandem were introduced on existing timings. On 13 April a new half-hourly service was inaugurated, intermediate calls being staggered and alternate trains giving fast London connections at Colchester. Frequency was reduced somewhat in the summer to avoid straining line capacity.

Through electric working to London became possible in late 1962, but it was 7 January 1963 before the ten coach main-line multiple-units appeared and 17 June before the revised time-table was introduced. By October 1989 this had evolved into a daily weekday service of twenty-four each way, built around a basic hourly provision, with the best trains scheduled at 82 minutes down and 87/88 up. Buffet cars were withdrawn in 1980 but from May 1986 light refreshments were again offered on a number of trains. Summer Saturday services to Clacton have been progressively whittled away from the initial three per hour to two and then one; the once numerous provincial through trains had already declined and had ended at the close of the 1967 season with that to Leicester. In May 1982 further changes affected Walton when division of trains at Thorpe-le-Soken was largely discontinued, a shuttle service providing the Walton link. One through weekday service was left until in May 1990 nine down and eleven up were restored, Clacton's share falling to twenty down and eighteen up.

Traffic not developing as hoped, the Colchester/Clacton/Walton services had to be subsidised to the extent of £284,000 in 1972 and £392,000 in 1973. At that time commuter traffic had not yet become a major element, and too much depended on the weather and its effect on day trippers; thus, while tickets collected at Clacton were 772,075 in 1959, the 1964 total was only 588,484 (comparable with the 589,693 of 1958). More significant for the future was Clacton's sale of season tickets, rising from 2,401 in 1958 to 2,874 in 1964 and 6,986 in 1975; a 1980 survey revealed 1,900 London passengers boarding early morning services, (567 at Clacton, 99 at Walton) of which the Walton direct service and six from Clacton arrive in the capital before 9.30 am. Here is a solid future; as if in confirmation a new electric traction maintenance depot opened at Clacton on 17 July 1971.

While the former THR lines have flourished, the Wivenhoe & Brightlingsea branch has now disappeared. Incorporated in 1861 to make Brightlingsea, a small harbour town on the Colne of 2,585 inhabitants in 1861, a place of 'considerable commercial importance', it was initially unable to raise sufficient capital. Only in 1864 when the GER, after blocking a proposed extension towards Clacton, offered one-third was the project enabled to proceed, the THR meanwhile having constructed the first quarter of a mile out of Wivenhoe (see above). Built by Munro the branch opened on 18 April 1866. Single track, without intermediate stations and with the swing bridge over Alresford Creek as the principal engineering feature, it was worked by the GER for 40 per cent of the receipts (except August 1876, a period of dispute, when the W&B hired stock and trains had to terminate short of Wivenhoe station), until purchased outright for £31,000 in June 1893. This was then a good bargain.

Inadequate depth had prevented harbour development at Brightlingsea and the quay begun by the W&B in 1866 remained unfinished, but the town had flourished as a yachting centre and resort for day trippers from Colchester and by 1901—on the last day of which the old station burnt down to the great pleasure of the townsfolk—had grown to a population of 4,501. In addition Pyfleet oysters and fishing had developed, bringing further traffic. However, being too much in the shadow of Clacton, the town's growth then virtually ceased, and in 1961 it numbered only 4,801. The branch continued to carry oysters, fish and trippers and, each November to March prior to 1939, despatched regular consignments of sprats in continental wagons to the train ferry at Harwich; but by the 1950s it was suffering badly from road competition. The whole section from the Hythe to Brightlingsea had always been susceptible to flood damage, notably in 1897 (on 29 November passengers on a branch train had to be rescued by boat), 1903, 1921 and 1928, and when on 31 January 1953, the night of the great storm and exceptionally high tide that inflicted heavy damage and loss of life all around the region's coast, three miles of the branch were washed away (in addition to blockage of the Hythe–Wivenhoe section) the opportunity was taken to propose total closure; but pleas for the interests of the town and the oyster trade led to resumption of services on 7 December. From 4 March 1957 diesel units were employed and the Colchester service was greatly improved, but by 1963 less than 600 a day were using the line and two-thirds of these were concentrated on six of the thirty or so trains. A bus service passed Alresford on the electrified Clacton line and freight could be handled more economically by road from Colchester; total closure occurred on 15 June 1964.

COLCHESTER TO IPSWICH

The decision of the ECR to terminate its line at Colchester was a major disappointment to Norfolk and Suffolk in general, but a matter of grave concern to the merchants of Ipswich and Norwich who were ever fearful of isolation. During 1839 the ECR proprietors in the two counties obtained a rule nisi in the Bail Court to compel fulfilment of their company's 'original contract with the public', and followed this with an application for a writ of Mandamus, but in 1840 Parliament's refusal to extend ECR powers beyond the July of that year effectively closed the issue. Initiative now passed to the districts most concerned, and in 1842 resulted in the incorporation of the Yarmouth & Norwich, and then, in 1843, the projection of the Norwich & Brandon, developments which threw Ipswich into consternation, heightened when it became clear that even if the ECR did extend to the Norwich & Brandon from Colchester the town could expect no more than a branch from Hadleigh. All representations proving vain, Ipswich did what probably the ECR had hoped from the start and produced its own scheme to connect the town with the ECR at Colchester. The leading spirit was John Chevallier Cobbold, an enterprising speculator from a wealthy Ipswich brewing and shipping family, a solicitor to the original ECR board.

Named the Eastern Union in reference to various current pro-
jections north of Ipswich, the new company was incorporated
on 19 July 1844.

Although only seventeen miles in length the EUR line presented many difficulties amongst which the negotiations for
entry into Colchester, the timber-pile viaducts over the two
arms of the Stour (the Cattawade bridges) and the high overline
road bridge of five 30 ft arches at Brantham (designed by Barnes
of Ipswich) were the principal sources of delay. In all, the line,
designed by Locke with Peter Bruff of Ipswich the resident
engineer, had cost £270,000 when it was opened for goods on
1 June and passengers on 15 June 1846. In the early days good
traffic was built up, but then, with the EUR's extension to Norwich (December 1849), ECR co-operation turned to rank obstruction. A revenue pool was negotiated on London–Norwich
traffic, but this the ECR, not content with its unjustifiable ratio
share of four in five, violated in both letter and spirit until, after
ineffectual recourse to litigation, a disgusted EUR repudiated it
in March 1851. The ECR declared its intention to 'leave no
means whatever untried to destroy "EU" traffic'; through bookings at Colchester were refused except at rates totally unremunerative to the EUR, and ECR carts from Colchester, Newmarket and Attleborough trespassed deeply into the latter's
territory, even to Ipswich itself.

Overall on the EUR receipts rose, from £111,000 in 1850 to
£132,000 in 1853, but so did expenses, from 49 to over 60 per
cent, and the capital debt could not be supported. Thus, despite
202,714 passengers and a freight revenue of £32,611 in the first
half of 1853, the EUR was obliged to capitulate on terms that

---

THE CAMBRIDGE MAIN LINE

*18 (top)   Railways have been a major benefit to education in rural
areas; in this Newport scene of 1959 boys of the local Grammar School
are about to board their special train for Elsenham, Stansted and towards
Bishop's Stortford. Note the relief goods line behind the island and the
agricultural merchant's siding beyond the down platform.*

*19 (bottom)   Transformation at Bishop's Stortford in August 1960.
Remodelling is nearly complete and suburban electrification to London
imminent. An express from Cambridge is entering the up platform*

72

made Cobbold tell Waddington, 'a strong minority of our board consider that you have done us'. The agreement, operative from 1 January 1854, was a tripartite one under which the ECR was to work the EUR and the Norfolk, sharing profits in a 5:1:1 ratio after deducting expenses at the actual rate on its own lines and at a fixed 46 per cent for those of its partners. The EUR was enabled to complain with some justice that although owning one-fifth of the lines it received only one-seventh of the profits, and that even this was dependent on the ECR's efficiency in cutting its own expenses; the fixed 46 per cent was also resented, as at the time the ECR level was believed, erroneously, to be only 41 per cent. Nor did the ECR endear itself to the EUR by charging 4¾ per cent interest on the £200,000 it lent for the redemption of preference stock, and by paying only £149,751 11s 6d for EUR rolling stock and ships when an independent assessment in 1853 had placed their value at £199,000. In the event misgivings were justified, the ECR persisting with high rates and inadequate stock and never paying the EUR more than £90,000 in a year to support a capital debt that by 1856 had reached £2,948,009.

After 1854, little distinguishes this section from that west of Colchester, other than the 1897 installation of water troughs at Halifax Junction (Ipswich) to facilitate the non-stop runs of the 'Cromer Express' between London and North Walsham, begun that year. Colour light signalling in 1984 and transfer to the new Colchester box (27–29 July 1984: with closure of the Manningtree box, Colchester no longer passed trains to it and then received them back) prepared the way for electrification, the new services being inaugurated on 13 May 1985. Local

---

CAMBRIDGE MAIN LINE BRANCHES

20 (top)   Saffron Walden station in 1956 looking towards Bartlow and with a push and pull unit at the platform. The promoters' hopes that this would become a busy through line into Suffolk never materialised

21 (centre)   Thaxted in 1951, the terminal of an undistinguished line that was open only from 1913 to 1953, and a representative of the 'Farmers' lines' mentioned in the text

22 (bottom)   Ware on the Hertford branch in 1956. The line was electrified in 1960

development has been minimal and in the agricultural slump of the 1880s rents fell as much as 60 per cent. Bentley, where in the 1876–7 winter a slip coach was detached for Hadleigh, closed to freight on 13 July 1964 and passengers on 7 November 1966; Ardleigh, from the 1890s gaining much traffic from local orchards and seed beds, closed for freight on 7 December 1964 and completely on 6 November 1967. Manningtree, where a railside quay was precluded by the EUR's need for economy, lost heavily to Mistley where there were such facilities, and despite GER cattle pens (1864), a residual river trade in coal, corn and timber, and a large maltings shrank in population from 1,255 to 872 between 1841 and 1901. Since the 1970s the town has attracted commuters—some 250 a day by 1980 but more since electrification—and in 1986 the former goods yard was converted into a car park. The 1981 population was 3,946. Brantham, near the Cattawade and enjoying both rail and water facilities, gained a large xylonite factory in 1887; this remained rail served until 1983, the private sidings being taken out of use on 20 November of that year.

The 7 mile single track of the Eastern Union & Hadleigh Junction from Bentley, incorporated in 1846 with a capital of £75,000, was opened to goods on 21 August 1847 and to passengers on 2 September. It was in essence an EUR venture to block the ECR route to Norwich and to provide the basis for a possible extension towards Lavenham; with this in mind works for double track and a cutting for an Ipswich-facing spur were provided. The branch was formally absorbed by the EUR in 1848. A handful of daily trains, for example five in 1892, sufficed throughout its life. Hadleigh's milling and malting prospered for a time and some coconut matting, clothing and machinery making were established but the railway did not prevent a fall in the town's population from 3,679 to 3,245 between 1841 and 1901. In the present century, proximity to Ipswich and the disadvantage of branch status as compared to a place on the main line like Woodbridge precluded recovery. A new bus service to Ipswich permitted withdrawal of branch passenger facilities on 29 February 1932, although goods services remained until 19 April 1965, a reminder that Hadleigh was for long a useful agricultural railhead and in earlier depression the railway an encouragement to fruit and horticulture in the area.

HARWICH

Commencing with that of the ECR, many railway projects were designed to reach the ancient port of Harwich, but not until 1847 did the Eastern Union obtain powers to build from Manningtree and provide a pier there. However, financial difficulties and ECR hostility indefinitely postponed the start of construction; powers were renewed in 1850 but only in 1853 when, foreshadowing general agreement, the ECR guaranteed a 4 per cent return on construction costs, did the EUR commence the work. Estimated as £100,000, expenditure in fact reached £177,000, and when opened on 15 August 1854 the branch proceeded to lose money. In the first half of 1859 receipts were down to £1,609 and closure was a possibility. In the autumn of 1854 the ECR had assumed control of the North of Europe Steamship Company's sailings to Antwerp and these and a Harwich to Ipswich boat service also lost heavily to the extent of £5,976 in the first full year alone.

In July 1863, however, the GER, overcoming strong opposition from vested interests elsewhere, was authorised to operate its own steamers from the Town Quay. Such a development was essential to the recovery of Harwich which had sunk to 3,829 inhabitants in 1841; new Ipswich docks (1842), the efforts of the Norfolk Railway and the ECR to develop Lowestoft, reduction of passage time to London on the Thames by steam navigation and the growing strength of the Dover to Calais service had all dealt it grievous blows in its years without rail transport. Revival to a population of 4,588 in 1861 indicates the value of the railway in stimulating general trade and fishing.

Shipping services directly developed by railway interests were now effectively to exploit the size, shelter and deep water of this fine natural port. At first, and until its own vessels became available during 1864-5, using chartered steamers, the GER inaugurated a weekly cargo service to Rotterdam in October 1863. On 13 June 1864 its own fleet began a weekly passenger service which, however, became thrice weekly in the following month. From 1 August 1864 the Rotterdam sailings were joined by those to Antwerp, at first once a week but becoming thrice weekly in 1872 and daily from 1882. Initially competition for sea traffic was severe and in 1866 the two GER routes carried only 9,350 passengers, but once established the company won a major share. Numerous factors including the economic expansion of Germany and improved continental rail and port facilities such as the 'New Waterway' of 1872 from the Maas to the Hook (allowing fixed Rotterdam schedules from 1874) and the new port at the Hook of Holland in 1893, supplemented GER efforts in providing luxurious ships and fast rail connections. In 1897 130,000 passengers were conveyed on GER vessels. In 1904 the Rotterdam link became thrice weekly and freight only, the daily passenger sailings transferring to the Hook; the latter continues today after disruption in two wars and their immediate aftermaths. The Antwerp route remained daily to 1939 but after the war was thrice weekly and in 1956, its patronage suffering from air competition and, through war losses, the use of admittedly inferior vessels, became freight only before finally ceasing on 31 May 1968. Between the wars there were weekend luxury cruises, in a brave attempt to attract custom to the port, and also, in 1921, a short-lived unsuccessful attempt to establish a summers-only Zeebruggë passenger service; Hook passenger traffic was showing remarkable increases, including one of some 8 per cent as between 1927 and 1928, before the recession in the 1930s.

The most important development, however, was the introduction of the train ferries to Zeebruggë from a berth near the old Continental Pier in Harwich on 24 April 1924; the LNER provided rail access but the service was jointly operated by Great Eastern Train Ferries Ltd and a Belgian counterpart until in 1933 the LNER purchased the former and its three ferries. Speed, security and reduced handling made this for many years the most consistently expanding element in port traffic, doubling between 1950 and 1960 alone. From 1968 to 1975 the number of wagons handled declined from 59,834 to 36,622 but ample compensation had been found in Roll on/Roll off TIR container traffic which had increased from a mere 775 units to 4,467 in 1975 in the same years. Container traffic continued to flourish and in May 1979 the Hamburg and Bremerhaven ferries were transferred to Parkeston Quay, but rationalisation and organisational changes (and reputedly the loss of money by the Harwich operation) culminated in the decision to concentrate all train ferry work on Dover (for Dunkirk) and the last sailing was on 31 January 1987.

General freight had always been a major element in the port's economy, growth being halted only by two World Wars and the depression years of the 1930s. In 1901 total trade was valued at £19.5 million but in 1960 at £144.3 million (just under 2 per cent of the national total), a remarkable rise even allowing for changing values. The 1960s saw further rises; between 1962 and 1964 imports grew from 349,904 tons to 376,268, and exports from 169,566 to 220,048 tons. At that time the railway retained much of the port traffic, in 1964 despatching inland 328,754 tons (of which 91,065 were food and drink, 65,707 agricultural produce) in wagon-load consignments of 1 ton and over. Then came the container revolution. On 18 March 1968, Parkeston Quay having been strengthened and provided with two 30 ton widespan cranes as part of an £8m development scheme, a twice daily container service was commenced to Zeebrugge in two new, purpose built cellular ships (Sea Freightliner I and II) that required a turn-round time of only five hours. By 1970 container throughput from all services had so grown that during 1971 a £500,000 extension scheme, involving two further goliath cranes and a 650 ft storage shed, was implemented to increase handling capacity by 50 per cent. Meanwhile, the original Freightliner terminal was developing links with London, Birmingham, Liverpool, Manchester, Swansea and Glasgow and, through them, virtually all major centres. A daily service with the Ford plant at Halewood was instituted. The number of ISO containers handled was 23,177 in 1968 but 103,644 in 1975, totals of RO/RO TIR containers increasing from 8,300 to 42,230. On 31 December 1985, however, the Freightliner Terminal at Parkeston Quay closed, most container traffic being retained but most being transferred to Felixstowe. Even so, demand remained and it was re-opened on 27 February 1989.

The railway's most obvious contribution to the rise of Harwich was Parkeston Quay itself, designed to allow the expansion of GER steamer services and attract foreign shipping lines. At Harwich, space for additional facilities was lacking in the 750 yd wide peninsula: further handicaps were the distance between the quay and the station and the irksome attitude of the corporation in such matters as the supply of fresh water. The new quay, authorised in July 1874 and named after C. H. Parkes, the GER chairman, was sited 1½ miles up river on the marshy Isle of Ray where there is deep water at all tides. Its construction involved the moving of much of a nearby hill for material to stabilise the marsh and provide foundations for the causeways. It cost over £500,000, and when completed in 1883 was 1,800 ft long, of timber construction (rebuilt in concrete by the LNER) and offered seven berths. Besides full warehouse and railway facilities a luxurious GER hotel followed; eventually closed in 1965 this was additional to that in Harwich which opened on 12 July 1865, closed between 1908 and 1912, was used as an army hospital in World War I, reopened as a hotel in 1919 and finally closed at the end of the 1923 summer, subsequently becoming the Town Hall and eventually (1989) flats. A small township of railway houses was built on the mainland. The quay was improved under an act of 1904, a stone section (now the centre) was added in 1911 and on 1 October 1934 it was extended again, to its present length of 3,947 ft.

Railway enterprise has long attracted independent foreign sailings to the port; in 1880 Royal Danish Mail (subsequently the United Shipping Company) began thrice-weekly services to Esbjerg, increasing the frequency to four in 1908 and continuing today, daily (except Mondays) in the summer and twice per week in winter. From 1884 to 1914 there was a service to Hamburg, operated until 1887 by H. J. Perlbach & Sons and then by General Steam Navigation, and from 1910 to 1914 the Thule Line provided a link to Gothenburg. On 1 January 1927 the Zeeland Shipping Company transferred its Flushing service to Parkeston Quay, and after the war changed its continental base to the Hook, so giving a daytime sailing additional to the long established night crossing. The overall pattern has continued to evolve, on 12 June 1984 the former Tor line moving its base from Felixstowe to Parkeston, until in 1989, apart from the Hook services (now jointly operated by Sealink and Zeeland lines, the former using the 'St Nicholas', a £40m ship commissioned in the spring of 1986 able to accommodate 2,100 passengers and 500 cars and, at 30,000 tons, twice the size of its predecessors), there are regular passenger sailings to Esbjerg, Gothenburg and Hamburg (by the Danish DFDS) and to Kristiansand and Oslo (the Norwegian Fred Olsen

line). The increase in passenger traffic is more than compensating for the loss of the train ferries and reduction in container
handling. In 1962 624,919 passengers passed through Parkeston Quay but even by 1975 this had doubled to 1,238,407, and
has continued to expand. A very significant area of continuing
growth has been that of passenger-accompanied cars, 57,495 in
1968 but 130,469 even by 1975. In response to all these trends a
new passenger terminal was opened in 1972 (a new parcels' and
ticket office followed on 12 June 1984) and the platforms lengthened at Parkeston Quay station, the latter permitting the
closure of Parkeston Quay West (opened 1 October 1934), after
some months of disuse, on 1 May 1972.

The nightly Hook boats were served successively by the
'Continental Express' (with restaurant facilities from 1904),
and, after 26 September 1927, the 'Hook Continental'. Progressively more luxurious corridor sets were provided in 1904,
1924 and 1938, and from July 1921 to 1939 two Pullman Cars
were added to the formation. By 1914 these trains were scheduled to run the 69 miles from London in only 82 minutes, a
standard recovered after the war until 1932 when heavier loads
brought slowing to 87. The 'Day Continental', named on 14
June 1947 and successor to the pre-1939 'Flushing Continental'
took 80 minutes, cut to 78 by the late 1970s when the 'Hook
Continental' had been advanced to 80. Antwerp passengers
were given their first corridor set in 1905 and Pullmans between
the wars on what was named by the LNER as the 'Antwerp
Continental', also designed to serve the short-lived Zeebrugge
link. Prior to 1939 the 'Scandinavian' (named the 'Esbjerg
Continental' until 15 May 1930) ran in the summers only,
winter passengers being conveyed by a portion detached from a
Yarmouth buffet-car express, but by 1977 running daily, but
unnamed, throughout the year. Amongst the first cross-country services of its kind was the unofficially named 'North Country Continental' introduced in 1883 running via Ipswich, Bury
and March, the first to admit third class passengers to its dining
car (introduced 1891), given its first corridor set in 1906 and
offering through sections to Birmingham (to 1939), York (to
1939: until 1914 the main portion), Glasgow (1922–3 only),
Liverpool (until 1963) and Manchester. Only wars and the
floods of 31 January 1953 (when the line was breached at two

points and at Dovercourt small craft were washed on to the track) disrupted these services.

Electrification of the branch, fully implemented from 12 May 1986, and the changed pattern of shipping, did bring fundamental alterations. Twenty daily services are provided by multiple units including an hourly service to London (90 minutes) and some to Ipswich. The two express boat trains, locomotive hauled, are allowed 70 minutes. For two years, from 31 May 1987, these were accorded EuroCity status, and given the names 'Admiral de Ruyter' (9.45 down and 18.45 up in 1988) and 'Benjamin Britten' (19.45 down and 7.40 up). Services to the Midlands and North-West have been greatly extended. In 1990 the 'Loreley' runs daily to Manchester and Liverpool, detaching a Birmingham portion at Peterborough, and the 'Brittania' to Nottingham. For a short time the 'European' ran to Glasgow and Edinburgh.

On the branch itself double track was provided to Mistley in 1866 and the Ipswich facing spur at Manningtree on 29 August 1882. On 6 September 1882 work was completed to provide double track throughout and the diversion of the line via Parkeston Quay; the now redundant section from a point 2$\frac{1}{2}$ miles east of Wrabness to near Dovercourt was closed on 15 March 1883 and subsequently lifted. From 14 January 1968 the section between Parkeston East and Harwich Town was worked as single track on the direction lever system, the down line being preserved as a through siding; the whole was resignalled in the autumn of 1985.

Harwich (including Parkeston and Dovercourt) had grown to a population of 15,076 in 1981 from 10,070 in 1901 when nearly 2,000 were employed by the railway and the docks. Fishing and cement making were two activities fostered by GER. Full freight and coal facilities were withdrawn on 4 April 1983, leaving the yard as a 'specific user' depot, principally the traffic, shared with Parkeston Quay, in cars (in 1975 71,935 trade cars were handled). From 1846 and the opening of the EUR, Dovercourt developed as a minor spa, its population rising from 813 to 3,894 between 1841 and 1901. After 1945 the transit camp established at Upper Dovercourt made Harwich the principal port for the British Army of the Rhine; for some years specials to London, Manchester and Edinburgh ran in connec-

tion with the almost daily leave boats. Along the Stour barge
building remained important and at Mistley, where a short,
steeply graded branch (strengthened in 1960) gave it the advantage over Manningtree as a minor river and coastal port,
large maltings and, after 1900, the making of fertilisers and
farm foods flourished. Little development occurred at Bradfield
where the station closed on 2 July 1956.

CHAPTER IV

Ipswich and East Suffolk

In Ipswich industrial and market growth came prior to the railways; in vigorous efforts to recover the prosperity lost with the ending of the woollen export trade, the Gipping (containing fifteen locks in 16 miles) had been made navigable to Stowmarket in 1798 at a cost of £26,000, and the Orwell so improved under an 1805 Act that larger vessels were no longer restricted to Downham Reach 3 miles below the town; the harbour had been developed from 1815, and in January 1842 32 acres of wet docks, with a quay frontage of 2,780 ft, were opened to the immediate encouragement of foreign trade. As a direct consequence of these measures shipbuilding had been revived, old industries such as malting, brewing and Ransome's engineering (founded in 1789 and installing steam machinery in 1831) expanded, and new ones, including paper making and tobacco processing, established. Population had grown from 11,277 to 25,264 between 1801 and 1841, and ease of access to the sea had so boosted the markets (where at times corn fetched as much as 6s a quarter more than in Norwich) that carriers regularly visited them from as far afield as Norfolk.

Only a railway was missing to drive the advantages home. Hopes were prematurely raised in the 1824 to 1826 period by such projects as the Norfolk, Suffolk & Essex Railroad (London to Norwich), the London & Ipswich and the Port of Ipswich & Suffolk (to Eye) in 1836 by the ECR and in 1837 by a scheme for a Bury St Edmunds line. From 1843 the tantalising ability to get to London and back in a day by rail from Colchester heightened desire. Finally the town turned to self-help, impelled by fears of Norwich, the refusal of the ECR to come to the town except by a branch (and even that by no means certain), hopes for further commercial expansion and by such contributory factors as the land speculations made in Felixstowe by various Ipswich men (Cobbold himself had opened a hotel there in 1839) in anticipation of the ECR. The progress of the previous forty years had made a sound basis of local capital available and ensured that the town could create for itself a comprehensive network. It was on the triple foundations of the railways, the docks and free trade that modern Ipswich was raised.

The EUR (Chapter III) terminated its line at a temporary station just south of Stoke Hill, subsequently the site of the engine sheds. Any inconvenience involved was intended to be short-lived for, as undertaken with the Corporation in 1846, the permanent station was to be on the line of the Ipswich & Bury, a company incorporated in 1845 with £400,000 capital and sharing with the EUR six directors (including Cobbold) and the same offices, secretary, engineer and contractor; such dualism was common, for amongst other advantages it avoided the failure of the whole in that of a part. The 26¼ miles line of the I&B (absorbed by the EUR on 1 January 1847 and formally amalgamated with it on 9 July), was designed to oust the influence of King's Lynn from the central districts: it opened to goods on 30 November 1846, formally on 7 December and to passengers on Christmas Eve. In Ipswich a 361 yd tunnel had been driven through Stoke Hill to the EUR at Halifax Junction, from where Bury trains were reversed in and out of the terminal, an arrangement that perforce continued for some years as financial difficulties and then, after 1854, haggling with the ECR over the cost, delayed until 1860 the completion of the permanent station, immediately north of the tunnel. At first it had only one long platform, but in 1883 the present island was added on the down side. A goods depot was opened in 1866 by the GER and there were also a docks branch (as today, the quayside rails were owned by the dock authorities) and a branch of 74 chains to the Orwell at Griffin's Wharf. Other railway amenities were to include regular GER steamer services to Harwich and Felixstowe and excursions on the Orwell, and, from 1905 to 1922, except from January 1917 to January 1920, a bus service to Shotley, which became the terminal of the Harwich motor-boat link that continued until 31 December 1961. Subsequent sections discuss the further growth of the network beyond Ipswich, in which the most important features were the line to Norwich (1849), the ability to reach the midlands and north without a detour via London (1854) and direct access to Lowestoft and Yarmouth (1859), Felixstowe (1877) and Harwich (in 1882 by the Manningtree North Curve). As a result, a huge area became tributary to Ipswich, which in its turn had progressively faster services from London, schedules falling from 115 minutes in 1874 to 84 by 1914 (Radical Alterations timetable), 80 by 1938 and 70 (67 by one up train) in the late 1970s.

Ipswich grew to a population of 32,914 in 1851, 37,950 in 1861 and 66,630 by 1901. Cheapness of land and labour, and the combination of excellent railway services and water facilities (the docks were steadily improved from 1852, and between 1877 and 1881 £80,000 was spent in providing accommodation for larger vessels), were powerful attractions to industry. In 1849 coprolite processing was transferred from Snape and in 1850 Fisons opened a fertiliser plant, reached by rail from the dock branch; other fertiliser firms, several from the Gipping valley, also moved into Ipswich and, from 1854, to former railway land at nearby Bramford. Other important developments included a silk mill (1855), stay and corset making (a factory instead of cottage industry from the 1870s and employing 600 by 1900), clothing, footwear, some laundry work (attracted from London by clean air as well as the general advantages) and the manufacture of sacking. Engineering was greatly expanded, and Ransome's (employing 900 men by 1855) not only began its present works in 1849 but in 1869 opened the Waterside works of Ransome & Rapier where particular emphasis was placed on the production of railway equipment, an aspect of the business that had mushroomed over the previous thirty years. By the 1890s the town had also become a leading milling and malting centre although, as with fertilisers, this perhaps owed more to water transport than to rail.

The docks were flourishing with up to 1,000 coastal sailings a year and regular links with Sweden, Norway and the Black Sea. In such trades as coal and corn (in the 1850s, when forty steam engines were at work in the town, 90,000 chaldrons of coal a year were being imported, and 300,000 quarters of corn exported), rail and coastal shipping facilities both complemented and stimulated the other. As a market also Ipswich boomed, each week drawing in thousands from wide areas of the country-side; as early as the 1850s 50,000 quarters of corn were changing hands annually in the town, but the Corn Exchange of 1850 soon became too small and had to be replaced in 1882. Rateable value jumped from £193,875 in 1884 to £339,213 in 1908 by which time real efforts had been made to improve the town's amenities and conditions, the latter long marred by much substandard housing that had grown up in association with the railways and docks.

Despite a marginal drop in population from the 123,312 of 1971 to 120,447 in 1981, modern Ipswich is a thriving provincial centre typifying the new East Anglia. Flourishing factory estates co-exist with the older engineering, brewing and agriculturally based industries, while the shops, sporting facilities and social life draw huge numbers from surrounding areas. The docks, modernised and extended, in 1988 handled nearly three million tonnes of imports and two million of exports, the former including 504,791 of petroleum. A container terminal opened on 13 November 1984 on Cliff Quay, a second following on the West Bank (aided by a government grant of £119,087). During 1988 194,810 containers were handled, some eight per cent involving the railway. In 1985 a large grain terminal was opened, rail services being introduced on 11 June 1985. Rail also has a share in the Ro/Ro traffic that has developed from 69,164 units in 1984 to 115,854 in 1988. Daily freight services link the town to both the Freightliner and Speedlink networks. For passengers, electric services to London became fully operational on 13 May 1985; in 1990 there are twenty-five daily weekday trains from London with a standard timing of 63 minutes but a best of 58. From 1983 to 1985 the station area was extensively remodelled. The site of the former Locomotive Depot (one of the four diesel depots in East Anglia) is used as a base for regional electrification works.

THE EAST SUFFOLK LINE

The line from Ipswich to Lowestoft and Yarmouth (South Town) began with the Halesworth, Beccles & Haddiscoe, a local venture incorporated in 1851 to join the river ports of Halesworth and Beccles to the Reedham–Lowestoft line of the

Norfolk Railway with which, in 1852, it was empowered to make a working agreement. Operated by the ECR, which leased the Norfolk Railway in 1848, its line, including the Beccles swing bridge, opened to goods on 20 November 1854 and to passengers on 4 December; by the end of the following June it was able to record a modest profit of £528. But meanwhile, in 1854, renamed the East Suffolk, it had been authorised to increase its capital to £450,000 and build southwards to Woodbridge where the EUR had undertaken to meet it from Ipswich by a line originally authorised in 1847 but never built and for which further powers were obtained in 1854. The ESR scheme also included branches to Leiston, Framlingham and Snape Bridge. To all this the ECR raised a howl of ineffectual protest, the general manager appearing at public meetings to speak against it, as it was too obvious that the new line would divide traffic with the Haughley to Norwich line which the ECR, after trying so hard to destroy it when in EUR hands, now controlled. It was essential that similar control be exercised over the ESR and the ECR agreed to work it but without the financial guarantees applicable to the original section.

A further reason for this caution lay in the activities of Sir Samuel Morton Peto. In furtherance of his far-reaching plans to elevate the status of Lowestoft (Chapter VIII), and recognising that the new line would afford more direct access to London than the existing route via Norwich, he not only became the principal subscriber to the Woodbridge extension but offered to lease the whole line for fourteen years at 6 per cent on a cost not exceeding £10,000 a mile; 3½ per cent was to be paid during construction. This in itself was innocuous, but in 1856 two newly-authorised companies, in both of which Peto had played a part, the Yarmouth & Haddiscoe and the Lowestoft & Beccles, accepted his proposal to lease them for twenty-one years at 6 per cent. At the same time he was feeling his way towards a line from Pitsea on the London, Tilbury & Southend (which he had on lease already) to Colchester, from where running powers would be sought over the EUR to Woodbridge. Thus, it was possible that a whole system from London to Yarmouth and Lowestoft could exist almost independently of the ECR.

The Pitsea line never materialised, but in 1856 Peto had gone on to start the process by which the Y&H and the L&B were amalgamated with the ESR, had revised his terms so that the whole line would be leased for twenty-one years and 6 per cent paid from 1 July 1857 whether open or not, and undertaken to provide double track from Yarmouth to Woodbridge, leaving only the Lowestoft to Beccles section and the branches as single. The general opening, with ECR operation, took place on 1 June 1859, the same day as the Ipswich to Woodbridge section, under Peto's guarantee: the lease in fact continued until 1861, when its termination was made a condition of entry into the GER.

Such absorption was desperately desired by the ESR proprietors who foresaw that the more powerful company would starve it of traffic and then, having ruined it, take it over on totally unfavourable terms. Two years had sufficed to expose the weaknesses of a line that above all owed its origin to the work of speculators such as Cobbold, who was in fact one of the directors. The situation had not changed since 1846 when Parliament had rejected the Ipswich, Norwich & Yarmouth project because of the sparsity of likely traffic. The ESR passed through extremely rural countryside and was faced on one side by competition from river and coastal navigation and on the other by that from the ECR's Norwich line; the numerous curves and steep gradients adopted in seeking the most economical means of traversing the river valleys and watersheds made it a slow and expensive line to work. All told, the ESR proprietors did well in 1862 to be awarded £340,000 in GER 4 per cent debentures and £335,000 in 4½ per cent preference shares, as well as ordinary shares to the value deemed appropriate to future revenue prospects by Captain Galton of the Board of Trade. In return, the GER was indemnified against the £86,488 simple contract debt still plaguing the company and all other liabilities.

Great ambition and high expenditure contrasted sadly with the line's future history; Lowestoft and Yarmouth (Chapter VIII) certainly grew but never sufficiently, except for peak holiday traffic, to justify two main-line approaches. There was little development between them and Ipswich and the whole area proved severely vulnerable in depression. Beccles, a railway crossroads, compensated for its lost river trade by an expansion of milling, malting, general and agricultural engineering, and in 1875 the advent of a London firm began its rise as a printing centre; but by 1901 its population had risen to only 6,898 from the 4,398 of 1851. Subsequently, pleasure boating, marine engineering and saw-milling became associated with the town, but in 1981 it still had no more than 8,903 inhabitants. During depression extensive local nurseries were established, and the section of movable platform swinging over the track to facilitate manual handling of heavy milk churns was a further reminder of the importance of this and other stations on the line over wide rural areas. This was particularly so at Halesworth, where large quantities of corn and flour were once despatched annually to London by rail. Local farmers supplied milk to Ilford; later, a factory was built near the station which until 19 April 1965 sent one or two tank-wagons of milk each day to London, the last regional survival of a once-extensive traffic. But despite this, Halesworth, where from 1922 to 1958 part of the station platforms swung over the tracks with the level-crossing gates, declined in population from 2,662 in 1851 to 2,253 in 1961, (1981: 3,927) little having come to make up for the lost Blyth trade. Saxmundham, a small market town, where again the staggered down platform was associated with a level crossing, registered a slight increase, but only from 1,180 to 1,543 over the same period (1981: 2,371). At Wickham Market the railway led to the remarkable growth of Whitmore's engineering works which, within a few years, founded a world market in mill and factory machinery before sudden collapse in the 1890s: nothing replaced it and the 1981 population of the town was only 2,611. Woodbridge, with its station near the harbour and a horse

---

EAST OF CAMBRIDGE

23 (top)   A train of horse-boxes between Cambridge and Newmarket in 1936. Six Mile Bottom should have been the junction for the Newmarket Railway's Cambridge branch, but when this opened in 1851 the original main line to Great Chesterford closed. The station closed in 1967

24 (centre)   Soham station in Great Eastern days. Note the variety of freight stock in the scene. This was the station destroyed by the explosion of an ammunition wagon in 1944

25 (bottom)   A Mildenhall branch train near Isleham in 1957 crossing typical Fenland country

tramway to the Sun Wharf, had already been injured as a market by the railway to Bury St Edmunds of 1846. The East Suffolk line permitted some recovery, but after providing an initial stimulus crippled trade through the harbour, so that overall the population fell from 5,161 to 4,403 between 1851 and 1901; some yachting and engineering, both owing something to the railway, later restored the position and helped to produce the 1971 level of 7,283 (in 1981: 7,224).

Not surprisingly with such a background services have always been fundamentally local in character and lightly loaded, an admixture of through London workings providing the backbone. In 1874 four stopping trains a day sufficed, three in each direction offering either London portions or connections; by 1883, and for some years to come, there were seven or eight daily trains including two or three through London services in each direction, the latter generally combining beyond Ipswich with a Norwich service. There was, however, a Mondays-only service each way between London and Yarmouth, taking 200 minutes, calling only at Ipswich and Beccles (for Lowestoft), and also at Halesworth from the summer of 1883. In the summer of 1904, when the seaside holiday habit had become firmly established, daily 150-minute non-stop runs were provided to and from Liverpool Street for both Yarmouth and Lowestoft. The latter train loaded badly, and in 1905 was combined with a Felixstowe portion, changed to Aldeburgh in the up direction in 1906; but the former continued until 1914, and after the war ran on Mondays, Fridays and Saturdays in the summers of 1927 to 1931 inclusive, in 147 minutes up; then, on Mondays and Fridays in the summers of 1932 to 1938, again took 150 minutes. In 1939, when of twelve daily up trains, nine provided through workings to London, five from Lowestoft and nine from Yar-

---

ELY: A FENLAND JUNCTION
26 (top)   A water-colour of about 1850 showing an up train approaching the level crossing on the Newmarket road prior to entering Ely station
27 (bottom)   A view in the latter days of steam looking south. The absence of development round the station and traces of the marsh on which it was built are clearly evident as is the position taken by the artist of 1850

mouth, it ran on Mondays and Fridays, with a Lowestoft portion attached during an advertised stop at Beccles; on Saturdays the run between London and Yarmouth was non-stop in both directions, the down train conveying a Lowestoft portion which worked on from Yarmouth via Gorleston. Under British Railways greater use was made of the line than ever before, traffic reaching a peak in the mid-1950s when up to twenty-five trains in each direction ran on summer Saturdays, including a holiday-camp special for Gorleston. From 5 June 1950 to 1958, the 'Easterling', running non-stop each way between London and Beccles, gave a daily summer service. Even winter services along the line reached ten or eleven daily in this period.

Summer Saturday traffic, itself declining from 1918, could not compensate for poor returns at all other times; moreover, fitted freight stock and diesel power, equalising speeds and increasing line capacity, were making the longer route via Norwich a viable alternative. Melton was closed to passengers on 2 May 1955 and Bealings on 17 September 1965 (after losing freight facilities on 19 April) and dmu operation was introduced from 5 January 1959, but the overall effect was marginal. Closure of the entire Yarmouth–Beccles section on 2 November 1959 (Yarmouth trains being diverted via Lowestoft) was no surprise. The threat still hung over the remainder. In 1963 a 45 mph speed limit was imposed to reduce track maintenance, and in March 1964 £40,000 a year saved by removal of staff from nine crossings, and booking facilities from six stations entirely and four partially. Even so 1965 costs (including the Aldeburgh branch) of £178,300 were still in excess of revenue at £154,800 and closure proposals were published. However, reprieve was won by the vigorous campaign of the East Suffolk Travellers Association and because of the undoubted hardship that would result in such an isolated area, and so only the Aldeburgh branch was closed (12 September 1966). The line was now designated a 'basic railway'. Track was largely singled (passing loops at Woodbridge, Saxmundham, Halesworth and Beccles), some forty level crossings were converted to automatic operation and, on 6 March 1967, conductor guards introduced on all local services, from November 1966 these numbering nine each way and second class only. Through London to Yarmouth South Town workings (eight up, ten down on summer Saturdays in 1966) were discontinued, but one express (with buffet car) to Lowestoft survived on weekdays, and initially four down and three up (two and one by 1976) on summer Saturdays. Freight between Beccles and Saxmundham ceased on 18 April 1966 although Brampton and Halesworth had lost their facilities earlier on 13 July 1964 and 19 April 1965 respectively.

For two months from 13 October 1980 revenue earning trials were conducted with the four-wheeled Leyland Railbus (LEV 1) but although local reaction was generally favourable this was not pursued. However, there followed the effective guarantee of the line's future, the pioneer use of Radio Electronic Token Block working, centred on Saxmundham, and giving radio contact between drivers and the three signalmen still required. Due in November 1985 but delayed by technical problems to 5 January 1986, this represented £1.25m in a total £1.6m investment, also involving continuous welded track (some from the York-Selby line and other from the GN&GE), automation of all level crossings (including reconversion of some from open to lifting barrier type), refurbishing of the line's dmu's (including new engines to give 600 hp per three car set) and completion of track singling, although leaving a double section from Halesworth to Darsham for crossing at speed. A 55 per cent return is expected. The last through London to Lowestoft working was withdrawn on 14 May 1984 (an alleged saving of £143,000 annually), but Melton station was formally reopened on 5 September 1984 (after two days in use) to share in the nine daily services each way.

Of the five branches, only that from Westerfield to Felixstowe remains intact. Opened to passengers on 1 May 1877 (freight a month later) together with a new pier and sea-wall, it was worked by the Felixstowe Railway & Pier Company of 1875, a property of Colonel George Tomline, the leading landowner in the area, and a forceful if eccentric personality who sought to create docks able to rival Harwich. At the time Felixstowe was still a village of less than 1,000 inhabitants despite coprolite working from 1843, a small flow of summer visitors since the completion of the EUR, and speculation such as Cobbold's 1839 hotel. Initially the company offered three daily services, terminating at an independent Westerfield station and worked by three tiny 2–4–0 tank engines, until on 1 September 1879 the GER assumed responsibility for operation, diverting trains to the main-line station at Westerfield and extending some of them to Ipswich. In the same year the local concern, renamed the Felixstowe Dock & Railway Company, was authorised to construct a dock basin. Completed in 1884 at a cost of £101,000, this enjoyed only moderate success, in 1892 one daily goods sufficing for the branch. The unexpected emergence of Felixstowe as a resort for fashionable visitors, including in 1891 the German Empress and her family, and for day trippers from Ipswich, gave a fillip to passenger traffic: seven trains a day were being provided in 1892, supplemented by GER steamer links with Ipswich and Harwich.

Confident in the line's future, the GER purchased the railway (but not the docks) in 1887 for £221,000, on 1 July 1898 opening the new Town station, central to the settlement that had developed on the cliffs rather than round the Beach (formerly Town) and Pier stations as Tomline had intended. As on the same day the section from Trimley to Beach station was closed, access now involved reversal in Town station. Traffic was carefully fostered. From the summer of 1905 to 1914 the formerly non-stop Lowestoft express called at Westerfield to detach a Felixstowe portion arriving in 117 minutes, a time bettered by two minutes from 1906 with a new train that detached a Clacton slip portion at Colchester. In 1920 the top-ranking Felixstowe Hotel was acquired by the GER; this was to remain railway property until sold in 1950. By 1936 excursion traffic had so developed that doubling of the track was planned, but war prevented this. In 1939 twenty-three daily summer services were provided (twenty-five on Sundays), but after 1945 patronage declined. There were still twenty trains daily in the summers of the 1960s, but by the late 1970s no more than a dozen; the branch by then closed on winter Sundays. Introduction of diesel multiple-units on 5 January 1959 ended through London workings, although with fast connections at Ipswich the capital remained within two hours journey time. Summer Saturday provincial trains (for example, from Sheffield) had also ceased. In 1965 99,743 tickets were collected at Town station but only 15,003 at Beach which, used in the summers only, closed entirely from 11 September 1967. Pier station, closed from 11 September 1939 to 3 June 1946 as a wartime economy, had finally closed on 2 July 1951, as had Orwell on 15 June 1959. In 1990 thirteen daily services were being provided and Town station had been reduced from four platforms to one, the site being for the most part incorporated into a shopping centre around Great Eastern Square. Felixstowe's 1981 population was 20,588.

Passenger decline, however, has been more than offset by the extraordinary rise of the docks from the obscurity of 1951, when Gordon Parker purchased them for £50,000, to major international status. In 1957 87,410 tons were handled, in 1965 630,000; the 1987 total was 12,706,863 tonnes. In 1957 18,522 containers were handled on the quayside but in 1988 913,178 in four modern terminals; indeed, since 1981, Felixstowe has been Britain's leading container port. Landguard Freightliner terminal opened on 28 November 1972, Beach Junction having been altered from 13 May 1970 ready to give direct access. The Trinity terminal, opened in October 1986 (since when it has been doubled in size) was given its own direct access by provision of a new 2,591 metres loop from near Trimley station to the original line at Beach Junction. This opened on 2 March 1987 at a cost of £1.9m of which the government had contributed forty per cent. Currently 170,000 containers annually are handled by the railway, including traffic transferred from Parkeston. Freightline services, supplemented by Speedlink, connect daily with London and destinations as far apart as Glasgow and Holyhead.

The single-track branch, 5 miles 5 furlongs long, from Campsea Ashe near Wickham Market to Framlingham was opened on 1 June 1859 as an ESR property. It was an undistinguished line on which five daily services sufficed in 1883, six in 1938. Speed restrictions and a very badly-placed terminal station made it readily susceptible to road competition and passenger services were finally withdrawn on 3 November 1952, although the Framlingham granaries and coal and beet traffic caused retention of a daily freight serving all stations except Parham until 19 April 1965; since then the track has been lifted. Framlingham, too near Ipswich and too dependent on agriculture, declined from 2,450 inhabitants to 2,005 between 1851 and 1961. Also opened by the ESR on the same day was the 1 mile 32 chains goods branch from Snape Junction, where the intended station was never built, to the maltings and small harbour, annually despatching 17,000 quarters of barley to London, of Snape. A daily goods train, formed by the diversion of a pick-up service from the main line, with all shunting at Snape done by horse, continued until 7 March 1960, in parts still along 30 ft rails laid in the 1880s. A 15 mph restriction applied even in GER days and wagons had to be propelled into Snape for lack of turn-round facilities there.

The Saxmundham to Aldeburgh branch was the other ESR construction from its main line. Initially intended to serve only Leiston, where Garrett's world-famed engineering works were established in 1778 and around which the town of 1,580 inhabitants in 1851, had grown (Garrett was an ESR director), it was opened on 1 June 1859. The same year, however, authority was obtained to extend to Aldeburgh, a small harbour and fishing town with a population of 1,627 in 1851, but growing in popularity with upper-class families as a resort; the extension was opened on 12 April 1860. Fishing was greatly boosted and as much as 70 tons of sprats and other catches were sometimes despatched by rail in a day; but by 1914 this and the surviving coastal trade had been crippled by shingle banks near the harbour. The GER and LNER both fostered the town with cheap rates and excursions, and from 1906 to 11 September 1939 one or two through coaches ran daily to and from Liverpool Street; very occasional visits were made by the 'Eastern Belle' touring train. On 29 July 1914 the growth of a garden village and country club led to the opening of Thorpeness Halt, but generally the area was too far from any centre and Aldeburgh station itself sited too inconveniently to attract day trippers, so the holiday trade has remained limited. Aldeburgh's 1981 population was only 2,911. At Leiston, with a crossing loop but only one platform, engineering was greatly expanded with the railway, Garrett's covering over 20 acres by 1907; besides the private sidings in the main works a short GER branch was built to a second plant. But little else developed to broaden the basis of the town's economy, and in 1981 its population ws no more than 5,133. This, and lack of major development at Aldeburgh, had confined daily services to levels fluctuating between five and nine, operated, with some through workings to Ipswich, by diesel units from June 1956. On 30 November 1959 Aldeburgh

lost its goods facilities, and in 1960 only the impending construction of the Sizewell power station won the line a five-years'
reprieve. In 1965 no more than 16,008 tickets were collected at
Aldeburgh, and on 12 September 1966, despite economies such
as reduced services and conductor guards, the branch closed.
Goods facilities were retained at Leiston until 7 May 1984;
Sizewell, however, with its gantry equipped siding, continues
to handle nuclear flasks (to and from Stratford) for the power
station.

From Halesworth and a platform alongside the main-line
station ran the independent 8¾ miles 3 ft gauge line of the
Southwold Railway, incorporated in 1876, and opened on 24
September 1879. The story that the materials and plant were
salvaged from the Woosung Railway of China is mythical. Its
purpose was to assist, by stimulation of fishing and of an inci-
pient holiday trade, the recovery of Southwold from the damage
done since the ESR had refused it a branch. Its presence certainly
led to considerable harbour improvements, and between 1908
and 1914 some 300 drifters were annually unloading there. The
holiday trade showed similar growth, three hotels being established between 1887 and 1900. Indeed, the line, despite its pic-
turesque character, its antique open coaches, its quaint locomotives and an apparent unconcern for the timetable that made
it a tourist attraction in itself, provided invaluable service to the
area, carrying coals and general merchandise in, and milk, other
farm produce and fish to the main line; 104,197 passengers and
12,824 tons of freight were conveyed in 1910, and from 1911 to
1913 ordinary dividends of 2 per cent were possible. During
World War I local army camps sustained traffic levels, but thereafter they steadily declined, while at the same time costs were
rising steeply (£3,000 between 1924 and 1925 alone); a 2 per
cent ordinary dividend was paid in 1922 but this was the last. In
1925 payment on the 5 per cent debentures ceased and 1926
brought the first working deficit, even if of only £4.

Bus competition was the immediate problem, improved road
services costing the line 10,000 passengers in 1926–7 and a further 25,000 in 1928 when the corporation allowed road coaches
to pick up within the town. But the roots of the trouble lay much
deeper. Lowestoft overshadowed Southwold (a GER bus service
between the two, operated from 1904 to 1913) and left the line

running in the wrong direction; the break of gauge and the need for transhipment of goods at Halesworth were fatal weaknesses in face of road competition (even earlier the Southwold gasworks near the line had relied on cheaper sea coal), as was the 16 mph speed limit when from 1928 buses were allowed 20 mph. The capital debt was too heavy, with construction costs of £8,504 per mile and such expenses as the 1907 rebuilding of Blyth swing bridge, to allow replacement of time-worn stock or the conversion to standard gauge first considered in 1899, together with an extension to Kessingland to meet a GER branch from Lowestoft. Lastly there were the company's own follies. One was the refusal to provide a harbour branch until 1914, by which time the war had destroyed the fishing. More serious were the rejections of offers of purchase from the GER and the LNER, in 1893 and 1923 respectively; in 1929 the LNER flatly refused to have it. After closure on 12 April 1929, the company remained in existence and track and stock lay derelict until removed for war salvage in 1941–2. Various schemes for revival have come to nothing and in 1971 Southwold, its harbour used only by yachts and other small craft despite the £60,000 expended on development between 1906 and 1932, had a population of only 1,998, a decrease of 111 from that of 1851.

FROM IPSWICH TOWARDS NORWICH

The Ipswich to Norwich line originated with the Ipswich & Bury Railway, incorporated in 1845 and opened for passengers to Haughley and Bury St Edmunds on 24 December 1846. In the latter year the company was authorised to raise a further £550,000 capital and extend from near Haughley, where on 9 July 1849 the first station was replaced by that at the junction, a mile to the east, to the independent Victoria terminal in Norwich, and a junction at Trowse with the Norfolk Railway. In January 1847 the plans passed to the EUR. Amidst fulsome praise of J. C. Cobbold by Norwich representatives, who warmly welcomed the prospect of a shorter route to London, construction, planned by Locke, supervised by Bruff and contracted for by Mackenzie & Brassey, commenced near Lakenham on 25 February 1847. Work also began at Haughley, and because of the extensive viaduct at Lakenham and the awkward slew bridge over the turnpike at Dunston, it was at the southern end that the greater progress was made. With a view to obtaining some return as soon as possible, sectional openings were made from the south, road conveyance being provided between Norwich and temporary terminals at Finningham (7 June 1848) and Burston (2 July 1849). A formal but premature opening of the final section took place on 7 November 1849 to fall within the Norwich mayoralty of Samuel Bignold, an EUR director who had given much practical assistance in the northern area, but only one line of rails was ready beyond Burston and it was 3 December before goods services began. Passenger trains were officially inaugurated on 12 December, but it is likely that some service had been offered in the previous nine days.

The effects of this line on company relationships have already been indicated in Chapter III. Traffic promised well but ECR obstruction at Colchester barred it from participation in through traffic between London and Norwich: for this the EUR was obliged to issue unremunerative rail/steamer tickets to London via Ipswich. After 1854 matters improved, but for London–Norwich traffic the emphasis continued to be on the Cambridge line. As late as 1874 there were only four daily trains each way, stopping at most stations and averaging 127 minutes down and 126 up over the $45\frac{1}{4}$ miles between Norwich Victoria and Ipswich; one daily express was provided to and from Norwich Thorpe. In the early 1880s, however, considerable changes were made, and by 1883 nine down and eight up trains were running daily. Semi-fasts were more frequent, and average times had fallen to 82 minutes down on Norwich Thorpe services ($46\frac{1}{4}$ miles) and to 107 on those to Victoria where the local services tended to concentrate. From the 1880s the story was one of steady acceleration, made possible by the relatively easy terrain (a short section of 1 in 84 between Trowse station and Trowse Upper Junction, $1\frac{3}{4}$ miles at 1 in 132 from Mellis and the $2\frac{1}{4}$ mile Haughley Bank of 1 in 131 are the severest gradients) and the absence of large intermediate centres. The Tivetshall water-troughs installed in 1896 were a particular benefit.

War years apart, both speed and frequency developed steadily. In the 1938 summer, fourteen down and fifteen up daily services averaged 79 and 80 minutes respectively, the expresses $56\frac{1}{2}$ and 56, with the best in both directions 48 by the 'East

Anglian'. The latter was not surpassed until September 1952 when the 'Broadsman' gave a 45 minute down run, reduced to 44 in June 1953, a timing achieved by four daily services in 1959 (when the best up trains were taking 45). By 1962 six down services required only 46 minutes and five up 45. With diesel haulage (as in 1977) times of 41 up and 43 down became standard for non-stop trains, 51 and 52 for those calling at Stowmarket and Diss. Electrification from Ipswich, logical in that the London–Norwich service was amongst the most profitable InterCity routes, was implemented from 11 May 1987 (although emus had been operating between Ipswich and Stowmarket since 5 August 1985)—the first electric train to Norwich had been an officers' special on 9 April. Now, standard times became 45 up and 42 down, the best being a mere 35 up; twenty-one down and twenty up weekday trains are now provided. There are only three surviving stations, Stowmarket and Diss, the former serving the junction for the Bury line and both regular calling points for the expresses, and Needham Market (which as Needham was closed on 2 January 1967 but then reopened on 6 December 1971) used by local services. Swainsthorpe closed on 5 July 1954, Bramford (apart from private sidings) on 2 May 1955. Claydon on 17 June 1963 and the remaining eight on 7 November 1966.

Stowmarket grew from 3,404 inhabitants in 1841 to 4,162 by 1901. The EUR destroyed its river trade by taking over the Gipping Navigation but its market status was enhanced and a series of industrial developments stimulated by the railway; before 1900 malting, the making of explosives and fertilisers and engineering (general and agricultural) were important, subsequently to be joined by printing, textiles, paint making and food processing. Now modern factory estates have added to the diversity and it has become, especially since 1987, a centre for commuters. The 1971 population was 8,676, that of 1981 10,910. Diss, with agricultural engineering after 1900, has experienced similar growth although only 5,423 in 1981. In 1848 land on the common was selling at £700 per acre in expectation of the railway but over-dependence on agriculture thwarted hopes. Local growers initially strengthened their ties with the Norwich markets but after 1890 those without glass proved unable to compete with growers at a greater distance who had.

Diss lost its Public Delivery Siding in January 1985 but retains its rail served grain depot. Local military installations in World War II brought much additional traffic, ticket sales of 40,000 in 1938 increasing to 330,000 in 1944. Today, as at Stowmarket, its station draws daily commuters from a wide scattering of local villages. The line's freight was essentially coal and agricultural produce, deliveries of the former to Claydon cement works ceasing only in 1983. At Barham is a road material depot, served to 28 February 1986 from Merehead and then, from 8 April, Mountsorrel. In World War II a petrol depot at Haughley received 681 trains from August 1939 to June 1944, 445 of them in the last six months.

Branch development has been minimal and generally unsuccessful in this totally rural area. Eye, once a prosperous market centre, began to decline when the main line passed it 3 miles to the west, and between 1851 and 1961 its population fell from 2,587 to 1,583. The locally promoted Mellis & Eye Railway of 1865 barely checked the trend. Opened on 2 April 1867 under GER operation it was absorbed by the latter in 1898. Its only intermediate station, Yaxley Halt, was opened on 20 December 1922. The line was finally closed to passengers on 2 February 1931, though freight, mainly coal and beet, continued until 13 July 1964

The Mid-Suffolk Light Railway, designed to alleviate agricultural depression in deeply rural Suffolk and provide readier access to the coast, was sanctioned by an Order of 1901 to build a standard-gauge line from Haughley to Halesworth (28 miles), with a branch from Kenton to Westerfield (14 miles), on a capital of £300,000. Physical connection with the GER was planned at each terminal, but that company long regarded its new neighbour with some suspicion, heightened when extensive purchase of Midland Railway stock by its chairman, Stevenson, wrongly aroused fears that the Midland might be looking to Southwold for development as a port.

Construction began in May 1902, but disputes with the contractor, Jackson, the discovery that marshland made the Halesworth approach unfeasible, and general financial embarrassment (the County Council refused a loan) delayed implementation of the first goods services between Haughley and Laxfield (19 miles) until 20 September 1904. Hopes were retained of reaching Halesworth: deviation plans were drawn up in both 1904 and 1907, and a further attempt was made in 1909 to extend towards it, but in the event nothing but a 2¼ mile extension to Cratfield in 1906 was achieved. Similarly, the branch from Kenton reached no farther than 2½ miles, to near Debenham: some facilities seem to have been available on this but there was never to be a regularly advertised service. By May 1907 all construction had ceased and, the £500 or so annual profit being totally inadequate to support the capital debt of a line that had cost some £9,630 per mile to build, the company was declared bankrupt and a receiver and manager appointed.

As a consequence the board rescinded its intention of withholding passenger services until the completion of the whole and, after a delay while the line was brought up to standard, these began between Haughley and Laxfield on 29 September 1908. The basic pattern of two or three trains daily remained throughout the line's life. In 1910 33,796 passengers and 33,464 tons of freight were carried, this yielding £5,132 but incurring costs of £4,695, a pitifully small return on a capital account that by the close of 1916 had reached £216,620. In February 1912 the Cratfield extension was closed beyond Laxfield Mills and during the war the branch track was lifted. After 1918 the situation steadily deteriorated with traffic failing and costs rising. From 1920 village traps met trains only by request and many fare concessions were withdrawn; in 1921 Sunday service ceased. In 1924 the LNER absorbed the line and the Official Receiver was withdrawn, but the speed limit of 25 mph and shunting delays left the way wide open for road competition. The 1939 war and the aerodrome at Mendlesham brought some revival but decline accelerated after 1945 and total closure came on 28 July 1952. Most of the track has now been lifted and the land sold.

More successful in joining the EUR and ESR routes was the Waveney Valley Railway. This began in 1851 as a 12¾ mile long, £40,000 project to link the EUR at Tivetshall with Bungay, a prosperous river terminal and market. Depression in railway securities caused delay and not until 1 December 1855 did the first section open to Harleston, the ECR working the line and providing five daily trains. As usual with the ECR the relationship was far from harmonious. The ECR grumbled at the inability to cover costs let alone show a profit, the WVR complained of mismanagement and unrealistic rates. Eventually the WVR was driven to undertake its own working, from 1861 until it was absorbed into the GER on 2 March 1863. Completion to Bungay had meanwhile been delayed by shortage of labour and materials even though the requisite funds had been raised. The river interest secured rejection of the application for further time beyond that sanctioned by Acts of 1855 and 1856, at which latter point authorised capital had risen to £120,000, and the company was obliged in 1859 to obtain a further Act permitting extension to Ditchingham, just beyond Bungay; in 1860 a continuation, originally sanctioned in 1853, to Beccles was reauthorised. Bungay was reached on 2 November 1860, Beccles on 2 March 1863.

The line led a placid and quietly useful existence with four to seven daily trains each way. Starston and Redenhall were closed as early as 1 August 1866 and Wortwell on 1 January 1878. In World War I services were withdrawn on 22 May 1916 from Earsham (until 1 August 1919) and Geldeston; the latter reopened as a halt on 14 September 1916, before being restored to station status on 2 October 1922. At Pulham Market a long siding to a farm was laid to serve an airship base of World War I and was used in World War II and until February 1958 for a later RAF base. Indeed in World War II the branch had its busiest time. Tivetshall, where a new connection to the main line and additional sidings were put in, and Earsham, which handled 200,000 tons of military stores, became the focal points for several air bases, and Ellingham had an Air Ministry petrol depot from March 1944.

After 1945 the whole area suffered a recession. Traffic, never high, fell steadily both through this and the effects of road competition, although at times the two daily freights, one from each end meeting at Harleston, where there was agricultural-implement making, could load quite substantially with beet, grain, coal, some government materials and general merchandise. Passenger services, however, were withdrawn on 5 January 1953. Goods facilities remained, and on 15 November 1954 a Light Railway Order was made operative for the line. But eventually this was not enough. On 1 February 1960 the line was severed by closure of the Harleston to Bungay section; on

3 August 1964 the Bungay–Ditchingham portion followed, on 19 April 1965 that on to Beccles, and finally the western section on 18 April 1966. The only centre markedly affected has been Bungay, with maltings, flour and saw-mills, an iron foundry and printing, but its 1961 population of 3,582, while up on the 3,359 of 1911 was down on the 3,841 of 1851; in 1981 it was 4,106.

CHAPTER V

Two Main Lines

ORIGINS

In 1821 William James, with the patronage of the Earl of Hardwicke, surveyed an Engine Railroad from the river navigation at Bishop's Stortford to the river near Cambridge as an alternative to a previously sanctioned canal, and followed this with proposals for railroad extensions to Norwich, King's Lynn and Lincoln. James's schemes were far too ambitious for the period and in the event neither railroad nor canal was built, but an important concept, that of linking London to northern coal and industry by way of Cambridge, had been initiated. It was taken up again in 1825 by the Northern Railroad Company, with John and George Rennie as surveyors, initially projecting a London to Cambridge line via the Lea Valley and Barkway, but evolving to include extensions to the proposed High Peak Railway at Cromford in Derbyshire and possibly Lincoln and York. National depression ruined this and delayed further activity until the reviving prosperity of the mid-1830s when, in 1833 and 1834, Nicholas Cundy surveyed a Grand Northern & Eastern Railway via Bishop's Stortford, and was followed in 1835 by Joseph Gibbs with his Great Northern by way of Dunmow. Both proposed a London to York line and both included a Norwich branch, Cundy's to run from Trumpington (immediately south of Cambridge), Gibbs's from near Saffron Walden. The first of these projects was facing oblivion when it captured the imagination of Handley, a Lincolnshire MP, who, with Cundy's concurrence, had the route resurveyed and slightly modified in 1835 by James Walker, engineer of the recently completed Leeds & Selby line with which it would be in contact, and then formed a new Northern & Eastern company.

The Great Northern complained bitterly, although unjustly,

that the N&E was 'only so varied ... as to make it distinct' and as a result had become 'tortuous to an extent which should never occur in a railway of this national importance', a view, however, which obscured the superiority of Walker's scheme of spreading the inclines over Gibbs's intention to 'concentrate the summits'. It was largely this weakness and the singular failure of the GNR to placate local prejudices, although an unusually large number of country estates were to be disturbed, that explained the defeat of its bill by 99 to 85 votes at the second reading in the Commons. But the Northern & Eastern itself was also in trouble. Already the incompleteness of surveys and land negotiations had caused restriction of its application to the line south of Cambridge (the continuation northwards was intended for 1837), and the opposition of the ECR brought rejection of the Norwich branch which was now to have been extended to Yarmouth. Thus, when incorporated on 4 July 1836, the same day as the ECR, the N&E was confined to a 53 mile line from Islington to Cambridge and a share capital of £1,200,000. Even so a 16 per cent return was anticipated from an estimated revenue of £199,530 2s 8d a year from passengers and £91,172 from freight, the latter excluding malt and flour and any part of the annual 256,000 tons attributed to the Lee and Stort navigations. Although these figures now seem wildly improbable especially as Cambridge had only 24,453 inhabitants in 1841, Ward, the chairman of the Commons Committee on the line, was so impressed that he bought shares and became a director.

Depression delayed the raising of capital and not until 1839, when the first trains should have been running, did construction commence, and even then only after an agreement with the ECR, sanctioned in 1839, whereby, to avoid a more expensive line and terminal, the N&E route was to be diverted from Tottenham into

---

NORWICH AND YARMOUTH
*28 (top)   The original Norwich station built by the Yarmouth &
Norwich company as shown in the ECR's Guide of 1851. The present
Thorpe station opened in 1886 on the nearside of the old structure, the
site of which is now occupied by the goods depot*
29 (bottom)   Between Yarmouth Vauxhall and the quays in 1951

Stratford from where running powers to Shoreditch would be exercised on payment of an annual rental of £7,000 plus various additional tolls. It followed that the N&E would now have to be built to the 5 ft gauge although a third rail from Stratford to Shoreditch was briefly considered. Construction began but in 1840 a further Act was obtained to permit abandonment beyond Bishop's Stortford. Opened in sections from the south and costing over £25,000 a mile, the N&E reached Broxbourne on 15 September 1840, Harlow on 9 August 1841, Spellbrook on 22 November 1841 and Bishop's Stortford on 16 May 1842. In the first half of this last year, despite an incomplete line for most of the period, sparse services and the ECR tolls which near London raised fares above omnibus levels, revenue totalled £28,985 and expenses only £15,626 so that a dividend of 2 per cent was possible. This, however, did not save the board from expulsion by a thoroughly restless proprietary made additionally anxious for its property by an 1841 revival of Gibbs's line to overtake the N&E to Cambridge (the Broxbourne to Hertford branch authorised in 1841 and completed in 1843 owed its origin to the need to gain locus standi in blocking such projects to the west), and J. U. Rastrick's East Anglian scheme of 1840–1 to appropriate the N&E's proposed route from just south of Cambridge through Newmarket and Thetford to Norwich and Yarmouth. The new board vigorously overhauled services and improved revenue. Moreover, in 1843, it secured both an extension Act for a line to Newport, a small Essex village but a potentially useful agricultural railhead and 9 miles nearer Cambridge, and an agreement with the ECR whereby the latter undertook management of freight traffic and granted a conditional reduction in tolls. This,

---

MIDLAND & GREAT NORTHERN RAILWAY STATIONS

30 (top)   Cromer Beach before 1923. Its central position gave it a great advantage over the GER station and it is now the only station in Cromer 31 (bottom)   Aylsham Town in Eastern & Midlands days; under magnification the second line of the timetable appears to give the date 1887. This station had to share the traffic of a small town with that of the GER on the Wroxham–County School branch. The Pickford's advertisement offers furniture removal by rail or road

however, was a prelude to a much closer union, agreed on 23 December 1843 and effective from 1 January 1844, whereby the ECR took the N&E on a 999 years lease (this passed to the GER in 1862 and continued until the dissolution of the N&E in 1902); the guaranteed rental was 5 per cent on the then-authorised capital, consolidated and revised since 1836, of £970,000 of which at that point £910,800 had actually been raised; subsequent modifications were made, in part to accommodate the Newport extension which were to bring the capital figure to £1,180,400.

Such a union, negotiated by G. P. Bidder, had become virtually inevitable during 1843. Although much improved, N&E prospects were still not good, and the ECR had sadly to recognise that even completion to Norwich could never produce sufficient traffic to recoup the massive capital expenditure already incurred to Colchester alone. The ECR's solution was to seek a major share in coal traffic to London and the south by means of a line from Peterborough to Lincoln, reached over an extended N&E. The opportunity came in 1843 when the projected Norwich & Brandon (Chapter VII) invited both the ECR and the N&E to meet it by extensions. Both were responsive, but the advantages all lay with the ECR which would have a shorter distance to build (Colchester to Thetford as opposed to Newport to Brandon), would acquire the shorter of the two London to Norwich routes so completed and could always strangle N&E traffic prospects at the London end. When faced by the generous terms offered by the ECR, the N&E had little option but to accept, for it could never hope to extend farther than Cambridge if the ECR went ahead by itself. The lease in force, the ECR obtained powers on 4 July 1844 to extend from Newport to Brandon with a branch from Ely to the London & Birmingham at Peterborough, additional capital of £960,000 being authorised. The N&E line was converted to 4 ft 8½ in in the late summer and autumn of 1844, and, after a formal opening on the previous day, the whole line from Bishop's Stortford to a temporary terminus at Norwich (Trowse) commenced public service on 30 July 1845.

Since 1 July 1840 a through route had existed between London and York by way of Rugby and Derby over the London & Birmingham, the Midland Counties or the Birmingham &

Derby Junction, the North Midland, the last to be completed, and the York & North Midland. George Hudson, promoting the York & North Midland in 1836 as an alternative to supporting either the N&E or GNR, had a major interest in the Derby and Rugby route through both the Y&NM and the Midland Railway, the latter being formed by the amalgamation of the three Derby companies in 1844. The circuitous route of 219 miles was unsatisfactory, however, and it could only be a matter of time before a more direct alternative was provided. Recognising this Hudson was concerned that either the Midland should provide it or that the new line should be so contrived as to do the least damage possible to his existing interests. Hence, in 1844, the Midland projected a 124 mile long line from Swinton to Boston and the ECR at or near March. For its part the ECR had sought unsuccessfully to come to terms with the projected Wakefield, Lincoln & Boston and extended its surveys from Lincoln to Doncaster. However, in July 1844, recognising that the Midland line would serve its purpose without cost to itself and apprehensive of the awesome power of the hostile London & Birmingham–Midland alliance it agreed, on the promise of a half share in all traffic with York and stations north, to divert its Peterborough branch through March and, withdrawing its own, support the Midland's bill; thus it joined Hudson against the common threat of the London & York.

This last company was formed by Lincolnshire interests in February 1844 as the Cambridge & York, and, basing itself on Walker's resurvey of his 1835 N&E route, had acquired its new title in May, after northern pressure for the shortest line possible had led to the adoption of a direct London approach from Peterborough. In the same month it absorbed the Great Northern, which had likewise been formed in February after Gibbs had shown his 1835 plans to Mowatt, an East Indian director, and Edmund Denison MP, and had then undergone similar evolution. 'Upwards of 9 per cent' on a capital of £4,500,000 was promised. Walker left the L&Y in May 1844 and was succeeded by Joseph Locke, who in August elected to take Gibbs's modified 'Towns' line by Grantham and Retford rather than Walker's more easterly 'Fens' route. However, in September Locke himself resigned and was replaced by William Cubitt of the Wakefield, Lincoln & Boston. This last company's proposed

line was then absorbed by the L&Y, leading to the inclusion of
the 86 mile loop from Peterborough to Bawtry (subsequently
Rossington when the Sheffield–Bawtry branch was rejected) via
Spalding, Boston and Lincoln. As entered the whole scheme
involved 327½ miles and a capital of £6¼ million, £5 million of
which had been underwritten by the close of 1844.

Two other companies completed the field. The Cambridge &
Lincoln, surveyed by Rendell, was formed rather belatedly
under Earl Fitzwilliam and a group of L&Y defectors when it
seemed that the choice of the 'Towns' line north of Peterborough
would leave Lincoln with no more than branch status. Hudson
favoured it, but only as insurance against the failure of the
Midland's bill and openly admitted that he would seek to prevent it being built. The Direct Northern was actually promoted
in London late in 1843 by Major Amsinck, and Farquhar, a
solicitor. Like the L&Y it proposed a King's Cross to York line,
surveyed by Sir John Rennie, but, being the earlier company,
refused to join its rival; a 9½ per cent return was promised.

Lord Dalhousie's Board of the 'Five Kings', charged with the
responsibility of advising Parliament on railway schemes due to
come before it, was badly misled by Hudson's prejudiced evidence against the validity of the L&Y's estimates, although it
went on to recommend not the Midland's scheme but rather the
Cambridge & Lincoln and the Lincoln to York section of the
Direct Northern. Thus encouraged the two latter combined
forces in March 1845, the DNR preparing a second alternative
bill for the contracted line; but not only was this technically
objectionable, in that insufficient notice was being given for
consideration in the 1845 session, but both the original bill and
that of the C&L were found to contain errors in their levels and
were therefore automatically rejected. Only the L&Y and the
Midland were now left.

For seventy days Committee X heard the L&Y evidence, supported by luminaries like Brunel and vigorously attacked by the
C&L and Hudson's men on grounds that the estimates were too
low, the gradients too steep and much else. On 23 July 1845 and
without the Midland's case being heard, the committee declared
the preamble proved. Credit for the success belonged primarily
to Baxter, who had organised the evidence brilliantly in refuting
Dalhousie's objections and giving proper emphasis to features

such as the 8s per ton reduction in London coal prices that would follow the L&Y's proposed ¾d per ton mile rate and his own scheme to bring coal to Doncaster by water. But Hudson was not a spent force. Using the dubious researches of the sycophantic Croucher he inveigled Bruce, the vice-chairman of the C&L, to petition Parliament that £500,000 of the L&Y shares had been subscribed by 'needy persons or paupers'. Bruce's 'Chaste Petition' could not be ignored and both houses appointed committees of inquiry. These showed only £74,200 to be in any kind of doubt and the Lords severely castigated Bruce for abusing the right of petition, but the damage was done, the L&Y bill being deferred to 1846.

In the time so gained, while in compliance with Standing Orders the L&Y registered its stock, Hudson first of all engineered the invitation that in October 1845 brought him to the chair of the ECR. Once there, in order to provide direct competition to the L&Y, he immediately launched a £4½ million scheme for a line from March to join the York & North Midland at Doncaster and the Leeds & Selby at South Milford, C&L proprietors having first option on the scrip in exchange for their own. Thus prepared, his next manœuvre, an insult to intelligence, was to offer amalgamation to the L&Y on terms that evolved to include six seats for the L&Y on a reconstituted board of eighteen, and the issue of £20 of ECR stock for each £50 of L&Y holding. His efforts were backed by carefully planted rumours that the L&Y would in fact cost nearly £10 million and by the Sise Lane Committee (April 1846) of L&Y proprietors (in all probability Hudson's agents who had purchased stock for the purpose) pleading with their fellows to accept Hudson's terms. Denison, however, motivated by both concern for his shareholders and personal dislike of Hudson, was a match for all such stratagems and on 5 May 1846 led the L&Y into union with the DNR, which had meanwhile prepared a fresh bill, and for the united scheme revived the title of Great Northern. Apart from gaining new assets and removing a competitor this move stilled the fears of many L&Y proprietors, for their shares, on which by far the greater part remained uncalled, were reduced in nominal value by one-half, those of the DNR by one-third.

The 1846 Parliamentary contest involved some anxious moments but was a relatively quiet affair, coloured principally in retrospect by rumours that the ECR had attempted bribery of MPs. But true or false it was the ECR bill that was withdrawn, and that of the GNR which, on 26 June 1846, received the Royal Assent. In all the L&Y and the DNR had expended £432,620 12s 1d to come this far. Now the £5,400,000 needed for construction had to be found and, although 5 per cent interest was to be paid on calls, the prospect was sufficiently daunting to drive the shares down to a discount.

BROXBOURNE TO CAMBRIDGE

The N&E line to Bishop's Stortford was completed on 16 May 1842 and to Brandon on 29 July 1845 (public services began on the 30th)—the section to Newport coming under the N&E Act of 1843, that to the north under the ECR's of 1844. This latter section, planned by Robert Stephenson and built by Grissell & Peto, presented few constructional difficulties. The tunnels at Audley End (456 yd) and Littlebury (407 yd), 352 yd apart, were little more than enclosed cuttings made necessary only by the insistence of Lord Braybrooke of Audley End Mansion on whose land they occurred and who was also responsible for their ornate portals; the ECR could count itself fortunate that an original demand for a third tunnel was dropped.

The line's early days were somewhat disturbed. South of Bishop's Stortford extra traffic caused considerable disruption, and although at the opening the *Illustrated London News* had claimed of the line to Cambridge that the 'carriages ran as smoothly as balls on a billiard table', it was only a few days before a down Norwich express came off the incline near Littlebury, killing one person and tearing up the track for 200 yd. On the other hand traffic developed quickly, although at 4s 9½d even the 'Parliamentary' single fare between London and Cambridge represented over half a working man's weekly wage (in 1855 the top of the range was the 13s 6d first-class express fare). Timings south of Cambridge were initially 120 minutes up and 110 down, with calls at Broxbourne and Wenden (renamed Audley End on 1 November 1848), rising to 127 and 114 respectively in October 1845 before falling in the early 1850s under the stimulus of EUR competition to 90 and 85. These latter schedules were only kept with difficulty as the condition of the

track deteriorated, and after EUR workings had been absorbed
by the ECR in 1854 there was considerable relaxation, so that by
the close of 1855 the best up train took 105 minutes, the best
down 115. Thereafter came some slight improvement, but in
1862 the fastest down service still required 98 minutes, a standard achieved in the up direction in 1858. So bad had the track
become in fact that in 1856 the Cambridge Town Council
deemed that 'it could not be used by the public without serious
risk' and petitioned for diversion of London services via Hitchin
and the GNR.

Until the 1950s this line constituted a major route to Norwich
and Yarmouth from London, although from the 1880s the fastest
journeys were all found on the Ipswich line; some indications of
relative frequency and times are given in Chapter VIII. From
1 July 1870 to 15 January 1917 the GER made regular use of
St Pancras, a *quid pro quo* for Midland Railway access to
London docks, reaching it over the Tottenham & Hampstead
Joint line (opened in 1868, the link being completed on
3 January 1870—for details see Volume 3 in this series), to which
both major companies had subscribed one-third of the capital;
in this way direct competition could be offered to the Great
Northern's Cambridge services from neighbouring King's Cross.
Up to nine down trains, three to Norwich, one to Hertford and
five to Tottenham, were run from St Pancras daily, the Norwich
trains usually combining at Bishop's Stortford, Cambridge, or,
more commonly, Ely with twin services from the GER terminal.
By 1914, however, only two expresses remained, together with
one service that brought through portions as far as Tottenham
to be attached to trains from Liverpool Street. With one regular
daily exception, up workings were principally by portions detached at Tottenham, the majority as slip coaches. GER specials,
notably for Newmarket races and Royal Trains, also used
St Pancras. The practice was revived briefly in the summers of
1922–3, with a daily restaurant-car express to and from Hunstanton, but in subsequent years lapsed entirely.

Additionally, from 1 September 1882 a thrice-daily service
ran between Liverpool Street and Doncaster via Cambridge,
and the Great Northern & Great Eastern Joint line from March
opened on 1 August 1882 (Chapter XI), augmenting the
through London coaches attached to certain March–Doncaster

trains. From 1 November 1892, running powers over the North
Eastern north of Shaftholme Junction having been obtained,
these trains were extended to York, thus establishing the 214¾
mile Cathedrals Route (Ely, Lincoln and York) in rather ineffectual competition with the GNR's 188 miles from King's
Cross. The York service remained thrice daily until July 1915
when it was reduced to a single train; in January 1917 this was
cut back to Doncaster and in May 1918 disappeared altogether.
There was never more than a fragmentary reinstatement of this
service. From October 1919 there was an up working from
Doncaster, briefly extended to run from York between 4 October 1920 and 6 April 1921 when it disappeared during the coal
strike; the last remnant of all was a Sundays-only train from
Doncaster to Liverpool Street that began in 1882 and continued
to 10 September 1939, apart from interruptions between May
1918 and July 1919 and during the labour troubles of 1921 and
1926.

By 1905 Cambridge was within 72 minutes of Liverpool
Street (74 up) and 71 of St Pancras, this placing the route
virtually beyond challenge by the GNR, although thereafter and
to 1914 the best times on the Liverpool Street line were increased to 76 minutes down and 78 up. Thornton, in October
1914, envisaged 70 minutes as a standard timing, but apart from
one 67-minute train on Thursday nights only, it was 27 September 1937 before 76 minutes was regularly bettered in the post-
war years, the achievement belonging to the newly introduced
thrice-daily (subsequently reduced) five-coach buffet-car service timed at 65 minutes each way. These ceased in 1939 and
thereafter it was 1953, with the advent of the 'Britannias', before
the best pre-1914 times were regularly bettered, the *Fenman*,
named in 1949 and with the main portion then running between
Hunstanton and Liverpool Street, taking 68 minutes non-stop
in each direction. In 1967–8 this train, by now to and from
King's Lynn only, was taking 70 minutes up and 67 down,
although the former was non-stop and the latter called at
Audley End. In 1977 the up train, now unnamed but still
non-stop, had been accelerated to 65 minutes, this reflecting
the general gain by expresses of eight minutes up and two
down, as compared with 1967/1968 following electrification of
the Lea Valley line in 1960 and reduction of through freight

traffic (see below), both contributing to smoother operation south of Bishop's Stortford. Prior to electrification the fastest-ever regular schedule was the 64 minutes up observed by a Sunday evening Norwich–London express between 14 June 1953 and 8 June 1958.

Although seemingly indifferent, the timings cited acquire a more favourable tinge when set against the operational difficulties of this line, particularly the predominance of curving double track, severe congestion at the London end (for measures such as the Stratford avoiding line of 22 June 1872 see Volume 3), the peculiar station layout at Cambridge (Chapter VI) and, until remodelling in 1960, the restrictive 'S' bends at Bishop's Stortford. Above all there had always been the problem of heavy freight traffic. Agricultural produce, manufactured goods and general merchandise to and from extensive areas of the eastern counties together constituted one major element. Over and beyond this had been massive through traffic between London and its docks and the northern and midland coal-mining and industrial areas. Through traffic received its first minor boost in autumn 1851 when the GNR offered the ECR a 20 per cent discount on all goods, except from London, handed to it at Peterborough for places that could also be reached by the Midland Railway; there was, however, no balancing benefit in the up direction, except that from 1852 the Midland handed large quantities of its coal to the ECR at Peterborough, a classic example of the benefits to be derived from being a third party in a major rivalry. Substantial increases naturally followed the opening of the GN&GE Joint line in 1882; by 1892 there were some twenty-eight up and twenty-seven down daily freights linking London with sorting centres at Peterborough (nine each way), March (five), Cambridge (six down, seven up), Norwich (two), Doncaster (three down, two up), Lincoln (one down, two up) and King's Lynn, as well as special coal and cattle services running as required. From December 1896 coal traffic was further stimulated, as by subscription to the Lancashire, Derbyshire & East Coast Railway, completed by 1898, the GER obtained direct access to the coal pits of north Derbyshire; but even with this the GER as a whole was still handling barely 2 per cent of national coal movement.

Along the Cambridge route coal and the movement of empty

wagons predominated but traffic in general merchandise was also heavy and it was between Spitalfields and Doncaster that the GER introduced its first fitted freights, twice daily and limited to twenty-five wagons in 1906. A further stimulant to traffic was the spread of industrial activity and market gardening northwards along the Lea Valley (Volume 3) to reach Broxbourne in the 1920s, and on 2 November 1959 leading to the inauguration of the 'Lea Valley Enterprise' loading from Tottenham to Broxbourne and running daily to Whitemoor for the midlands and north. During the 1950s there were still some thirty daily freights each way, but after April 1966 many fast through workings other than block loads of coal and returning empties were diverted to the former Great Northern and London & North Western lines. In 1989 less than ten through freight services a day were routed this way in either direction.

Despite the heavy freight flow, the line's inferiority to the Great Northern main line and the eventual preference of the GER for the Colchester route to Norwich discouraged investment. The LNER provided loops at Harlow, Spellbrook, Littlebury, Whittlesford and elsewhere, and after 1945 some colour light signalling was installed, but not until 21 November 1960 when suburban electrification and colour light signalling were extended from Broxbourne to Bishop's Stortford (where the station was remodelled to allow faster through running) did the line receive major attention. For some years there was indecision as to the next step, but growing commuter settlement north of Stortford, the growth of Cambridge and the threat posed by the M11 to existing traffic, led to the decision (announced in January 1984) to extend electrification to Cambridge. Services, not timetabled, began on 19 January 1987, with full implementation on 1 May. In 1990 there are thirty-eight daily weekday services, the fastest down in 62 minutes, and up in 65.

Bishop's Stortford, 4,682 inhabitants in 1841, soon lost its river trade but, remaining a malting and market centre, gained brick and sack making and some engineering. The 1921 population was only 8,858, but by 1981, with a thriving industrial estate and based on the excellence of the rail service to London, a developing role as a commuter centre, it had grown to 22,807. Each weekday in 1989 over fifty trains left for Liverpool Street, the expresses from the Cambridge line requiring 38/45 minutes, the stopping services some 50. As between 1959 (the last full year of steam) and 1964 issue of season tickets nearly doubled from 11,885 to 22,955; 1975 figures were 10,390 weekly, 9,564 monthly and quarterly and 844 annual but since then the upward trend has been sustained.

Harlow, designated for New Town development in 1947, had barely 4,500 inhabitants in 1950 but 79,253 by 1981. A splendid new station, with triple 50 ft lift towers, glass walled booking office and glazed overbridge was opened on 13 July 1960 on a four acre site (part once occupied by Burnt Mill station); parking space for 400 cars was provided to serve commuters (by 1979 1,500 daily); stone trains from Westbury began on 21 July 1987. The original Harlow now became Harlow Mill. An area freight depot was opened in 1964. Broxbourne and Hoddesdon have grown massively to a joint 1981 population of 79,253. A new station was opened on 3 November 1960, 100 yards south of the old GER structure. Goods facilities were withdrawn completely on 1 December 1986 except for a coal only Public Delivery Siding. The rail served power station closed in the early 1980s but the site was adopted as a depot by Redland Aggregates, receiving road stone from Mountsorrel.

North of Bishop's Stortford each station became a focal point for agriculture and its ancilliary industries, as testified at Newport by the 1853 former maltings adjacent to the station and the flour mills at Audley End, Shelford and Whittlesford. There was also the Sawston Paper Mill, much enlarged from 1917, served by a nest of sidings although Towgood, its owner, vetoed all GER proposals to build a station. Modern freight is concentrated on the oil depot at Stansted (serving the airport), Whittlesford grain depot and chemical sidings and the chemical works at Great Chesterford. All the stations have a basic hourly service to London and Cambridge, augmented in peak hours. Commuter usage is heavy and increasing; at Audley End, which draws from a huge area, parking space was increased in October 1985 to 500 cars. Just north of Stortford, Stansted (1981 population 5,496) is the starting point for a new 1½ mile branch from a triangular junction just north of the station to Stansted airport, where it will burrow under the runways and emerge into a new station beneath the terminal buildings.

Authorised in 1986 this is scheduled for completion in 1991 (when it is estimated the airport will have 8m annual users) at a cost of £40m.

As a historical footnote, mention should be made of the extensive use of slip coaches by the GER on this line. At various times these existed at Tottenham (for St Pancras), Waltham Cross, Broxbourne (for Hertford), Harlow, Bishop's Stortford, Audley End and, briefly, from 1914 to 13 January 1917, Newport for Saffron Walden, so avoiding the double reversal necessary at Audley End, where the junction lay south of the station. The villages were also included by the GER in many London excursions.

CAMBRIDGE LINE BRANCHES TO THE EAST

The 18 mile long Bishop's Stortford, Dunmow & Braintree branch was authorised in 1861 and was saved from financial ruin by absorption into the GER in 1865. It was opened on 22 February 1869, but without what would have been an invaluable agricultural branch from Dunmow to Epping. Apart from a beet-sugar factory established at Felstead in the 1920s the line brought little development and Dunmow, uncomfortably squeezed as a market by both Braintree and Bishop's Stortford, actually declined from 2,976 inhabitants in 1861 to 2,730 in 1901 after experiencing an initial slight rise. Passenger services were usually some five a day, latterly seven, until withdrawal (apart from occasional seaside excursions) on 3 March 1952. Coal, beet and general freight continued throughout until 18 April 1966 when the Felstead to Dunmow section and Takeley closed entirely (Rayne had closed on 7 December 1964). The rest followed in stages: Easton Lodge to Dunmow on 1 April 1969, Braintree to Felstead on 20 June 1970 and, finally, Bishop's Stortford to Easton Lodge on 17 February 1972. It may be added that in the Victorian era the line carried many distinguished passengers to Easton Lodge, a station specially provided near the home of the Earl and Countess of Warwick, and that in July 1960 it was used to test the prototype 'Road-Railer' of British Railways.

To its north lay the 5½ mile long Elsenham & Thaxted Light Railway, promoted by local interests to save Thaxted from further decline for lack of a railway (population had fallen from 2,556 to 1,659 between 1851 and 1901) and to assist badly depressed local agriculture. Receiving financial help from the GER and the Treasury, the line was sanctioned in 1906, begun in 1911 and opened under GER operation on 1 April 1913. The five daily services, one usually mixed, and carrying a tow rope for shunting at Sibleys, the one proper station (there were also three halts), were at first well patronised, but a 25 mph restriction, the anachronistic six-wheeled coaches with end-steps (replaced by corridor stock only in 1948) and the need for rebooking at Elsenham left the branch helpless before road competition. Passenger facilities were withdrawn on 15 September 1952, the freight services on 1 June 1953, since when almost all traces of the line, which never had any signals, have disappeared.

Like Thaxted the market town of Saffron Walden had suffered from having no railway, population falling from 5,911 to 5,474 between 1851 and 1861 alone as trade was drawn from the town to Cambridge and Bishop's Stortford; ECR proposals in 1861 to build from Shelford to Haverhill foreshadowed further losses. Initiative was taken by the Gibsons, a rich Quaker banking family of the town, who earlier had unsuccessfully sought an ECR branch; the persistent legend that the Quakers had caused the ECR to bypass Walden is completely without foundation. The Saffron Walden Railway, incorporated in 1861, opened to the town from Audley End on 23 November 1865 and was extended, under a second Act of 1863, to the GER at Bartlow on 22 October 1866. By 1869 issued capital had risen to £150,000, far too much for meagre local patronage to support. The GER, which had subscribed to the company and worked it from the opening, refused to divert through traffic for Suffolk over it (the junction at Bartlow in fact faced Cambridge), and the company, kept going only by loans from Gibsons' bank, was obliged to save itself from its creditors by the unusual expedient of having its secretary, to whom it owed money for land, file a petition of bankruptcy against it to gain the protection of an Official Receiver. This situation remained until 1877 when on 1 January the GER purchased the line outright for £70,750 in stock, but continued to run it purely as a country branch. Under it and the LNER, services evolved to some six daily over the whole route, with a further dozen running between Saffron Walden and the

Great Eastern Railway.

DAY EXCURSION TO LONDON
AND BACK.

FORESTERS' FETE
AT THE
CRYSTAL PALACE.

On TUESDAY, AUGUST 18th, 1868,
A CHEAP EXCURSION TRAIN
TO
LONDON AND BACK

WILL RUN AS UNDER:—

From	Train at	Fares to London and back.	
		First Class.	Covered Cars.
	morn.	s. d.	s. d.
Cambridge	6 15		
Whittlesford	6 30	8 0	4 0
Saffron Walden......	6 30		
Audley End	6 45	7 0	3 6
Newport...............	6 55		
Stanstead	7 10		
Bishop's Stortford ...	7 25	6 0	3 0
Sawbridgeworth......	7 35		
Harlow	7 43	5 0	2 6
London, arr. about	9 0		

Returning from London at 8.0 p.m. the same day.

No Luggage allowed, except a Small Bag or Parcel carried by the Owner.

S. SWARBRICK,
General Manager.

London, July 28th, 1868.

PRINTED AT THE COMPANY'S WORKS, STRATFORD

A typical excursion

main line. Saffron Walden was enabled to survive as a market
with a group of small industries such as malting and a cement
works (1870s), and population had recovered to 5,914 by 1901.
The 7,817 of 1961 largely reflected London commuter settlement,
although engineering is amongst several recently established
activities; the Acrow Company in fact provided its own halt on
25 March 1957 where certain services made unadvertised calls.
Diesel railbuses took over from the old push-and-pull trains on
7 July 1958 (subsequently diesel multiple-units were used), but
traffic, never heavy, was falling badly away, and after passenger
services had been withdrawn on 7 September the line closed completely on 28 December 1964. Undoubtedly its busiest period
had been in the war when between August 1939 and March
1944 498 trains were received at the Walden petroleum dump.

RAILWAYS TO HERTFORD

The intensely rural nature of the country traversed by the Cambridge line is reflected in that only one branch (other than those
in the immediate vicinity of Cambridge) was built to the west,
that from Broxbourne to Hertford. Authorised in 1841 this was
to gain *locus standi* for the Northern & Eastern in opposing any
independent London to Cambridge promotion through the
neighbourhood of Ware; although only 7 miles in length,
shortage of capital and the reluctance of the turnpike trustees to
allow their road at Ware to be crossed on the level delayed its
completion until 31 October 1843. Constructed as single track
on the 5 ft gauge, conversion to 4 ft 8½ in in the early autumn of
1844 involved a total stoppage, but generally traffic developed
well, for although Hertford was only a small market and river
port on the Lee it was the focal point for a large area and
supported its own foundries, maltings and breweries.

The ECR remained the sole rail link until 1858. On 1 March of
that year the independent Hertford & Welwyn Junction, incorporated in 1854, commenced services from the GNR main line at
Welwyn to Cowbridge station, beyond which there was a freight
link to the ECR and running powers to Ware. The opening was,
however, without the dock which the H&WJ had been required
to provide to protect the river interest. The company was closely
involved with the Luton, Dunstable & Welwyn Junction (incor-

porated in 1855 but as yet incomplete) and on 28 June 1858 the
two amalgamated as the Hertford, Luton & Dunstable. In
effect, the HL&D linked the ECR, GNR and L&NWR main lines,
although the GNR, following unsuccessful lease negotiations between the LD&WJ, and the L&NWR and fearful that the latter
might yet enter its territory, successfully blocked the intention of
the HL&D to cross its main line by a bridge. On the other hand
neither GNR nor ECR was disposed to jeopardise the 1852 truce
by competition for the relatively insignificant traffic between
London and Hertford. In January 1858 the two companies,
after each had been approached for terms, formed a joint committee to work the line, granting mutual safeguards for through
rates and arranging that the GNR should pay the ECR two-thirds
of the revenue it derived from London–Hertford bookings.
Slightly modified this remained in force until 1860 when terminated at the request of the HL&D, whose line was completed on
1 September of that year by the opening of the section from
Luton to Welwyn. Operation of the whole route was handed
exclusively to the GNR which absorbed the company on 12 June
1861, paying a fixed dividend of 3½ per cent on £55,000 for the
Hertford to Welwyn section, 4½ per cent on £70,000 for the rest.
The GNR's main-line trains ceased to call at Welwyn Junction on
1 September 1860, the station then closing; in 1868 and 1876
respectively the Dunstable and Hertford branches were extended
into Hatfield. The necessity to reverse there vitiated the value of
the Welwyn to Broxbourne line as a means whereby cross-
country traffic could avoid London, but it did provide the GNR
with access to the docks and for a time carried a not incon-

WEST NORFOLK

*32 (top)   A royal occasion at Lynn with the Mayor presenting an
address to the Prince and Princess of Wales, probably in 1863. The
station is that of 1846 built by the Lynn & Ely on what was then the
edge of the town. (The hotel still stands, but the artist mis-spelt East
Anglian as East Anglican!)*

*33 (bottom)   East Dereham in 1911. The through platforms were used
by the Norwich to Wells service, the bay by King's Lynn trains. The
juxtaposition of station and rural industry is typical of the region*

siderable traffic to and from the midlands. An 1859 proposal by Denison to incorporate the H&WJ section in a loop to be completed by extension from Wood Green to Hertingfordbury and so relieve main-line congestion did not materialise.

In terms of speed the GNR approach to Hertford from London could never hope to compete with the route via Broxbourne, nor did the branch from Welwyn stimulate any local development. Traffic was ever sparse, even in 1904–5 when experiments were made with steam rail-motors, in connection with which temporary halts, where ordinary trains did not call, were opened at Attimore Hall (closed to passengers on 1 July 1905, to freight on 4 May 1964) and Hatfield Hyde (closed completely on 1 July 1905). The little justification that the line possessed was largely lost on 2 June 1924, when passenger services commenced on the Hertford Loop (below), Cowbridge closing except for freight, and passenger services being extended into the new North station. However, the LNER persevered in the hope that residential settlement might still come, and as late as 1939 nine up, eight down daily services were being provided. Passenger facilities were finally withdrawn on 18 June 1951, freight continuing to unstaffed public sidings at Hertingfordbury and Cole Green until 5 March 1962 and 1 August 1962 respectively. The line remained in use for rubbish trains to Holwell Pit until total closure on 23 May 1966.

Up to 1924 the Broxbourne line had gone from strength to strength, services increasing from eleven up, twelve down daily in 1874 to twenty-four down by 1892 when there were twelve through Liverpool Street workings and one to St Pancras in times of 75 minutes or less; for some years a slip portion from the

---

DISAPPOINTED HOPES

34 (top) Mundesley station in 1963, a substantial building of 1898 opened by the Norfolk & Suffolk Joint Committee in expectation of a holiday traffic that never really developed, and closed in 1964

35 (bottom) A 1966 view of the highly ornate Newmarket goods depot opened as its terminal by the Newmarket & Chesterfield Railway in 1848; although very inconvenient it was used by passengers until the opening of the present through station in 1902

SAFFRON WALDEN RAILWAY

TIME TABLE.

SEPTEMBER, 1872.

DOWN TRAINS.

FROM	Week Days						Sundays		
	Par.y 1 2 3	morn 1 2 3	morn 1 2 3	even 1 2 3	even 1 2 3	even 1 2 3	morn 1 2 3	Par.ly 1 2 3	even 1 2 3
LONDON....dep.	6 45	8 0	..	2 0	4 0	9 0	6 90	..	9 0
STRATFORD	6 58	8 11	..	2 15	4 15	9 51	6 41	..	9 47
BROXBOURNE ..	7 50	8 39	1 39	3 39	6 35	10 23	7 27	2 53	10 19
BPS. STORTFORD	8 29	9 7	2 12	4 15	7 16	..	8 8	3 33	..
STANSTEAD	8 37	9 12	4 22	5 25	* *	..	8 17	3 44	..
ELSENHAM	8 44	..	4 29	..	..	..	8 23	3 51	..
NEWPORT	8 53	..	4 38	4 38	..	..	8 33	4 4	..
Bartlow ....departure	..	8 55	11 10	5 12	6 45	..	..	..	..
S. Walden....ditto	..	9 15	12 25 4 20	5 25	7 15	..	..	..	..
Audley End.... arrival	..	9 22	12 32	4 37	5 32	7 22	..	..	..
AUDLEY END junc.	8 59 9	9 28 12 37	4 44	5 44	7 36	10 45	8 39	..	4 11 10 41
Audley End..departure	..	9 35 12 42 4 48	5 50	7 38	..	..	..	..	..
S Walden .... arrival	..	9 42 12 49 4 55	5 57	7 45	..	..	..	..	..
Bartlow ....ditto	..	9 54 1 4 5 7	6 10	..	..	..	..	..	..
CHESTERFORD ..	9 8	12 46 4 53	5 53	7 45	10 54	..	8 48	4 22 10 50	
WHITTLESFORD ..	9 16	12 54 5 9	* *	8 10	..	..	8 56	4 33	
SHELFORD	9 23	1 5 20	6 30	11 16	..	..	9 4	4 42	
CAMBRIDGE	9 40 9 57	1 20 6 15	7 1	12 0	..	..	9 15	4 55 11 12	
ELY	10 22 10 29	1 50 6 40	7 40	1 45	..	..	..	5 55 12 0	
PETERBORO'	12 20	3 30	9 10	2 35	..	..	..	7 35 1 45	
NORWICH	1 0	3 55	9 55	2 35	..	..	..	8 20 2 35	
YARMOUTH	2 25	4 55	..	3 30	..	..	..	9 30 3 30	

UP TRAINS.

FROM	Week Days						Sundays		
	1 2 3 morn	morn	Par.ly morn	morn	even	eve 1 2 3	even 1 2 3	1 2 3 morn	Par.ly 1 2 3 even	1 2 3 even
YARMOUTH	..	..	7 15 10 40	4 0	..	..	..	12 35 8 40	
NORWICH	..	..	..	3 0	4 10 0	..	..	1 45 10 0	
PETERBOROUGH ..	..	..	11 25	3 0	4 40 10 58	..	..	2 45 10 58	
ELY	7 10	9 0	9 12 45	4 23	6 10 12 30	9 50	4 20 12 30	
CAMBRIDGE	7 18	9 7	9 45 1 37	5 10	6 53 1 20	9 58	5 20 1 20	
SHELFORD	7 25	9 14	9 54 1 37	5 17	..	10 6	5 29	
WHITTLESFORD ..	7 33	9 22	10 2 1 41	5 24	..	10 6	5 38	
CHESTERFORD ..	..	..	10 11 1 52	5 33	7 16	10 15	5 47	
Bartlow ....departure	..	8 55	9 58 1 33 5 12	6 45	..	..	..	
S. Walden .... ditto	7 30	9 15	10 10 1 48	5 25	7 16	..	..	
Audley End.... arrival	7 37	9 22	10 17 1 55	5 32	7 22	..	..	
AUDLEY END junc.	7 42	9 31	10 23 2	5 43	7 26	1 56	10 26	5 58 1 56
Audley End.. departure	7 58	9 35	10 28 2 5	5 50	7 38	..	..	
S. Walden .... arrival	8 5	9 42	10 35 2 12	5 57	7 45	..	..	
Bartlow ....ditto	8 25	9 54	10 50 ..	6 10	..	..	..	
NEWPORT	7 47	..	10 29 2 6	5 48	..	..	10 32	6 4
ELSENHAM	7 57	..	10 41	2 6	..	..	10 43	6 16
STANSTEAD	8 3	9 45	10 48 2 19	6 2	7 40	..	10 50	6 23
BPS. STORTFORD	8 11	9 53	11 0 2 27	6 11	7 54 2 30	11 0	6 33 2 30	
BROXBOURNE ..	8 47	10 21	11 42 2 56	6 46	8 23 3 9	11 37	7 15 3 9	
STRATFORD	..	..	12 20	..	8 4 0	12 31	7 53 4 0	
LONDON	9 36	10 59	12 30 3 36	7 30	9 10 4 15	12 45	7 53 4 15	

PRINTED BY J. M. YOUNGMAN.

* will stop when required, notice being given at the preceding Station.

§ These Trains run To and From Bartlow on Thursdays only.

An independent company under Great Eastern operation

11.05 am down York comprised one of the workings. Hertford's markets (with a new Corn Exchange in 1859 and a covered market in 1889) and industries had expanded and the overall level of traffic had justified a 300 yd extension towards the town centre in February 1888 (the present East station), but, despite some residential growth the 1921 population was still only 10,702.

The Hertford Loop, described in Volume 3, was authorised in 1898 to run from the Enfield branch (April 1871) to Langley Junction. It sought to relieve main-line congestion, without the expense of widening Welwyn Viaduct and providing new tunnels, while at the same time opening up a new area. It was not begun until 1905 and did not open to Cuffley until 4 April 1910. North of there lengthy viaducts at Horn's Mill and near Hertford, and the 2,684 yd Ponsbourne Tunnel (the longest in the eastern counties and the last major bore through clay to be built by traditional English methods) further delayed what at best had been only half-hearted construction. From 1914 the war caused shortages of both labour and materials and it was 4 March 1918 before goods services commenced on a single line of rails, without a crossing loop for 15 miles, between Cuffley and Langley Junction. This extension was doubled on 23 December 1920, but passenger facilities were withheld until 2 June 1924. Hertford North station, not quite complete at the openings, was provided with two island platforms, but one track, used by Hatfield trains, was removed when these trains were withdrawn, a further token of the contrast between railway hopes and the actual growth of the town. A service was provided to Finsbury Park and King's Cross with some peak-hour trains using Moorgate or Broad Street. By 1939 there were twenty-four down, and twenty-three up services daily; from the mid-1960s diesel multiple units provided a basic half-hourly service augmented at peak times, a pattern perpetuated after electrification from Moorgate and King's Cross to Hertford (a £35m scheme) on 3 October 1977 and throughout the loop on 6 February 1978, except that one each hour was extended beyond Hertford to Stevenage.

North of Hertford the sparsely populated countryside and the existence of a main road running parallel to the railway and into the town centre militated against passenger traffic from the first; some five daily services by rail-motors were provided until total withdrawal on 10 September 1939. Since 1945 the northern section of the loop has remained invaluable for diversions at times of main-line blockage and for through freight (eleven up and nine down in 1965, principally coal and returning empties). Passenger traffic, however, has been confined to an early morning King's Cross to Hitchin service that ran until 5 March 1967, a Wednesday-nights-only Huntingdon service that ceased after 12 June 1963, a handful of summer-Saturday specials as from Enfield to Skegness and, from 5 March 1962 a diesel multiple-unit service that was initially five down and four up trains between Hertford and Stevenage or Hitchin, introduced at peak hours to accommodate workers in the rapidly growing industries of northern Hertfordshire; with electrification this provision has continued, plus the hourly Stevenage train to and from King's Cross, some extending to Huntingdon or Peterborough.

By 1961 Hertford had acquired a diverse range of light industries and the commuter element had swollen, but population was still no more than 15,734. However, its value as a focal point and the potential for further growth were deemed sufficient to justify electrification of the Broxbourne branch on 21 November 1960, when colour-light signals and continuous track circuiting were installed and the East station platforms were lengthened to take eight-coach trains. Service frequency was made half-hourly at off-peak times and every twenty minutes at peak hours. In 1981 Hertford's population was 21,412.

The Broxbourne line had its own branch, the 13¾ miles Ware, Hadham & Buntingford from St Margarets (despite the title the opposition of the landowners prevented it going from Ware). It was brought into existence by the efforts of Mickley of Buntingford and other local men, being authorised in 1858 to save Buntingford from further decline occasioned by loss of road traffic and its isolated position between two main lines (ECR plans of 1846 to steal GNR traffic by a loop from Shelford to Ware through Buntingford were rejected at Standing Orders in 1848 by the Commons). It was rescued from imminent ruin by the financial intervention of the ECR in 1861, opened under GER operation on 3 July 1863 and was purchased by it on 1 September 1868.

The terms of £1 of GER 5 per cent preference stock for £10 of its own ordinary shares reflected accurately the perilous nature of its infancy, but with characteristic efficiency the GER set to work to exploit the agricultural potential and subsequently that for some residential development. Traffic so grew that in 1884 Mardock, Widford and Westmill ceased to be conditional calls, in 1890 mixed trains were discontinued and in 1892 Braughing was made a crossing point additional to Hadham. By 1914 there were eleven daily passenger trains, and agricultural traffic and developments such as the 1901 flour mill at Standon could support up to three freight services a day. Residential growth in the area was increasing, and from 1922 a handful of peak-hour through-coach workings with Liverpool Street were evolved. These, latterly two up and three down in a branch total of nine each way, ceased from 15 June 1959 when a single diesel multiple-unit took over the line. By then, however, freight had declined and local passenger patronage was falling away. Sunday services had ceased from 25 September 1955 and from 21 November 1960 only morning and evening trains, nine overall, with extras on Saturdays, were run, giving London connections of 72 to 76 minutes. The inevitable passenger closure occurred on 16 November 1964, that for freight on 20 September 1965.

THE GNR MAIN LINE

Requiring deviation powers at Peterborough (Chapter XI), the GNR began construction with the northern 'Loop' line through Spalding and Boston, completed on 17 October 1848. The principal contract (in all there were four) for the King's Cross to Peterborough section was taken by Thomas Brassey in November 1846 after Cubitt had completed his final surveys. Progress was relatively slow, for although between five and six thousand men were employed funds were scarce and some major works were unavoidable, these including nine tunnels south of Knebworth (of which Welwyn North and South, the two relevant to this text, were 1,046 and 446 yd long respectively), and the 519 yd Welwyn Viaduct of forty arches over the Mimram near Welwyn. A particular difficulty was the crossing of 3 miles of fenland marsh at Whittlesey Mere, where alternate layers of faggots and peat had to be laid to displace the moisture; Ballard, Brassey's agent, whose idea it was, kept down the cost of this expensive operation by shrewdly making simultaneous bulk purchases of timber over a wide area before prices could be raised against him. The line, fast and straight with a ruling gradient, except near London, of only 1 in 200, opened from a temporary terminus at Maiden Lane on 7 August 1850 (freight followed on 12 December), before extension to King's Cross on 14 October 1852.

At first, faced by determined competition from the LNWR and the MR (members of the Euston Square Confederacy to 1854 and, with the GNR, of the Octuple pooling agreement of 1851 for traffic north of York) traffic developed only slowly, although by March 1851 the GNR system as a whole was earning £36 per mile per week and the Great Exhibition of that year brought thousands of excursionists into London by the line. Initially eight daily trains each way (two south of Hitchin only) were run, becoming twelve by 1852 when all but three were slow; meanwhile best times to Peterborough had fallen from 150 to 100 minutes. Coal traffic, flowing from the spring of 1851 after settlement of disputes with the South Yorkshire and earning £2,000 a week by 1852, proved the saving grace, the GNR acting both as merchant and carrier until 1860 when, as the result of a Chancery suit sought by disgruntled private interests, it was forced to suspend direct sales; meanwhile, coal prices in London had fallen by 13s to 17s a ton.

Activity on the line was further increased from 1 February 1858 when, by agreement of December 1857, the Midland Railway began to exercise running powers into King's Cross from its Bedford to Hitchin branch (authorised in 1853, opened 8 May 1857); freight working started in August 1858 after expansion of the GNR's terminal facilities. By 1862 Midland passenger services had risen from four to seven daily each way, those of the GNR to twenty-three including the Manchester expresses begun on 1 August 1857 by agreement with the Manchester, Sheffield & Lincolnshire. Relationships between the GNR and Midland, at best uneasy, steadily deteriorated, the former resenting coal brought over its lines by another company, the latter growing increasingly bitter at the constant delays imposed on its trains— 2,400 freight and 1,000 passenger trains in 1862 alone. The GNR offered to provide two additional tracks south of Hitchin if the tolls paid by the Midland were raised from £20,000 to £60,000 a year, but the latter craved independence and in 1863 secured powers for an extension line from Bedford to St Pancras; this opened to freight on 7–8 September 1867 and to passengers on 1 October 1868, ending what had become an impossible situation exacerbated by the imminence of GNR suburban development (Volume 3).

By August 1873 King's Cross was handling 193 trains a day including some twenty main-line services each way; this latter total had doubled by 1893 when the tracks had also to be shared with some fifty daily freights in each direction. By 1867 regular express timings to Peterborough had been cut to 97 minutes, although as early as 1857 the then new Manchester expresses had taken only 95, falling further to 86 by 1895; in 1898 ten down and eight up needed only 85 to 94 minutes between London and Peterborough. Probably the fastest journey of the nineteenth century was the 72 minutes achieved on 21 August 1895 in the Race to Aberdeen, and the speediest steam hauled run ever the 55 minutes on the down trial run of the 'Silver Jubilee' on 27 September 1935. By 1939 with some thirty-five daily trains in each direction, the non-stop at speeds (81 to 86 minutes down) were only slightly better than in GNR days but generally with much heavier tare weights. After the war steam locomotives eventually achieved a regular 75 minutes timing, diesel engines as little as 61. High Speed Trains, introduced in May 1978 brought further cuts; in 1982/3 one down service was allowed only 49½ minutes for the 76¼ miles, an average speed of nearly 92½ mph.

High speeds and heavy frequency have gone hand in hand with safety, the line's reputation for this originally forming in 1851 when Queen Victoria and Prince Albert used it on their way to Scotland. Serious mishaps are to a certain extent occasionally inevitable, but in fact there have been very few south of Peterborough. The most dramatic was that in Welwyn North Tunnel on the night of 9–10 June 1866, when a Midland goods hit a down train of empty coal wagons halted in the tunnel by a burst boiler tube, the wreckage being struck by an up meat express; all three were destroyed by fire (the smell of roasting meat is said to have spread for miles around), but only two men were killed, the guard of the first GNR train and a friend stealing an illicit ride in his van. Eight died at Hatfield on 26 December 1870 in a derailment caused by a broken coach tyre, and thirteen at Abbot's Ripton on 21 January 1876 when the up 'Scotsman' overran snow-clogged signals falsely showing clear and hit a goods train setting back into a siding to allow it passage—a down Leeds express could not be warned in time to avoid the wreckage. A result of this last disaster was the adoption of somersault signals by the GNR and, generally, of the principle that a signal's normal indication should be danger. In the same year, on 23 December, four died in a collision at Arlesey. Another major accident was on 15 June 1935 when a misunderstanding between signalmen allowed a Leeds express to collide at 70 mph with the rear of a Newcastle train slowly moving from a signal halt at Welwyn; fourteen were killed. In its latter days the GNR began the installation of yellow-light distant signals, the LNER completing the work before, in July 1935, introducing colour-light signals and closing twenty-four boxes between King's Cross and Peterborough. Under British Rail the Automatic Warning System had been installed throughout the route by March 1960. In 1978/79 the provision of colour-light signals between Sandy and Holme was a prelude to the control of the 56 miles from the former to Stoke Tunnel by the new £1½m signal-box commissioned at Peterborough on 2 December 1972; this shares with King's Cross and Doncaster the responsibility for the whole line south of York.

Congestion had ever been a problem on the GNR line. Volume 3 of this series has described the efforts at alleviation south of Potter's Bar, at which point the opening of a new two-island-platform station (1955) in place of the former two platform building, and a second double track tunnel (1,214 yards) finished on 3 May 1959, completed a process begun in 1867 to provide quadruple track to Welwyn Viaduct, 21 miles from King's Cross. The expense of widening the latter remained prohibitive but work brought to conclusion at Sandy. Holme, Huntingdon and elsewhere by the summer of 1978 gave 43 miles of continuous quadruple track from Woolmer Green (2½ miles north of the viaduct) to Conington. Earlier, in 1923/24, the Offord to Huntingdon section had been widened with the building of a new bridge over the Ouse, and from 1928, with capitalisation of the recently repealed Passenger Tax, a number of refuge sidings had been provided.

Electrification of the East Coast main line was first proposed in the 1955 Modernisation Plan (see Postscript), but it was 1977 before the King's Cross suburban area was converted and 1984 before the larger scheme was approved. Once accepted, however, progress was rapid, resignalling work having been already done, and the first multiple-unit services were running to Huntingdon, although not timetabled, from 4 November 1986, the full implementation to Peterborough following on 11 May 1987. The HSTs meanwhile continued the northern express services. Crew training and testing of the Class 91 electric locomotives began in August 1988, regular workings in the October. Power from the National Grid is obtained at Hornsey.

By 1939 commuter settlement had spread to Potter's Bar, then the terminal for twelve daily services, including some from Broad Street and the North London line first introduced in August 1877. After the war settlement pushed steadily northwards; in the 1959 remodelling of suburban services Hatfield became the terminal for fifteen trains a day (from seven) and Welwyn Garden City for twenty-seven (from five); with electrification the latter's share is over forty daily. In the same years, Hitchin, junction for the Cambridge and Bedford lines (the latter closed to passengers on 1 January 1962, freight on 28 December 1964), has seen daily services rise from thirty-three to over eighty. In 1964 461,106 tickets were collected and 185,00 issued (the discrepancy a reflection of the town's market status); by 1974, however, there were 800 daily commuters, rising to 1,000 in 1979 and still increasing. In 1965 a siding was laid to the gas-reforming plant at Cadwell, train-loads of virgin naptha being received from Fawley; in 1989 Hitchin was a coal concentration centre. The town, with aero-engineering and a variety of more recent industries has grown from 13,525 in 1921 to 30,317 by 1981. Stevenage, the first development under the 1946 New Towns Act, 5,038 in 1921 but 74,381 in 1981, formerly with rail links to various new factories, was given a new station on 23 July 1973 (a mile south of the original) with an overhead passage to the town centre. In 1965 185,326 ordinary tickets were issued and 5,934 season, but in 1979 there were already 1,700 daily commuters with many coming in to work in the town's modern factory estates. To the south, settlement at Watton-at-Stone led to the provision of an entirely new station during 1982, a joint venture of British Rail and the

Hertfordshire County Council. Development at Welwyn Garden City was begun by a private company in 1919 but taken over by the state in 1948; the 1921 population was only 950, 18,314 in 1951 but 40,496 by 1981. In 1965 301,716 ordinary and 12,673 season tickets were sold and 442,138 collected, but now there are 2,000 London commuters a day. In the year to September 1965 24,536 wagons were handled in the yard but the diverse modern industries, electronic engineering and food preparation predominating, are road served.

The original Welwyn Garden City station, a wooden, single platform halt on the Dunstable branch, opened on 16 August 1920, the main-line station, partly on the site of Welwyn Junction (closed in 1860—see page 124), following on 20 September 1926. When on 20 February 1966 the collapse of an overline bridge at Hatfield blocked access to Luton (closed beyond Blackbridge Sidings from 3 January) a new connection was put in from Welwyn Garden City on 26 April.

Nearby, Welwyn, a farming centre of 1,400 inhabitants in 1851, has modern settlement, by 1979 providing some 300 daily commuters; the 1971 population was 8,134. Hatfield, its station rebuilt in 1972/3 and with 900 London commuters daily in 1979, was in 1851 a small market town of under 4,000, and only 5,695 in 1921; in the 1930s, however, aero-engineering was the first of several important industries to be attracted to the town. In 1948 it was selected for New Town development and by 1981 had grown to 25,180. The branch to St. Albans (authorised in 1862 and absorbed by the GNR on 1 November 1883) closed on 1 October 1951, that to Dunstable to passengers on 26 April 1965 and the Hertford line (see above) in 1951, but in 1965 the station issued 150,919 ordinary and 5,957 season tickets, collecting 183,628; in the twelve months to September 1965 Hatfield's up-yard (remodelled 1955) and Marshmoor together handled 13,841 wagons. Elsewhere, south of Hitchin, only Knebworth, the site of King's Cross Control in World War II, with 3,500 inhabitants in 1971, has failed to share in the dramatic post-war expansion of its neighbours on and through the railway.

Although the area between Hitchin and Peterborough remains predominantly agricultural, electrification has made the five stations focal points for intensive growth, many houses

having been built in anticipation. The May 1989 timetable
offered 2,500 extra seats per week and a twice hourly off-peak
service to King's Cross, Huntingdon being the terminus for
one. Within three months of electrification revenue at Biggleswade (growing 9,605 to 10,594 from 1971 to 1981) increased
eleven per cent; at Sandy (5,277 to 7,544), with grain and
fertiliser rail depots, twenty-two; at St. Neot's (15,204 to
21,185), where 44,563 wagons were handled in the twelve
months to September 1965, mainly in connection with Barford
Power Station, fifty-six; and at Huntingdon (16,577 to 17,557)
twenty-one per cent. The fifth station is Arlesey, originally
Arlesey & Henlow, closed to passengers on 5 January 1959 and
completely on 28 November 1960, but reopened on 3 October
1988 at a cost of £630,000, shared between BR and the local
authorities concerned. Other stations, not so fortunate, were
Tempsford, closed to passengers on 5 November 1956 and
Abbot's Ripton on 15 September 1958; both these became
unstaffed public sidings on 9 July 1962, the former closing
entirely on 1 March 1965. Three Counties lost its passenger
service on 5 January 1959, Offord & Buckden on 2 February
1959 (becoming an unstaffed public siding on 9 July 1962
before final closure on 26 April 1965—there had been a large
steam mill and manure works once served by rail), Holme and
Yaxley & Farcett, both on 6 April 1959, the latter closing to
freight on 1 November 1965.

Huntingdon, the service and employment centre for a wide
area, its station rebuilt in 1959/60, now only 39 minutes from
London was a key point in early railway history. The first
arrival, on 17 August 1847, a short branch from the ECR at St
Ives, was the Ely & Huntington (launched as the Ely & Bedford it never reached Ely, and the Rugby & Huntingdon with
which it hoped to join was abortive). The E&H in 1847 became
part of the East Anglian, based on King's Lynn, which in turn
was in 1851 briefly leased to the GNR. During this the line was
extended from the first terminal at Godmanchester to a south
facing junction 13 chains south of the GNR station (opened 7
August 1850). So suspect were EAR finances that the contractor
took twenty-three coaches and a quantity of rails as a security
before beginning the work. Opened on 29 October 1851 the link
was of little use as the EAR was now leased to the ECR. However,

on 21 February 1866 the Midland Railway, working the Kettering, Thrapstone & Huntington (absorbing it in 1897), reached the town with a direct link to the E&H (now GER) and a north facing spur to the GNR; a service to Cambridge was instituted from 1 March. On 1 May 1883 the E&H became part of the GN&GER Joint line to the north; the MR spur was lifted, that to the St Ives line doubled and resited to give an easier curve. A new station was opened to GNR design with three curving platforms. Known from 1 July 1923 as Huntingdon East, this closed on 18 September 1959 after being used on Fridays only (11 September was the last) since withdrawal of the Cambridge to Kettering service on 15 June 1959.

CHAPTER VI

The Cambridge Region

CAMBRIDGE

Without a serious rival within 20 miles, route centre, river port and market, for many the natural gateway to the eastern counties, Cambridge was an obvious focal point for railway promotion, quite apart from its possible significance as an intermediate stage to the north. Anticipation of the Northern & Eastern in 1836 precipitated a whole range of projects including the Oxford & Cambridge and the Cambridge Transverse Railway (Bury St Edmunds to Market Harborough), and, after a period of relative quiescence, the pattern was repeated from 1844 with the sanctioning of the ECR extension from Newport to Brandon. In this second outburst of activity duplication and even triplication were implied in schemes that proposed direct links with Worcester, Oxford, Northampton, Bedford, Bury St Edmunds, Colchester, Harwich, Lincoln and Hull amongst many other places. A Cambridge Town Meeting of 19 November 1845, at which George Hudson, busily engaged in making friends for his 1846 ECR northern extension, was prominent, extended a wide welcome to many of the promotions, but, as was only to be expected, the vast majority of them failed utterly. Even so, on 30 July 1845 the ECR placed the town on a through route between London and Norwich, and by 1885 an extensive network had brought not only the GER but also the Great Northern, Midland and London & North Western into the town's station.

Freed from clogging dependence on King's Lynn and river transport in general, Cambridge was enabled to exploit its many advantages, to which were now added an abundance of cheap rural labour and the availability of national markets. In 1857 market facilities in the town had to be enlarged, and a £20,000 Corn Exchange was opened in 1876, reflecting extensive London

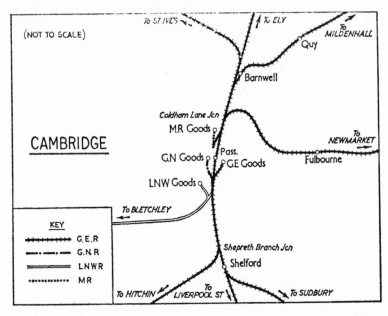

trade; a £19,000 cattle market followed in 1885. Meanwhile
two imponderables had been settled. Many had been hopeful
that river and rail would complement each other, but in fact
river trade disappeared almost completely within a few years
and the 1851 Census showed that many families connected with
the navigation had already left the town. The second matter
was the apprehension of many in 1845 that the siting of the
station a mile from the town centre (where land that was at the
same time firm, undeveloped and cheap had proved unobtain-
able) might vitiate railway benefits; in fact the town grew towards the railway, the bulk of the new or expanded industries,
including iron and brass foundries, brewing, malting, milling,
cement making, bricks and tiles and a tobacco manufactory,
being found between the station and the town centre. By 1901
the population was 47,731 and growing fast under the additional
stimulus of agricultural depression. The 1971 total was 98,840.

   In the late 1980s, (estimated population in 1987 just over
100,000), the university and markets are as important as ever
but the town is also a major centre of light industry with
printing, scientific instrument making (1881), electronics, elec-

trical engineering and plastics just a few of the activities. Railway freight has declined (the upper yard closed on 31 January 1966) but an oil terminal and coal concentration depot remain. During 1965 1,425,211 tickets were collected at the station but this has increased with the population and revived status as an interchange point. Both routes to London are now electrified, that to Liverpool Street providing (1990) thirty-eight daily trains, the best in 62 minutes, and the line to King's Cross thirty-two with the fastest in 57. A £7m resignalling project, authorised in 1978, has brought (by stages) 56 route miles (Bishop's Stortford to Ely and from Royston) under the control of Cambridge's power-operated box, opened on 16/17 April 1982.

When opened the station was described by the *Railway Chronicle* as a 'long, flat and handsome brick building ... consisting of a double series of arcades', one side enclosing the trains on the one and only platform, the other road carriages; Sancton Wood's main block survives today although in extended form. Within four months of the opening on 30 July 1845, local interests were pressing for a more central station or enlargement of the existing one and the provision of a branch to the town centre; the ECR was in fact prepared to include this last concept in an 1847 bill until the university objected to the disturbance of its calm. This was neither the first nor the last occasion on which the university had a decisive voice; it had counted a lot in the 1836 victory of the Northern & Eastern, had had much to say in the discussions and decision-making of 1845 and was to influence subsequent discussions on routes into Cambridge and matters affecting the station. Its power was sufficient to secure the introduction of certain curious restrictive clauses from 1844 into a number of local railway Acts, for example that of the Newmarket & Chesterford in 1846. No person was to be picked up or set down within 3 miles of Cambridge between 10 am and 5 pm on a Sunday except when a train was running late; moreover, university officials were empowered to enlist the co-operation of railway staff in identifying members of the university on the station, and if any such did not hold the degree of Master of Arts or Bachelor of Medicine or Civil Law could order the company not to carry him for 24 hours even if the fare had been paid. Any failure to comply or attempt at evasion (dropping passengers between stations was specified) made the company concerned liable to a £5 fine payable to Addenbrooke's Hospital or some designated charity. Although repeated in new Acts until at least 1864 these clauses were virtually a dead letter from the first, but it was 1908 before they were finally repealed.

During 1848, presumably while repairs were effected on the main platform, a temporary wooden island platform was erected on the up side at a cost of £273 18s 6d; precise dates are not known, but 1847 illustrations did not show it and an 1849 ECR report referred to it as 'now removed'. However, the ECR was finding difficulties in coping with increasing traffic and public feeling was growing strong against the inconvenience of a single platform, and so in 1850 a wooden island was restored. This soon became more unpopular than the former arrangement because of the very steep footbridge by which it was approached (and the dark subway for luggage), and on 16 November 1863 the GER removed it for good, partly to gain goodwill, at the same time extending the original platform to 1,200 ft.

Since then the basic principle has remained unchanged. A double platform bay has been added at each end (the first at the south end to accommodate services from the GNR's Hitchin line) and the main platform, with a scissor crossing at the centre, is now 1,650 ft long, handling down services at the north end, up trains at the south. Twice since 1863 this layout has been threatened. In 1886 Parliament responded to local feeling by rejecting GER plans for a completely new £130,000 two-platform station, on the grounds that realignment of the Newmarket branch (a troublesome line curving over all the outside tracks within the northern platform limits) involved taking part of Coldham Common; it was in vain that the GER offered other land in compensation. In 1893 Parliament relented by allowing part of the common to be used for a new junction to provide an easier

---

FENLAND SCENES
36 (top)　Spalding station as built by the Great Northern in 1848
37 (bottom)　Wisbech & Upwell Tramway at Outwell in 1929. Note the enclosed motion and the fender, necessary for working alongside public roads

curve to the branch (this opened on 17 May 1896, the original section out of Cambridge then closing); but this time local feeling ran strongly in favour of keeping the highly individual layout of the station itself. From 1908 numerous alterations have been made, most recently a £650,000 refurbishment completed on 23 March 1987, but none has altered the basic plan; the classical facade has not only been retained but restored. All electric signalling (reducing the boxes from five to two) was installed between July and September 1926 when, because of the developing beet traffic Cambridge had become a Control Centre. The GNR locomotive shed was closed in January 1931 (after being 'turn-round' since 1923), the GER LPD was replaced by the Coldham Lane diesel depot in September 1958; the dmu depot closed in May 1987.

SOUTH AND EAST OF CAMBRIDGE

The main ECR line from London (Chapter V), opened on 30 July 1845, gave at best a circuitous approach to Norwich and for some years a means of shortening the distance was eagerly sought. The most important of these was the Newmarket & Chesterford, a £350,000 incorporation of 1846, with Robert Stephenson and Braithwaite as its engineers. Initially it was for a 16¾ mile main line from Newmarket to Great Chesterford, with an 8½ mile branch from Six Mile Bottom to Cambridge, but in 1847 further powers were obtained for an extension to the Norfolk Railway at Thetford with branches to Ely and Bury St Edmunds. Cambridge, to be by-passed by through traffic, strongly opposed the scheme, as did the ECR, but their resistance

---

GREAT NORTHERN AND PETERBOROUGH
38 (top)   A northbound express on the notorious bottleneck of Welwyn Viaduct in 1962
39 (bottom)   A 1961 view of Peterborough North station from the south. The dog's leg curve, the cramped facilities and the 1913 Crescent road bridge, which replaced a level crossing and was designed for a realigned main line, are clearly seen. The Midland Railway's Crescent yard and box, closed in 1960, are opposite the outer face of the island platform

was outweighed by public convenience and the enthusiastic support of Newmarket and the Jockey Club.

Financial and legal difficulties delayed the Cambridge branch and no immediate start could be made on the 1847 extensions, but the main line went ahead, opening to goods on 3 January 1848 and passengers on 4 April; through services to Shoreditch were offered, in times ranging from 140 to 170 minutes. At first the Newmarket (an abbreviated title taken in 1847) worked itself with six locomotives (appropriately named after famous race-horses), the ECR, hopeful of its collapse, having declined all offers to lease or purchase the line. In May 1848 assumption of Norfolk Railway working by the ECR removed one threat to the latter, but the danger remained that the Royston & Hitchin (see below) might still be tempted to extend to Great Chesterford, so allowing the GNR into the area. In fact the R&H much preferred the cheaper alternative of continuing to Cambridge, but the risk for Hudson was too great and in October 1848 the ECR took the Newmarket on lease. However, in the following February Hudson fell, and the ECR proprietors repudiated the agreement, although allowing the continuance of ECR operation at rates totally ruinous to the smaller concern.

In resentment, the Newmarket turned again to the Norfolk, still legally independent, arranging a joint committee and the diversion of all through traffic to the Newmarket line from Thetford, although this had so far not even been begun. Compelled to be more amenable the ECR offered the Newmarket proprietors the same terms as its own on condition that the 1847 extensions were abandoned. Before an answer had been returned the Norfolk finally surrendered to the ECR, total amalgamation being agreed. The Newmarket and the East Anglian both opposed this, but Parliament, while rejecting full union, gave retrospective sanction to a lease agreement between the two. A feeble threat to extend to Royston was the only response left to the Newmarket.

The company was, however, in no position to sustain this game of power politics. Race traffic alone was not enough and the ECR's poor services and excessive charges had produced a perilous financial situation; the branch remained unfinished and even if funds could be found completion was deemed to rest on the GNR's choice of a Cambridge terminal, the very possibility of which was itself extremely uncertain (see below). Traffic remained 'utterly inadequate' and working costs impossible to bear; from 1 July to 9 September 1850 all services were suspended, being resumed only after negotiation of a fairer agreement with the ECR (from which stock was hired) and the election of a new board. The latter, with Cecil Fane in the chair, adopted a realistic policy. On 28 May 1851 agreement was reached with the ECR whereby on completion of the Cambridge branch the whole line, other than the Bury St Edmunds extension which was still to be undertaken, and for which further powers were obtained in 1852, would be taken over by the ECR at a guaranteed 3 per cent rental on the £350,000 capital, subject to a maximum ECR subsidy of £5,000 in any one year. With ECR help and by taking a line of rails from the main line the branch was completed on 9 October 1851; on the same day the 11½ mile section of main line from Six Mile Bottom to Great Chesterford was closed entirely. Powers to dismantle this section were obtained in 1858.

The completion of the branch, followed on 1 April 1854 by the Newmarket's extension to Bury St Edmunds, established the link between Ipswich and Cambridge that was so important to the growth of both. The section west of Newmarket (for the overall pattern of services see Chapter VII) remained entirely rural, Fulbourn (with a large grain silo near the station) and Six Mile Bottom closing on 2 January 1967 when Dullingham became an unstaffed halt. Newmarket, to 20 September 1989 with a rail served grain depot, remains the 'Racing Capital of England', world renowned for its racing (eight annual meetings) and horse-breeding, and with over half of the adult males in the 1961 population of 11,227 employed in connection with horses. Its 1981 population was 16,235.

The original terminal station of the Newmarket & Chesterford was a highly ornate structure, becoming a goods depot in April 1902 (used until 1967) when, at his own expense, Colonel McCalmont provided a handsome through station that ended the tedious necessity for reversal on to the Bury St Edmunds line; spoil from the hillside excavated to make room for this was used in railway embankments then under construction in north Norfolk. Race traffic used to be very heavy; in 1874, for example, trains run in connection with the One Thousand and

Two Thousand Guineas included six departures from Bishopsgate and St Pancras (arriving as three), two first-class specials
(later Pullmans were used) from St Pancras, and an excursion
from Norwich. In April 1885 a special station (Warren Hill) was
opened at the east end of Warren Hill Tunnel (really a roofed-in
cutting but with its single-track bore of 1,100 yd the longest
tunnel on the GER) to relieve pressure on race days, but since
1945 special traffic has greatly declined and the station is now
closed and the track lifted; the town station itself has been an
unstaffed halt since 2 January 1967 and no effort has been made
to replace the buildings on the up side destroyed by fire.

Immediately east of Warren Hill a triangular junction gives
access to both the Bury St Edmunds line and that to Ely. As
Ipswich grew, a more direct approach to the north than that via
Cambridge became an urgent necessity. Local traffic also
needed better accommodation: as late as 1856 the Lark Navigation was still making £30,000 a year, although in winter as
many as ten days could be consumed between Bury St Edmunds
and King's Lynn. The gap in the railway map left vacant by the
failure of the Newmarket to build to Ely as authorised in 1847
was eventually filled on 1 September 1879 by the 13½ mile long
Ely & Newmarket, incorporated in 1875 with a £100,000 capital and successively worked, leased on a £5,000 annual rental
(1 January 1888) and then absorbed (1898) by the GER. Local
services, operated by diesel multiple-units from 3 November
1958 but withdrawn between Ely and Newmarket on 13 September 1965, were early supplemented by through trains such
as the 'North Country Continental' and, in later years, other
workings linking the midlands and north with Ipswich, Harwich, Colchester and Clacton. Considerable through freight also
developed in connection with Ipswich and Harwich, but it was
June 1938 before the LNER, stimulated by heavy traffic, particularly in green peas and perishable produce from Colchester
and Ipswich to the north, doubled the 6 miles between Soham
and Snailwell Junction. Above all the line is remembered for the
events of the early hours of 2 June 1944 when the front wagon,
containing forty 500 lb bombs, of a Whitemoor to Earl's Colne
ammunition train caught fire near Soham. With incredible
courage, Driver Gimbert and Fireman Nightall detached the
blazing van and ran it forward in an effort to get it clear of the

town area. At 1.43 am, however, it exploded in Soham station, killing Fireman Nightall and a signalman and badly injuring Driver Gimbert. As it was the station was destroyed and 700 houses badly damaged, but the action of the engine crew, justly rewarded by the George Cross and LNER medal for both men, had undoubtedly saved a whole town from total annihilation.

Bisecting the Ely to Newmarket line at Fordham Junction was the 19 miles of single track from Barnwell Junction (Cambridge) to Mildenhall, opened to Fordham on 2 June 1884 and throughout on 1 April 1885. Built by the GER to stimulate local agriculture and foster other developments, this branch served a sparsely populated area already bounded by more important through lines. It came too late to save Mildenhall, in 1851 a prosperous river port of 4,374 inhabitants, from the decline occasioned by lack of a railway and agricultural depression; and for the greater part of its history the branch ran at a loss. In 1892 five daily services, one down being mixed, were provided, by 1953 only three. From 7 July 1958 railbuses were introduced to seek improvement on an adverse operating ratio of eight to one, but neither these nor the subsequent diesel multiple-units, nor a handful of daily journeys between Mildenhall and Ely and Newmarket succeeded, and on 18 June 1962 trains were withdrawn, to effect an annual saving of £13,615. A daily freight service continued from Cambridge (except at the three halts) until 13 July 1964, when all but the section between Fordham Junction and Burwell, where some light industry had developed and the population had grown to 2,734 in 1961, was closed entirely; this last section was closed on 19 April 1965. The giant air base at Mildenhall, largely responsible for the growth of civil population to 7,132 in 1961, had given the branch enhanced status in World War II, but afterwards Shippea Hill, between Ely and Norwich, often proved the more convenient station.

WEST AND NORTH OF CAMBRIDGE

Although supported by both universities the Oxford & Cambridge promotion of 1846 (73 miles of single track via Hitchin and Dunstable, planned by Locke) emerged from the Lords as nothing more than the 13 mile Royston & Hitchin, with an authorised capital of £800,000, a sum subsequently reduced.

The GNR readily appreciated the potential of this for providing its own access to Cambridge and an 1847 Act sanctioned a lease on completion, although at the same time extension to a separate Cambridge station with a spur to the ECR was rejected. The same disappointment was encountered in 1848, although this time authorisation was obtained for continuation to Shepreth and a junction with the ECR's Cambridge to Bedford line, sanctioned in 1847 as one of Hudson's attempts to strangle future GNR traffic but not yet commenced. Meanwhile the ECR's Shelford to Ware loop, another attempt to block the GNR, after being held over in Parliament from 1847 had been rejected at Standing Orders in 1848; an ECR proposal for a branch to a central Cambridge station had been dropped earlier.

The Hitchin to Royston section, double track as required by the Lords, opened on 21 October 1850 under a 6 per cent GNR guarantee (a level necessary to keep out the ECR and others), and was extended to Shepreth on 1 August 1851; overall the works had cost no more than £3,500 per mile. On the latter date the GNR inaugurated a service of five daily omnibuses between the trains and Cambridge (taking 40 minutes for the 9 miles), the fastest combined journey from King's Cross being 130 minutes by the 9.15 am northern express, but although fares were lower than on the ECR it is hardly surprising that the venture did not prove viable.

Although the R&H possessed reserve powers to build from Shelford to Shepreth if the ECR dallied unreasonably over the purchase of land, the latter prevaricated as long as it dared. In 1850, supported by the university because land required for the Botanic Gardens was threatened, it had little difficulty in causin the rejection of the independent Cambridge to Shepreth Junction: this, backed by the GNR, would have gone to a separate Cambridge terminal, but in 1851 the R&H not only put forward similar proposals but also, and this was the most alarming feature, sought a branch to the Newmarket Railway. The bill was defeated, the university objecting this time because the new line would go too near to St Peter's College, but meanwhile, the ECR, fearing to take further risks, had put the construction of the Shelford to Shepreth line well in hand, completing it on 1 August 1851. On 1 April 1852, an end-on junction having been laid and the GNR being glad to relieve itself of an unprofitable obligation of nearly £15,000 a year, the ECR assumed a fourteen-year lease of the R&H, receiving the branch revenue and 60 per cent of that deriving from it south of Hitchin. Three daily services, subsequently four, with two on Sundays, were provided between Cambridge and Hitchin.

As the lease period drew on the GNR revived its efforts to gain entry·into Cambridge. It was aided in this by the presence of the Bedford & Cambridge line. This was locally promoted in 1860, and between Sandy (where connection with the GNR was intended) and Potton took over the route of the private railway owned by Captain Sir William Peel (opened to freight on 23 June 1857 and to passengers in April 1858). The line began passenger services to Cambridge on 7 July 1862 (freight on 1 August) under, a prelude to absorption in 1865, LNWR operation. This and the cordiality then existing between the GNR and LNWR allowed the former to exert pressures impossible to resist on the GER during 1864. Two schemes were advanced. One envisaged running powers from Shepreth to Cambridge, doubling of the track between Shepreth and the main line, use of the GER station and a 1 mile extension to a separate terminal; the other was to be an extension from Shepreth to the Bedford & Cambridge, $1\frac{1}{2}$ miles east of Lord's Bridge, with running powers from there to the outskirts of Cambridge, from where a 2 mile branch would run to the town centre. Either way the GER would suffer, and the outcome was an 1864 Act conceding to the GNR an effective compromise—full running powers to Cambridge station, where all facilities and a separate platform would be provided; double track capable of carrying express services was promised between Shepreth and Shelford by 31 March 1866, the last day of the lease, on the expiration of which the R&H would be returned to the GNR. Financial difficulties prevented fulfilment of this undertaking until 1867, a source of some bitterness to the GNR, which was also resentful of the condition of the track to Hitchin despite requirements laid down after inspection by its officers in December 1865. Feelings were not improved when, on 3 July 1866, sleepers 'in the last stage of rottenness' and in any case too few contributed materially to a derailment near Royston in which two locomotive men were killed and nine passengers injured.

Even so the GNR, which finally absorbed the company on

1 July 1897, had introduced an express service between King's Cross and Cambridge (95 minutes, then 90 down, 100 up) from 1 April 1866. By 1883 up journeys of 75 minutes were possible but GER acceleration ended the possibility of effective competition and the GNR, while maintaining good speeds (in 1898 there were six down and five up trains in times of 77 to 82 minutes), wisely determined to concentrate on the development of traffic at intermediate points as much as at Cambridge itself. This policy has generally been adhered to since, although in May 1932 five daily 'Cambridge Buffet Expresses' (originally 'Garden Cities Expresses'), were introduced, at first taking 82 minutes down and 77 up but from July 1932 taking 75 and 72 minutes respectively; suspended in 1939 but restored on 6 December 1948, four daily each way in times of 82 to 90 minutes, these brought the line enduring popularity. In 1978 Royston became the terminal for King's Cross suburban electrification, the logical extension to Cambridge, belatedly authorised in 1987 (see Postscript), following on 16 May 1988.

Harston was closed on 17 June 1963, but at Letchworth, Baldock (6,679 in 1981) and Royston (11,799), where there is a rail served grain depot, considerable post-war residential and industrial growth has occurred. At Letchworth, the world's first Garden City, founded in 1903, regular passenger services were provided at a wooden halt from 15 April 1905; a goods depot was added on 19 August 1907, and a permanent station on 18 May 1913. Population had grown to 31,835 by 1981 and many of its industries (principally engineering, printing, food preparation and the making of clothing and furniture) had developed alongside the railway. As early as 1965 Letchworth despatched 64,197 tons of freight in full wagon loads and 8,554 in smaller consignments, while the station issued 151,295 ordinary and 2,795 season tickets, collecting 168,015. At Foxton a $1\frac{1}{2}$ mile branch, sanctioned by a 1920 Light Railway Order, serves the Barrington Cement works (coal fired) where new sidings were installed in 1984.

No comparable development has occurred between Cambridge and Sandy except for the settlement of Bedford workers in Potton. In 1955 the branch was selected for development as a major cross-country route that would link four main lines, those formerly belonging to the GER, GNR, MR and GWR, but although a flyover was actually built at Bletchley the proposals were dropped. Closure was foreshadowed in 1959 but averted by the introduction of diesel multiple-units in that year, and local hopes were boosted when the Beeching Report recommended no more than the pruning of certain intermediate stations. However, in December 1963 total closure was again mooted, an annual revenue of £102,200 being offset by expenses of £199,700. This was approved but while freight facilities were withdrawn on 18 April 1966 adequate alternative bus routes proved difficult to arrange, and through passenger trains did not cease until 1 January 1968. Passenger services now survive only between Bedford St Johns and Bletchley.

The line from Chesterton Junction, where until about October 1850 there was a station to serve what was a small market town with substantial river trade, and the site of a large permanent-way depot, to St Ives was authorised to the ECR in 1845 and opened on 17 August 1847. St Ives station was shared by the Ely & Huntingdon which opened from there to Godmanchester (Huntingdon) on the same day and over which the ECR had running powers. On 1 February 1848 the St Ives to March link (Chapter XI) was opened for goods, giving new significance to the Chesterton branch by virtue of through freight traffic, further intensified with the opening of the GN&GE Joint line in 1882. The local effect of the branch was to destroy the river trade of St Ives in corn, malt and coal and to bring the town, in 1850 still an important cattle market, firmly into the Cambridge sphere: so that, despite being the junction for four lines (that to Ely was the fourth) St Ives was arrested in growth and even in 1961 contained only 4,082 inhabitants. Agricultural depression was very severe in the area and the population of the St Ives Union declined by 1,180 in the decade to 1901 alone, but the branch did encourage extensive horticultural development around Cottenham, served by Oakington station, during the 1890s, and further fruit growing in the St Ives and Histon districts. In 1875 a small jam factory had opened at Histon, being deliberately sited alongside the railway in case success justified subsequent expansion. It did, and in 1907, for example, the GER carried 14,800 tons of fruit and jam in connection with the factory, so earning £14,000. This, and the settlement of Cambridge commuters along the line had allowed continuation of passenger services between Cambridge and St Ives on the 'basic' railway principle, conductor guards being employed from 6 March 1967, even though workings north of St Ives, including through services by diesel multiple-units (introduced on 3 November 1958) to Peterborough, Wisbech, King's Lynn and Hunstanton ceased from 6 March 1967, but closure came on 5 October 1970; the Kettering to Cambridge services were withdrawn on 15 June 1959. In 1990 sand for King's Cross, is still carried from Fen Drayton.

The Ely and Huntingdon (the Ely & Bedford until its aims were restricted in Parliament), was an 1845 extension of the Lynn & Ely (Chapter X) designed to link Lynn with the Bedford & London & Birmingham (to Bletchley, incorporated in 1845 and opened in 1846). It promised a 9 per cent return on a capital of £270,000, but was singularly ill-fated. Construction began in November 1846 on the St Ives to Huntingdon section at the direct insistence of Hudson, who was currently negotiating an ECR lease of the Lynn lines and as ever was primarily concerned to cut across GNR traffic streams, in this case by a junction with the projected Rugby & Huntingdon. The lease did not materialise but the 4¾ miles section was built at the fantastic cost of £130,000 per mile, a sum attributable in the main to the luxury of double track (later singled) and the series of heavy single-track wooden viaducts over the Ouse. Hudson had further insisted on an immediate start on the Lynn & Ely's Wisbech branch (Chapter X), knowing full well that this would require diversion of E&H funds and, as happened, preclude completion to Ely. In this way he hoped to prevent a possible route for the GNR into Norfolk and at the same time leave the isolated E&H completely dependent on the ECR.

Separated from the main body of the East Anglian Railways (formed in 1847 by amalgamation of the E&H, the L&E and the Lynn & Dereham), the ECR had no option but to work the line. At first six daily trains were provided, but revenue was so poor that on 1 October 1849, by which time only one train was run, all services ceased. The EAR was reduced to using a horse-drawn tram which attracted the attention of the Railway Commissioners because it could not maintain the average 12 mph required by Gladstone's Railway Act of 1844. However, the folly of forcing a possibly useful line into closure and the contrary fear that the EAR might be leased by the GNR, which would then complete it to Ely, caused the ECR to resume freight operation and then, from 1 January 1850, two daily passenger services. In 1851 a GNR lease of the EAR (with access via Wisbech— see Chapter XI) did become a short-lived reality, but despite the new spur to the former's main line (Chapter V) the St Ives to Huntingdon section was virtually devoid of traffic, and when in 1852 it was returned to the ECR it was for some time used primarily as a siding.

The situation did not radically improve until 1 March 1866 when the Midland Railway, under an agreement of 26 June 1864 and having reached Huntingdon on 21 January 1866, commenced a Kettering and Cambridge passenger service via St Ives and Chesterton Junction after freight had begun on 21 February. Further activity came after 1 May 1883 when the Huntingdon to St Ives section became the southern portion of the GN&GE Joint Committee's northern line leading to March, Lincoln and Doncaster (Chapter XI). In later years, although local traffic always remained poor, the line was recognised as a useful but secondary cross-country link, which by 1939 had thirteen daily trains (four of which were LMS services) each way. By 1953, however, the total was down to three (although in the 1950s a summer-Saturdays Birmingham–Clacton service came this way), and on 15 June 1959 the Kettering service ceased. Huntingdon East closed on 18 September of the same year and Godmanchester entirely on 4 June 1962.

The intention of linking St Ives and Ely was belatedly achieved in 1878 by means of a branch from Needingworth Junction on the March line. The first stage had been the incorporation in June 1864 of the £36,000 7 mile Ely, Haddenham & Sutton, opening under GER operation (that company had subscribed one-third of the capital) on 16 April 1866. Early traffic was thin, as third-class facilities were restricted to the Parliamentary trains and the normal return fare from Ely to Sutton was 2s at a time when local wages were under 10s a week. In 1876 powers were obtained by what was now renamed the Ely & St Ives to improve its prospects by an 8½ mile extension to Holywell-cum-Needingworth with £60,000 additional capital. This opened on 10 May 1878 under a 999 year lease to the GER, agreed in 1876 and ratified in 1879, and finally was absorbed by it in 1898. Services were improved, but the area suffered badly in depression, with rentals around Bluntisham falling 40 per cent. The already sparse population generally declined, Haddenham falling from 2,103 inhabitants to 1,686 between 1841 and 1901. Local wages for agricultural workers were still no more than 12s a week at the turn of the century. Little significant development occurred thereafter and on 2 February 1931 the LNER withdrew passenger facilities, although half-day excursions to London were run at times until 1939. During the 1950s there were two annual trains, one each to Hunstanton and Yarmouth, from Bluntisham, Earith Bridge, Sutton and Haddenham. Sugar-beet, root crops and fruit long provided fair, although seasonal, revenue, but on 6 October 1958 Earith Bridge was closed and the track through the station lifted, the section to it from Sutton being used as a siding. Services from Ely to Sutton and from St Ives to the mill at Bluntisham remained until 13 July and 5 October 1964 respectively.

In 1845 the people of Ely were said to be 'almost in ecstacy at the idea of having a first class station in the city'; it may be added that the station in question was built on a marshy swamp and in fact was to cost the ECR £81,500, although on the whole this was a worthwhile investment. Besides the main line (1845), there were branches to Lynn (1847, Chapter X), Peterborough (1847, Chapter XI), Sutton (1866) and Newmarket (1879), and the station became a busy interchange point with much complicated marshalling of train portions, especially under the GER. On 1 October 1890 the West Curve was laid in to permit through freight running between the Norwich and Peterborough lines without reversal in the station. In later years this was used increasingly by through passenger services, particularly Norfolk coast holiday expresses, until in 1966 it reverted to its original function. Ely flourished with its railways although, after remaining 'tolerably brisk' into the 1860s, river trade was lost. The new Corn Exchange (1847) symbolised expanding markets, and from 1841 to 1901 population grew from 6,825 to 7,713. Local growers, London markets now in easy reach, turned to fruit, asparagus and vegetables; as late as 1966 a five year contract, later renewed, was signed for the despatch of fruit and flowers from the city. Agricultural engineering and jam making developed, followed in 1924 by one of the largest beet refineries in the country, rail fed and by 1933 handling 240,000 tons annually. This closed in the 1980s but the site was adapted as a rail distribution depot in 1989. With its modernised station, Ely remains an important interchange point, although in 1989 there was only a handful of London season ticket holders. In 1989 a Section 8 grant of £775,000 was announced for RMC Roadstone to develop stone traffic from Doves Hole to 165,000 tonnes per annum. Electrification from Cambridge to King's Lynn via Ely is, in 1990, in hand. The town's 1981 population was 10,268.

CHAPTER VII

The Central Districts

Before the demise of the majority, the railways of the central districts, those of northern Essex, West Suffolk and south Norfolk, had many features in common. All but one, that between Norwich and Ely, were essentially secondary lines, tending to winding courses at the dictates of valleys and hills, and generally sharing a placid existence of service to agriculture (corn, cattle, fruit, beet and vegetables) and countless scattered communities. For reasons suggested in the first chapter population has always been relatively small and in West Suffolk actually declined during the nineteenth century. The various small towns have undergone considerable evolution since the railways came, but only Bury St Edmunds achieved any notable expansion before World War II, and fundamental changes in the others derive principally from London 'overspill' schemes of the last thirty years in which the railways as such have played little part.

Overall, the effects of the railways were vitiated by overdependence on agriculture, which allowed the depression to bite more deeply here than elsewhere in the region. At Newton and Great Waldingfield, for example, two villages in the area of the Stour Valley line, rentals in the early 1900s fell from the £35 per acre of 1874 to £5, and peas from the former were fetching only £10 a ton instead of £60 as a few years earlier. Farmers found it cheaper to use horses than steam machinery, small men were too poor to buy sheep where once there had been thousands, and farms could lie vacant for two years between tenants. The absence of large centres and the indirectness of routes to London prevented the degree of specialisation that saved many in other parts of the region. Opportunities for the establishment of alternative economic activities were rendered fewer by the increasing dominance of Ipswich, Colchester, Cambridge, Norwich and London, a dominance due in no small measure to the railways.

THE STOUR AND COLNE VALLEYS

In 1846 the Colchester, Stour Valley, Sudbury & Halstead was incorporated to raise £250,000 and construct a 12 mile line from the ECR at Marks Tey to Sudbury, a market and silk town of some 5,000 inhabitants at the head of the Stour navigation, with a 5¾ mile branch from Chappel to the silk-weaving centre of Halstead, and also the Hythe line in Colchester (Chapter III); a future lease to the Ipswich & Bury was authorised. In effect this was a direct challenge to the Stour Navigation, which offered to sell itself to the railway company for £30,000, refused a counter-offer of £1,000, and went on to expend large sums in reducing the number of its locks to fifteen, and the first step into the central districts. Indeed, in 1847 extensions to Clare, Lavenham and Bury St Edmunds were sanctioned, and dropped only when the Eastern Union (which had amalgamated with the Ipswich & Bury) pressed its own Stowmarket to Sudbury proposal. The Sudbury line was built by the contractor, Jackson, for double track in anticipation of the extensions and included the 1,066 ft Chappel Viaduct that consumed 7,000,000 bricks. Together with the Hythe branch it cost £286,646 and so prevented a start on the Halstead link, although the company was successful in fighting off a line from Braintree to there backed by the ECR; another casualty of high expenditure was the west-facing junction at Marks Tey. The Sudbury line was formally opened on 2 July 1849 on a 999 year lease to the Eastern Union at an annual rental of £9,500, a figure revised in 1855 to vary with revenue and bear a closer relationship to the line's cost. It was finally absorbed by the GER on 1 July 1898.

On 9 August 1865 the line was extended beyond Sudbury, where a new station was built west of the town and the former terminal became a goods depot, to Long Melford, from where on the same day a branch was opened to Bury St Edmunds, and to Haverhill, in contact with the Cambridge main line at Shelford since 1 June. Besides the creation of a new through route, the aim of the ECR, which originated the extension in 1860, had been to cripple the Colne Valley Railway (below), but on the latter's completion to Haverhill in 1865, and after early disputes

had been settled, the two evolved harmoniously. A complex of
local services developed between Marks Tey, the Colne Valley
(independent until 1923), Bury St Edmunds and Cambridge,
supplemented under the GER by through London coaches detached by slip at Marks Tey. Through working, restricted by
engineering considerations and by the competition of the
superior Ipswich–Bury St Edmunds route, remained minimal.
World War II was an exception, for various air bases were
served, the line was kept open all night, a facing junction from
the up main was put in at Marks Tey (hitherto trains from
Colchester had had to reverse from the up main to the down
main to gain access) and Chappel received 103 special petrol
trains in the first six months of 1944 alone. Other elements of
through working have included a few holiday expresses and
excursions for Clacton, and some freight between Colchester
and Peterborough, later March. The small value placed on the
line for this kind of traffic was emphasised by the rate at which
electric-token working was introduced: the section between
Bartlow and Shelford was so equipped between 1893 and 1895,
that between Marks Tey and Chappel in 1900 and between
Sudbury and Clare in 1901, but the Chappel–Sudbury and Long
Melford–Bury sections waited until 1916, and that between
Bartlow and Clare until 1931.

Local traffic was always light and diminished further as road
competition, aided by the long distances with many calls that
the trains had to cover, was felt; subsidiary traffic sources were
lost with the closures of the Long Melford to Bury St Edmunds
line and the Colne Valley Railway to passenger traffic on 10
April 1961 and 1 January 1962 respectively. The latter closure
left only the basic Colchester to Cambridge service (some four
trains daily making the complete journey, others travelling
shorter distances from each terminal), operated by diesel multiple-units from 1 January 1959, and with conductor guards,
except for Marks Tey, Sudbury and Haverhill, from 28 January
1963; Sudbury and Haverhill themselves became unstaffed halts
on 14 August 1966. Apart from a daily service from Colchester
to Halstead (on the Colne Valley line) which was withdrawn on
19 April 1965 and a daily conditional train between Sudbury
and Bures, withdrawn on 28 December 1964, freight services
south of Sudbury ceased on 2 November 1964; to the north of

Sudbury withdrawal was finally effected on 31 October 1966.
By this time annual revenue amounted to £32,000, costs to
£77,700. Total closure was intended for 31 December 1966 but
the Minister of Transport refused permission for the Sudbury to
Marks Tey section in view of commuter needs and development
at the former. Matters were further delayed while five local
councils debated the question of a subsidy guarantee of £26,000
a year, a sum raised to £52,000 when the track was found to be
in such a state that £22,000 would be needed for each of the
next ten years. Support was not forthcoming and the Sudbury
to Shelford line closed on 6 March 1967. In 1990 there are
sixteen down trains (one from Colchester) and seventeen up
(two to Colchester) daily.

Sudbury grew in population from 5,225 to 7,109 (including
400 silk weavers) between 1841 and 1901; milling, malting,
brick making, horsehair seating and coconut matting compensating for lost river trade, although this, dependent on Sudbury
bricks and lime, local mills and some up-river coal and timber,
retained a precarious existence, aided by steam barges and
reduced rates, to 1916. Depression caused contraction of the
town, though the coming of a number of modern light industries led to some revival. It had a population of 8,166 in 1971
and continues to grow. A very similar pattern has been followed
at Haverhill, served also from Audley End (Chapter V) and by
the CVR, the town developing textiles, bricks, an iron works
(1878), horsehair weaving and coconut matting, and growing
from 2,535 inhabitants in 1851 to 4,862 in 1901; a new Corn
Exchange was completed in 1889. In 1939 its population was
down to 3,714, but it had recovered to 5,445 in 1961 with new
factory and housing estates, and by 1981 had reached 9,883
although all rail links had then been severed. Elsewhere, Long
Melford, in 1851 the largest village in Suffolk, with 2,587
inhabitants, had 700 employed in horsehair weaving by 1901 as
well as milling, malting and a foundry; but population was only
3,080, trade having been drawn to Bury St Edmunds, Colchester and Cambridge through the railways. At Glemsford an
essence factory received coal by a private siding.

The Colne Valley Railway, independent to 1923 although
never paying a dividend on its ordinary shares, was incorporated
in 1856 with £40,000 capital to link Halstead, where men like

Hornor and Brewster were the leading promoters, to the Sudbury line at Chappel. The original choice of Braintree for the southern terminal was strongly opposed by the three companies with interests in the Sudbury line, the CSVS&H which had built it, the EUR which had leased it and the ECR which had taken over the latter's commitments in 1854. The CVR was opened to a temporary terminus at Halstead on 16 April 1860, after long disputes with the ECR which had sought to avoid laying the Chappel junction, a manœuvre designed to bring the independent concern to heel as quickly as possible. Extensions to Haverhill, authorised in 1859 when at first plans to continue to Audley End via Saffron Walden were entertained, followed in stages to Hedingham on 1 July 1861, Yeldham on 26 May 1862 and Haverhill itself on 10 May 1863. The GER reached the town on 1 June 1865, whereupon the CVR ceased its subsidy on a Cambridge omnibus service; on the same day, a physical connection between the two lines, authorised in 1863, was established by the GER.

At first relations with the GER were strained, provoking the CVR to various futile attempts to extend to Colchester and Cambridge, the latter as a prelude to lease by the LNWR, to prevent continuation of the Sudbury line by building branches from Birdbrook to Clare and Wixoe (these were authorised in 1863 but not implemented) and to obtain running powers to Cambridge, Colchester and Harwich. At the end, however, the CVR was left with no security other than the clause it had had inserted

---

40 (top)   Anglia East. A September evening in 1989 and commuters leave a down train at Hatfield Peverel station on the Chelmsford–Colchester section. The electronic destination board, digital clock, the neat shelter on the down platform and the general air of tidiness are characteristic of the modern image

41 (bottom)   Witham station in November 1989 looking towards London, the unit on the left having terminated here, is waiting to return to Liverpool Street. Braintree branch services use the platform face on the far right. Extensive car parking facilities are provided but reaching the trains involves a long walk by the main road (just beyond the houses) and then down by the side of the station

in the GER's Act of Incorporation (1862) that the GER must take the line over and work it for 50 per cent of the receipts whenever so required, an obligation, however, that was neatly side-stepped both in 1887 and 1914. On the other hand, after 1869, common sense led to the development of a mutually satisfactory *modus vivendi* in which through rates, exchange facilities, running powers to Marks Tey (for attachment to GER services), use of Haverhill GER station and of Stratford works for heavy repairs were amicably conceded.

Traffic was inevitably too small to support a capital debt that in early years had risen to over £212,000 (£516,245 in 1916) and despite expedients such as letting the line on contract between 1865 and 1867, one lessee being Sir Daniel Gooch, and an enterprising programme of excursions and cheap rates, the company fell bankrupt in 1874 and remained in the hands of the Official Receiver until 1885 when it was permitted to break free by issue of further stock in settlement of claims. The apogee came between 1900 and 1913.

In 1913, for example, when five locomotives, twelve coaches and 177 goods vehicles were owned, 161,404 ordinary passengers (there were also 134 season and 1,744 weekly ticket holders), 29,874 tons of general freight, 132 of coal, 11,926 of other minerals and 13,018 head of livestock were carried to produce an operational profit of £3,600. Much of the traffic derived from local development inspired by the railway, particularly from the growth of Haverhill, and from the greatly expanded brick yards

---

42 (top)   Anglia West. Newport station in December 1989 as a train on the hourly Cambridge to Liverpool Street stopping service arrives at the up platform. This view should be compared with that of thirty years earlier on page 71

43 (bottom)   Anglia East. August 1989 and an afternoon train on the hourly service from Wickford to Southminster stands at Woodham Ferrers station. The extensive car park may be discerned alongside the original GER station building of 1889, still in use although with a number of modern features. The crossing is typical of many throughout the region and when installed caused a strong local demand, including a sit-in, for gates. This view should be compared with that of 1911 on page 17 to appreciate just how the railway scene has changed

at Hedingham (where there was also a factory siding) which at one time required thirty or forty wagons a day and led the company to provide forty new ones in 1901 and a fifth locomotive in 1909. At Earl's Colne (so named in 1905 after opening in 1882 as Ford Gate and then becoming Colne when the original station of that name closed on 1 May 1889, before reopening as White Colne, on 1 April 1908) a small engineering works grew and in 1903 its owner, a Mr Hunt, gave land and lent money at 4 per cent for station development, and a private siding served a gravel working. From 1870 to 1899 Halstead had a paper mill but generally the town did not flourish, use of the 1865 Corn Exchange and the railway's cattle pens falling far below expectation. After 1900, however, brick yards were established and in 1906 the CVR opened a small but well-equipped works there, closing the original at Haverhill. Only recently has Halstead, with 6,463 persons in 1961 and new housing and factory estates, really developed. By 1971 it had 7,632.

In 1919 revenue was £36,656 but costs were climbing, renewals were necessary, and since 1914 the National Steam Car Company had been running in competition. Cessation of winter Sunday services (from December 1921 to September 1928) and a 10 per cent wages cut (1922) helped only a little and in 1923 absorption into the LNER came as a welcome escape from wellnigh insoluble problems. Services remained at four or five a day, but Haverhill (CVR) was closed to passenger traffic on 14 July 1924 (for most of its history it had been used only by the very few passenger trains without GER connections), stock was replaced (except for two of the three bogie coaches acquired in 1906), Halstead works and depot were closed and the five locomotives were either withdrawn or dispersed by 1930. Weakness of the bridges and the general superiority of the Sudbury line largely prevented the development of through working by the LNER although there were a number of through excursions, mainly to Clacton. The war brought heavy traffic to air bases at Halstead and Birdbrook and others near the line (for example, 2,971 wagons of bombs were consigned to White Colne and 3,959 to Earl's Colne for USAF fields alone in the three summer months of 1944), but after 1945 traffic of all kinds fell steadily away and by the 1950s even the Hedingham installations were derelict. There was just not enough to share with the Sudbury line, and the extension of most services from 1944 to Marks Tey, and the use of diesel multiple-units or railbuses from 1 January 1959, made little appreciable difference. Passenger services were withdrawn on 1 January 1962, the section between Yeldham and Haverhill closing completely (this included Birdbrook where there was an extensive grain store in the yard); freight services between Halstead and Yeldham ceased on 28 December 1964 and the line closed completely on 19 April 1965, the same day as the link between the Haverhill stations.

RAILWAYS TO BURY ST EDMUNDS

Although its population was only 12,538 in 1841 Bury St Edmunds, the market centre for a huge area and well equipped with flourishing mills, maltings, tanneries and foundries, was a rich commercial prize to be contested for by King's Lynn, which sent 10,000 tons or more of coals, merchandise and wines to it each year along the Ouse and Lark, and by Ipswich, anxious to expand the trade of its new docks. The issue was resolved in favour of Ipswich with the opening of the Ipswich & Bury line (for its origins see Chapter IV) to freight on 30 November 1846 and passengers on 24 December; by the latter date coal prices in the town had already fallen by 10 to 15 per cent. In 1848 the Corn Exchange was enlarged, a gas company was formed in 1849 and by 1851 population was up to 13,900. Meanwhile, the rout of Lynn interests had been confirmed by the 1847 failure in Parliament of the Ely & Bury St Edmunds as an extension of the Lynn & Ely.

In 1847 Newmarket Railway extensions were sanctioned to Ely, Thetford and Bury St Edmunds, the Ipswich & Bury, hopeful of reaching Cambridge and Ely, having meanwhile been persuaded to be content with a spur to the new lines from Kentford. However, the Newmarket encountered insuperable difficulties (Chapter VI), and not until 1 April 1854 was the Bury line opened under ECR operation. Through traffic between Cambridge and Ipswich at once developed, increasing substantially east of Bury from 1 September 1879 with the opening of the Newmarket–Ely line, to which access could be gained over the Chippenham Curve without entering Newmarket. By 1883 twelve daily trains were running over whole or part of the line, including the through working between London and Bury made obligatory, on the town's representations, in the GER's 1862 Act; from 1949 this ran as a portion of the 'Fenman', then separately, and finally as the 11.00 pm down, before ceasing early in the 1980s. Over the years a wide range of through journeys have been possible from Bury, including destinations such as Glasgow and Edinburgh and the various towns served by the summer Saturday trains between Clacton, the Midlands and the North. These have all ceased but in 1989 there were five daily trains to Manchester (including the 'Britannia') three extending to Liverpool (the 'Loreley' as the successor to the 'North Country Continental'), one to Barrow (Blackpool on Saturdays), and three to Birmingham; in the opposite direction the counterparts were Harwich and Colchester. The basic service remains Peterborough and Cambridge to Ipswich. Although coal traffic ceased on 6 August 1984, and the beet refinery sidings were lifted in 1985, Bury is a Speedlink depot, and the line, resignalled in 1983, an important route to Harwich and Felixstowe. Apart from Bury and Newmarket there has been little local development other than granaries and related activities. On 2 January 1967, overall revenue producing £88,400 against annual costs of £123,600, the intermediate stations were closed except for Kennett, Thurston and Elmswell, which like Newmarket and Dullingham (Chapter VI) became unstaffed halts.

Feeding Bury St Edmunds and this important cross-country line was the single-track branch from Long Melford, originally authorised to the ECR in 1861, re-enacted in 1862 to the GER, and opened by the GER on 9 August 1865 in association with the Stour Valley extensions. A handful of local services sufficed throughout its history, some running to and from Marks Tey supplemented by the occasional holiday express (for example, Leicester to Clacton in 1959); diesel multiple-units were introduced on 2 November 1959 (although there had been one daily since 1 May) but passenger facilities, lost at Bury East Gate as early as 1 May 1909, were withdrawn on 10 April 1961; freight continued between Bury and Lavenham until 19 April 1965 but the track to the south was lifted in 1962. The branch had completely failed to preserve the markets of Lavenham from decline; coconut matting and horsehair weaving replaced silk and wool, but population rose only from 1,811 in 1851 to 2,018 in 1901 and was a mere 1,305 in 1961.

The last line to Bury St Edmunds, once promising an importance it never acquired, was the Bury St Edmunds & Thetford (12¾ miles), incorporated in 1865, but, encountering serious difficulty in raising capital; it was not completed until 1 March 1876, when it opened under Thetford & Watton operation. This latter company was an 1866 incorporation with authority to raise £45,000 and construct 9 miles from the main line at Roudham Junction (see below) to the small Norfolk village of Watton; freight services, worked until 22 July by a contractor, began on 26 January 1869 and passenger services (four daily) followed on 18 October 1869. In the same year the Watton & Swaffham was authorised to raise £62,000 and continue over the 9½ miles to the GER's King's Lynn–Dereham line at Swaffham; like the B&T it was empowered to enter into agreement with the GER. Also like the B&T it found difficulty in raising capital, and not until 20 September 1875 did goods traffic begin (passenger on 15 November 1875). In 1873 the T&W, the only one of the three actually open, obtained powers to work the Bury line, to be reached over the GER main line, and to construct a spur to it at Thetford Bridge (the station and spur were opened on 15 November 1875). It was also authorised to raise £21,300 and subscribe £10,000 to the Watton & Swaffham, which it was now to work on completion. The elements were thus present for a single-company line, feeding and fed by the main Ely to Norwich route, striking through the heart of the eastern counties and reaching Marks Tey over the Sudbury line. However, in 1878 the Commons rejected an amalgamation bill and the route itself never had a chance to develop. By 1878 the B&T, with £89,672 already raised, was still £25,000 short of its liabilities and gladly accepted the GER's offer to purchase the whole for £33,000 of 4 per cent stock and £75,000 ordinary shares. The two northern companies were in little better shape and on 1 August 1879 handed their workings over to the GER, following this on 1 January 1880 with a formal lease: under this an increasing annual rental was to be paid from a basis of £1,500 in 1880 until in 1888 the W&S was receiving £2,250 a year and in 1891 the T&W £2,550, levels to be permanent thereafter. The GER ended through workings from Bury to Swaffham almost at once, and on 1 September 1880 the Thetford Bridge spur was closed. In 1898 both companies were totally absorbed by the GER. Meanwhile, indeed from 1880, the histories of the two branches had become quite distinct, that of the Thetford–Swaffham section being considered in the next section.

The Bury to Thetford branch, restricted to speeds of 30 mph and 40 ton locomotives until the mid-1890s, was despite its early pretensions no more than a very quiet rural branch, except in the two world wars. In the first a large military camp opened near Barnham in 1916 and the station handled large quantities of tanks, troops and stores; in the second Barnham had special sidings for a new ICI factory on the Bury side and others for one of the largest bomb dumps in the country to its north, the latter handling 720,000 tons during the war years in 132,729 wagon loads. Peace fully exposed the paucity of traffic: passenger services ended on 8 June 1953, freight on 27 June 1960. By 1963 the track was lifted; at the Thetford end part of its bed now lies under a modern road while Thetford Bridge station became a Youth Hostel and then a County Council road depot.

By the time of this closure Bury St Edmunds had extracted the benefits of its four lines (plus a GER bus service to Stanton in 1908) to the full. Since the early developments mentioned above, malting, brewing, milling and agricultural-implement making had all flourished, the markets had expanded, from 1878 the Suffolk Regiment barracks had been located in the town and from 1881 to 1935 a large public school was contributing traffic. By 1901 population was 16,255, in part reflecting Bury's establishment as a high-class, residential town. In 1925 it acquired what subsequently became the largest sugar-beet factory in the country, the four railways having played a significant part in this, and since 1945 the largest maltings. The 1981 population was 28,914 and will rise further as industrial and housing estates are developed to accommodate 10,000 Londoners; engineering, malting, brewing and agricultural-implement making, printing and sugar-beet are amongst the principal activities; in the markets some 200,000 or so fat and store livestock are still handled annually.

ELY TO NORWICH

The 36¾ mile Norwich & Brandon, incorporated in 1844 with a capital of £380,000, formed the second stage of the east-west trunk route, now combined with a London line, begun by the two Stephensons with the Yarmouth & Norwich. The latter company backed the N&B and amalgamated with it on 30 June 1845 to form the Norfolk Railway. The N&B was built by Grissell & Peto and opened with double track on 30 July 1845, the same day as the ECR's Newport to Brandon extension; belated re-assessment of Thetford's importance led to a deviation through the town which at first was to have been served by a branch. London–Norwich services began at once, extending to Yarmouth after completion of the Trowse Swing Bridge on 15 December 1845 allowed entry into Thorpe and a junction with the Y&N line. Early services comprised five a day each way of which two were expresses; 4½ hours was the best time from Norwich to London and third-class passengers were offered covered accommodation from Yarmouth on the 5.30 am service which took exactly seven hours over its journey. The *Norfolk Chronicle* claimed that travel could not be 'rendered more comfortable than it is on the Norfolk Railway', and indeed the line quickly established itself; some of the effects on road transport have been indicated in Chapter I. An important subsidiary aspect was the availability of the railway telegraph to private persons so that from November 1846 London market prices could be 'expressed' to Norwich to the great benefit of the city's business.

A number of excursions used the line, these including an experimental trip between London and Rotterdam via Yarmouth on 9 July 1846. It was an experience the participants would scarcely forget. The down journey was uneventful, 215 minutes being spent on the railway, but on the return the ship encountered bad weather, the crew was the worse for drink and the ship got off course; the train left Yarmouth extremely late, and to crown all misfortunes the locomotive boiler burst near Ely and the wretched passengers had to alight and walk into the city. More successful, if bizarre, was the excursion from London for those who wished to watch the hanging of the murderer

Rush at Norwich Castle; the train was halted at Wymondham where police turned off a number of undesirable characters, whose presence had been notified by telegraph.

Sharp deterioration of service set in from 8 May 1848 when the ECR, replacing existing staff with its own, introducing new regulations, closing Brandon locomotive depot and revising fares, took the Norfolk on lease, so saving it from financial 'perdition'. Already on 12 December 1845 the 'excessive' speed of 55 mph had caused a derailment near Thetford in which the engine crew died, and under the ECR mishaps became much more frequent. Two were killed on 30 December 1854 when a fast cattle train struck the rear of the up mail that had already been standing 23 minutes while repairs were effected on the locomotive, and on 9 November 1856 the engine of the down 'Parliamentary' broke a leading tyre between Thetford and Harling, derailing and overturning the train and killing the driver; a few minutes later an up goods hit the wreckage but fortunately the collision was slight. Meanwhile public disquiet was mounting, culminating in November 1855 in the appointment of a committee of inquiry by Norwich City Council. On 7 December this reported most unfavourably on the ECR, leading the Board of Trade to conduct its own investigations and the conclusion that the line was insecure and dangerous. Remedial works, involving bridge and viaduct restoration as well as track renovation, were taken in hand at great expense during 1856-7.

Services were still five daily each way in 1874, but by 1892 had risen to seven down, eight up, including the Mail and five other London trains in each direction, along with seven down and ten up goods trains, three of the latter continuing to London; there was additional movement between Thetford and Roudham Junction, and between Wymondham (junction for Wells and King's Lynn—Chapter X) and Norwich. Under the LNER passenger services rose to thirteen or fourteen on ordinary weekdays by 1939, seven being London trains of which the majority combined with Lynn and Hunstanton portions south of Ely. Gradual concentration of such expresses on Lynn from the late 1950s left the Ely-Norwich line with a stopping service of multiple diesel-units, this being revised, speeded and, for the most part, extended to Cambridge on 2 January 1967. On 6 March conductor guards were introduced except for Ely and

Thetford and 'basic' railway operation adopted. Summer traffic to the Norfolk coast from the Midlands and North, long a feature, was increased by the closure of the M&GNR route (Chapter IX), but by 1989 had itself been superseded in importance by regular cross country links between Norwich and Liverpool (four daily) and Birmingham (eight), supplementing Sheringham/Yarmouth/Lowestoft/Norwich to Cambridge/ Peterborough stopping services.

Along the line, Thetford, a railway crossroads, given a new station in 1890, has gained the most. Growing to 4,613 by 1901 it became a major malting centre and acquired a large engineering plant. The latter failed in 1932 but canning developed, followed, in connection with London resettlement, by a variety of modern factories; even so the goods yard closed in November 1983. Population increased from 13,727 to 19,591 between 1971 and 1981. Wymondham, a rail distribution centre for cement, took up horsehair weaving and brush making, but population fell from 5,177 in 1851 to 4,794 by 1911; revival around a new staple industry of turnery followed and the 1981 total, boosted by recent housing and factory estates, was 9,811. At Brandon (6,609 in 1981), once a centre for rabbit skins and, after 1900, saw milling, the goods yard was reinstated in August 1986 to accommodate Redland timber and tile traffic transferred from East Dereham. A half-mile branch was laid in 1986 to a bulk grain depot at Eccles Road. Formerly, by 1900, Attleborough had offered cider traffic from a works near the station, and between Thetford and Brandon there was a railside manure works.

The line served many military bases in World War II. At Thetford extra sidings were laid in for petroleum trains, 594 of which were received (280 in 1943) before the laying of a pipeline in March 1944, and for extensive periods from 1941 to 1944 two or three daily trains of army tanks were handled for the nearby Breckland training grounds; issue of tickets was 110,939 in 1944 as compared with 21,418 in 1938. Shippea Hill (Mildenhall Road to 1 April 1885, then Burnt Fen to 1 May 1905) was the station for several air bases and today still serves that at Mildenhall. Attleborough yard was several times enlarged when, as at Harling Road, where a new stores depot was built, three bases were being supplied. Additional sidings were provided at Hethersett (where the station closed on 31 January 1966 as revenue was only £200 a year, costs £700) for petroleum, and for bombs at Brandon.

The Swaffham branch, the origins of which have been traced in a previous section, left the main line at Roudham Junction, an isolated station built with the branch. On 1 October 1902 this was officially designated as an exchange point only, and, apart from brief resumption during the coal strike from 6 April to 2 October 1921, main-line trains ceased to call on 1 March 1920; the station closed to advertised public services on 1 May 1932, although subsequently branch trains frequently made unadvertised stops there. Controversy exists as to whether normal tickets were ever issued to or from Roudham Junction. Probably they were not, except perhaps in the early days of independent working by the Thetford & Watton to 1880—certainly the station did not appear in GER fare tables although other places on the branch did even before their total absorption by that company.

Known locally, like others of its kind, as the 'Crab & Winkle', the line had a particular charm. In latter years it was noted for the remarkable care bestowed on the upkeep of its stations—Wretham & Hockham regularly won prizes after 1937 and Stow Bedon from 1958 to 1963—but the masterpiece was the station name and locomotive outline cut into the hedge at Watton. The branch's busiest days were again in World War II, with an RAF base at Watton and a cement centre for aerodrome construction near Roudham. In peace, however, many useful functions were fulfilled; schoolchildren made great use of it and the two Sunday-night trains to Thetford (withdrawn in 1959) were well patronised by servicemen returning from weekend leave for many years after the war. In the 1920s at Stow Bedon as much as £100 a week would be taken for parcels alone, much of the traffic there, as at all the stations, being in dead poultry and eggs; as late as 1963 some 180 trucks of sugar-beet were leaving Holme Hale annually. However, for forty years or more the line suffered from local belief that closure was imminent and few cared to become dependent on it; the climax of this was reached when the Beeching Report cited it in detail as an example of the need for pruning, £28,900 a year to be saved despite the use of diesel multiple-units. Closure to passengers finally came on

15 June 1964, although freight continued between Swaffham and Watton until 19 April 1965.

From Wymondham ran a 6¾ mile branch to the former Eastern Union line at Forncett, Ashwellthorpe being the only intermediate station. This was a GER branch opened on 2 May 1881 to afford a relief route between East Suffolk and Norfolk and so reduce the congestion around Norwich. Almost certainly double track from the first (indisputably so by 1890), it normally carried some seven passenger trains a day each way. For some years around the turn of the century one included a through portion from Liverpool Street to Wells, the development of an earlier service from Forncett only, continuing via Dereham. Freight usage under the GER was light, despite the purpose of the branch, and comprised little more than an Ipswich to Peterborough train with no return working, and a daily service each way between Beccles and Wells. In World War I it had heavy military traffic, but from 10 September 1939 passenger services were suspended and never reinstated; freight continued only until 4 August 1951. The track was lifted in February 1952 except for a portion at Wymondham used at first for storing cripples, and subsequently for burning the frames of old coaches, the frames and loose metal filling several trains a week to a private yard at Trowse (Norwich), where many locomotives were also being broken up for scrap. This last section did not finally close until 3 August 1976.

CHAPTER VIII

Norwich, Yarmouth and Lowestoft

FROM NORWICH TO THE COAST

On 7 February 1835 a 'moveable panorama' of the Liverpool & Manchester Railway exhibited in the Theatre Royal gave Norwich its first view of the railway world and no doubt served to raise enthusiasm if not capital for the ECR. The ECR's failure in fact left Norwich in a sorry plight. Despite the 'New Cut' of 1833 to the sea at Lowestoft, coal prices remained high and, coupled with reaction against the introduction of new machinery, left the city's textile industries in decline before northern competition. Some 8,000 in an 1841 population of 62,344 were still employed in the mills and factories but unemployment was rife. Yarmouth, between which and Norwich goods worth £40,000 passed annually, had suffered by both the 'New Cut' and steam navigation which had reduced shipping time to London. Lowestoft, with 4,837 inhabitants in 1841, was shortly to gain a new harbour, but at this time was of little significance.

Undoubtedly these factors weighed with George and Robert Stephenson in 1841 when Yarmouth was selected as the starting point for a grand east-to-west trunk route, the first phase of which was to be a 20½ mile, £200,000 line to Norwich along the Yare valley via Reedham. Other projects were being considered in the same period, but it was this Yarmouth & Norwich that was incorporated in June 1842. Again Norwich displayed short-sighted reluctance to invest, and the scheme was nearly abandoned before a solution was found in the device of letting contracts only on condition that a large part of the price be paid as stock; in this way over half of the sum needed was raised. Work began in April 1843, the 50 chain diversion of the Yare between Trowse Hythe and Wensum Reach, undertaken in preference to building a bridge, being started in the following month. Grissell

& Peto, with the latter as resident engineer, employed 1,500 men on the contract. No tunnels or major works were involved and, after a ceremonial opening on 30 April 1844, a daily service of four trains began on 1 May, 1,015 passengers being carried on the first day. Completion was thus within the target of eighteen months, although the cost had been nearer £10,000 a mile than the £7,000 estimated. One of the original stations was the isolated Berney Arms, built only because of Berney's condition of sale that a station should be provided there in perpetuity. However, he had omitted to specify that trains should stop, and when in 1850 the ECR discontinued calls through lack of traffic, years of dispute, compromise and litigation ensued, until in 1860 the courts finally declared in Berney's favour, services having meanwhile been restored in 1855.

The line offered journeys in 50 minutes, although for a time it held the national sprint record of 1 mile in 44 seconds. Speed was of especial value on 22 February 1851 when a seamen's riot was brewing in Yarmouth and a train of troops and police rushed there from Norwich prevented the development of a really serious situation. Ordinary return fares were 5s, 4s and 2s, but on occasion came far below these levels. A nonconformist excursion to the sea from Attleborough (on the Brandon line) and Norwich on 30 June 1846 cost only 1s for adults and 3d for a child and attracted some 6,000 passengers, while on the previous day a 7s 6d excursion to London, on which fourth class was provided, carried 1,500 out of Yarmouth. In general the company, the Norfolk Railway from 1845, adhered to the principle enunciated before an 1846 Parliamentary Committee by Robert Stephenson that 'you increase your income by diminishing your fares' to the point below which further reductions cause actual loss of revenue. By application of the same policy inroads were also being made on the water traffic conveyed by Norfolk wherries, sailing craft of 15 to 40 tons on the Yare, Bure, Waveney and the Broads, although there were still a hundred or so of these vessels in the 1880s and they were not finally ousted until the advent of steam and diesel navigation. Adverse weather gave an edge to railway competition, for example in August 1844 when a consignment of 60 cwt of tea was transferred to the railway, but the latter's exposed position did not always allow it to escape entirely. It was cut by floods in December 1849 and

January 1855, and in January 1881 the down Mail, already four hours late, was stuck in the snow near Buckenham for six hours: the combined efforts of five locomotives and sixty men proving ineffectual, it was eventually returned to Norwich.

Progress was generally retarded by the ECR's assumption of the line in 1848, and even by the early 1870s there were still only some six or seven daily services each way, including Lowestoft trains and portions. Yarmouth, however, was beginning its rise as a resort and within a few years additional traffic had justified the 11 mile long single-track relief line from Brundall to Breydon Junction via the small country town (subsequently a point of entry to the Broads) of Acle, reducing the distance to the coast by 2 miles. Opened from the Yarmouth end to Acle on 12 March 1883, it was completed on 1 June of the same year. By 1892 nine daily services were using the new line to Yarmouth, eight the original, which also carried the Lowestoft trains and, west of Whitlingham Junction, those between Norwich and Cromer (Chapter IX) and which had been doubled as far as Reedham.

From Brundall to Reedham had been double track since 1866 at least, and a further section, from Norwich to Whitlingham, had been laid and awaited inspection when on 10 September 1874, after years of perfect safety under Cooke & Wheatstone instruments installed in 1848, an appalling head-on collision near Thorpe village took the lives of twenty-one passengers and four company servants and cost the GER some £40,000 in compensation. The tragedy involved the 8.40 pm up Mail from Yarmouth and Lowestoft, with thirteen carriages travelling at 30 to 35 mph, and the fourteen-carriage 5 pm London to Yarmouth express. They met with a crash like 'a peal of thunder', each making speed in the belief that the other was being held for it. It was the down train that was in the wrong place as the result of serious confusion at Thorpe station in Norwich, where Cooper, the night inspector, had called the Mail up from Brundall but then told Parker, a day inspector, that he had not done so and allowed him to despatch the express. Robson, the telegraph clerk, had contrary to the rules transmitted to Brundall the permission for the Mail to proceed without obtaining Cooper's signature to verify the instruction; technically this perhaps cleared Cooper, except that he had returned to Robson specifically to cancel the previous message. The difficulty in apportioning blame was indicated when first the City Coroner's jury indicted both Cooper and Robson for manslaughter, then the County Coroner found against Robson only, and finally at Norwich Assizes (April 1875) it was Robson who was acquitted and Cooper who was imprisoned for eight months.

From the 1890s holiday traffic rose steadily, peaking between the wars, as the Broads (200 miles of navigable waterways and some fifty lakes of up to 400 acres) became a major attraction; Brundall Gardens Halt was opened in 1924 to serve them. By 1939 twelve daily trains each way (including London portions) were running via Acle, ten by Reedham; additional services ran in the summer with many Bank Holiday Extras—forty-six on August Monday 1939. After 1945 such levels would never be repeated, but summer Saturday expresses from the midlands and north remained; intensification of this traffic following the closure of the M&GNR led in May 1960 to track circuiting and colour light signals throughout the Acle line.

Diversion of through Yarmouth traffic from the East Suffolk was another element, until in May 1984 weekday locomotive-hauled workings ceased. Meanwhile, summer Saturday holiday workings had also been evolving until in 1988, with the exception of three London services, the basic daily links with Cambridge, Birmingham and Liverpool were enough; in 1977 there had been seven London–Yarmouth workings. Despite a small commuter element local usage has remained low. Whitlingham (site of a cement depot until 1987) closed entirely on 19 September 1955 and from 6 March 1967 all stations were unmanned. In 1990 the Yarmouth service is twenty-three up, twenty-four down but with many extended far beyond the line. In 1983 the Reedham–Yarmouth line was threatened with closure; 29 October 1985 was published as the date but a combination of user groups and local authorities undertook to provide an annual £52,500 (half the cost of track maintenance and renewals) and the section was saved. Cantley beet factory, opened 1912, and continuously operative from 1920, is still rail linked.

The 11¼ mile Reedham to Lowestoft branch, sanctioned in 1845 as the second stage of the Lowestoft Railway & Harbour promotion of 1844, opened to goods on 3 May and passengers on 1 July 1847. Sir Samuel Morton Peto, 'the maker of Lowestoft' and its lord of the manor, was the chairman and principal shareholder of the overall project, and it was envisaged that Lowestoft fish and imports would be despatched as far afield as Manchester. The hopes were not groundless, for on 9 May 1846 alone eighteen vessels from Lowestoft lay in Norwich with coke, coal and general merchandise for the railway station, and in 1845 the efforts of the company had already provided Lowestoft with a harbour containing 3,000 ft of wharf frontage, powered cranes, a bucket dredging machine, fishing facilities and a pier with double-track tramway and a turntable at each end. In 1846 the Norfolk Railway assumed a lease of the Lowestoft company and also took over the feeble Norwich & Lowestoft Navigation, which since 1844 had also been owned by Peto, and over which the railway had provided swing bridges at Reedham and Somerleyton.

In 1848 the ECR acquired control and set out to make Lowestoft a major port. Recognising that London-bound German cattle landed there would be saved twelve hours on the water, special rates of 5s a head were offered, to the fury of English farmers who had to pay 12s for an equivalent distance. The coal firm of Priors (later renamed the Norfolk & Eastern) was granted concession rates of $\frac{1}{2}$d per ton mile plus 25 per cent for the hire of wagons for inland conveyance, with a guaranteed reduction if lower rates were ever offered to anyone else on the ECR; it was the resentment of King's Lynn at this that led representatives of the East Anglian Railways on the ECR board to engineer the proprietors' revolt of 1855–6 which finally displaced Waddington from the chair. Waddington's critics also made much of the extensive capital expenditure by the ECR on Lowestoft (by 1856 this had reached £118,703 on the line, £196,369 on the harbour) which they described as a 'ruinous adjunct' detrimental to Yarmouth; but although immediate loss was involved the policy in the long run was sound. The number of vessels docking in Lowestoft rose from 410 (totalling 21,730 tons) in 1845 to 1,636 (134,944 tons) in 1851, and between the latter year and 1853 foreign arrivals increased from 85 to 144. The North of Europe Steam Navigation Company, of which Peto was vice-chairman, opened its main depot in the town and established regular steam sailings to Denmark; in 1853 its ships landed, *inter alia*, 14,998 oxen, 10,886 sheep, 1,370 casks of butter, 300 barrels of beef and pork, 1,100 quarters of grain and

115,000 cheeses, the bulk of which was forwarded to London by rail. Timber and stone imports grew and the entry of coal led to extensive coking ovens. Also, by 1860, the railway had precipitated the transference of the principal fishing activities from luggers to the 'half and half' boats that were able to set out and return fully loaded in a day. In 1851 77,999 packages of fish left by rail, but 13,030 tons of it left in 1860 and 17,340 in 1864.

LOWESTOFT

The Norfolk Railway retained its monopoly at Lowestoft until 1 June 1859 when Peto's Lowestoft & Beccles entered the town over a swing bridge at Oulton Broad (originally named Carlton Colville), the junction for a 1¾ mile freight line to the south bank of Lowestoft harbour, with a spur to Kirkley goods and coal depot, to join the Reedham line ½ mile from the terminal. On the same day the Yarmouth & Haddiscoe had opened, a spur from Haddiscoe Low Level to Fleet Junction affording direct access from Ipswich to both the Norfolk Railway and Yarmouth, the latter over the single-track St Olave's swing bridge. On 1 June 1872 a new link between Marsh Junction on the Norfolk line and Swing Bridge Junction on the Yarmouth side of Haddiscoe High Level established through communication between Yarmouth and Lowestoft. A service of four trains daily, three on Wednesdays, was introduced, but the route was circuitous and was almost entirely supplanted from 13 July 1903 when the Norfolk & Suffolk Joint Committee (formed in 1898 for the development of the region's north-east coast by the Midland & Great Northern Joint Railway and the GER) opened the direct coastal link between the two towns. On 9 May 1904 the original Haddiscoe on the Reedham line was closed except for the goods depot and replaced by the present Low Level station some 700 yd nearer Lowestoft; this was conveniently sited adjacent to the old Herringfleet Exchange station on the Beccles–Yarmouth line, which now had its platforms raised and other improvements made, and was renamed Haddiscoe. The western curve at Haddiscoe was never used by a regular passenger service, while the eastern spur, used by a handful of summer trains until 8 September 1934, was finally lifted in January 1939. Meanwhile, in September 1926, the manually operated single-

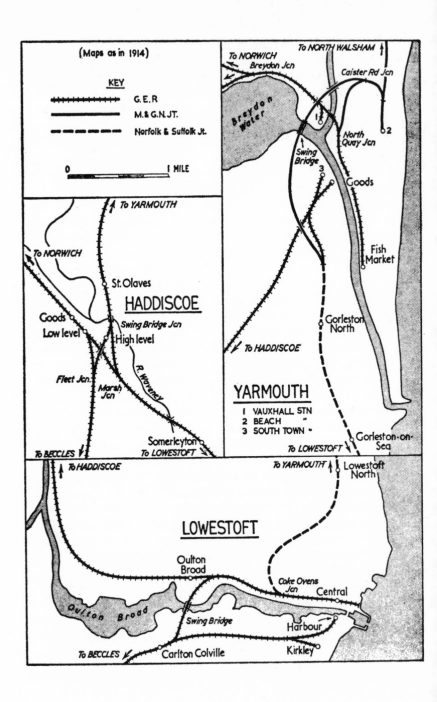

(Maps as in 1914)

KEY

┼┼┼┼┼┼┼┼┼┼┼┼ G.E.R

──────────── M.& G.N.JT.

── ── ── ── ── Norfolk & Suffolk Jt.

0 _____ 1 MILE

To YARMOUTH

To NORWICH

St. Olaves

HADDISCOE

Goods
Low level

Swing Bridge Jcn

High level

Fleet Jcn.

Marsh
Jcn

R. Waveney

To BECCLES

Somerleyton
To LOWESTOFT

To NORWICH
Breydon Jcn

To NORTH WALSHAM

Caister Rd Jcn

Breydon
Water

1

2

North
Quay Jcn

Swing
Bridge

3

Goods

Fish
Market

Gorleston
North

To HADDISCOE

YARMOUTH

1 VAUXHALL STN
2 BEACH "
3 SOUTH TOWN "

Gorleston-on-
Sea

To LOWESTOFT

To HADDISCOE

To YARMOUTH

Lowestoft
North

LOWESTOFT

Oulton
Broad

Coke Ovens
Jcn

Central

Oulton Broad

Swing Bridge

Harbour

To BECCLES

Carlton Colville

Kirkley

track swing bridge at St Olave's had been replaced by a double-track power-operated structure which continued in use until 2 November 1959, when, apart from the Fleet Junction to Aldeby stub retained for beet traffic until the end of the 1964–5 season (and for a short while the section outside Yarmouth), the line from Beccles to Yarmouth (South Town) was closed.

Traffic for the latter was diverted through Lowestoft, where the station was rebuilt in 1961, and over the coastal line. Since 1903 this has helped to develop a considerable holiday trade at Corton, Hopton and Gorleston (population 4,892 in 1961). In preparation for the additional traffic, bridges were strengthened and track improved, but the typical imbalance between summer and winter patronage dogged the line; from 12 September 1966 the intermediate stations became unstaffed halts and then on 4 May 1970 the line, including Yarmouth South Town, closed. Through traffic was discussed in Chapter IV and services between 1903 and 1953 from the M&GN at Yarmouth are mentioned below.

Railway enterprise, including a bus service to Southwold from 18 July 1904 to January 1913 and also one to Oulton Broad, continued at Lowestoft under the GER, which provided a spacious fish market (1865), reached by a street tramway, and curing houses. The harbour was further enlarged and improved, especially in 1883 and 1892, and the company opened a second pier complete with a concert hall and reading room, as well as being responsible for such developments as the new road bridge over Lake Lothing in 1897. By 1892 the harbour represented an investment of £320,000 and covered 20 acres; nearly 1,000 fishing boats were registered there and Yarmouth's trawling trade had been absorbed. In the early years of this century between 50,000 and 60,000 tons of fish valued at over £500,000 were being landed annually, of which five-sixths were forwarded by rail, half of it to London which annually consumed some 60,000 to 80,000 tons from Lowestoft and Yarmouth combined. In 1903 foreign trade brought 354 arrivals (totalling 58,245 tons burthen) and 168 departures (43,816 tons), coastal sailings 1,168 (112,222 tons) and 1,189 (123,663 tons) respectively; in 1902 the value of imports was £168,089, timber and coal being pre-eminent as in early days, and that of exports £249,712. Some held that the results, good as they were and especially so in view of continual silting problems, constituted an inadequate return on capital, but no one could complain of the emergence of the town as a resort.

Even in 1854 the ECR included Lowestoft in its 'Family Tickets' scheme of reduced rates (for example, 21s or 17s per person from Cambridge) and the GER continued to foster such traffic. From the 1850s many houses were built and the 'new town' of South Lowestoft grew rapidly; fine hanging gardens, bathing machines, the GER pier and many other amenities were provided, and overall the town was improved, gas and water being installed in 1853, electricity in 1903. The town was also receiving recognition as a good base from which to enter the Broads. Such developments were materially forwarded by the quality of rail service from London, times falling from 205 minutes in 1863 to 190 in 1888, and to 150 in 1904 when for one summer a non-stop express was run (Chapter IV); by the last date there were also through summer workings from Liverpool and Birmingham. Each summer something in excess of 100,000 visitors spend a week's holiday or more in the town and there are at least as many day trippers.

Excellent rail and water facilities early attracted initiative and capital to the town. Food processing, ship building, engineering (marine, general and precision) are amongst others that are to be found today, many extending back into the last century and owing much to the railways. Even the frozen food industry, a post-war addition, for many years despatched much of its output by rail. In 1989 there was still a daily Speedlink service to the town. The port, much developed, includes amongst its many functions that of base for off-shore North Sea Gas production. Continental competition and fish migration have destroyed the herring industry, which until the 1960s still brought the Scottish drifters into the town, but expansion of the whitefish trade has compensated; in 1960 18,000 tons were landed and by 1968 it was worth £2m per annum. In October 1987 a new fish market opened but, sadly, the once intensive rail carriage of fish ceased in 1972 latterly with two nightly vans of offal. The port's container terminal is essentially road served, and the Denmark Road coal depot closed on 23 January 1989.

A subsidiary source of local employment for sixty men or so

was, until closure in the 1960s, the GER sleeper depot opened in 1914 on a reclaimed mud bank in Lake Lothing. It eventually covered 13 acres and had a capacity of 450,000 sleepers and a 1,000 ft wharf where ships could unload directly; in its latter years, when there was also a pre-cast concrete sleeper depot employing 100 and covering 2½ acres, it supplied over half of the Eastern Region, two or three special trains leaving it each week.

GREAT YARMOUTH

Great Yarmouth, historically the port of Norwich, was intended in 1836 to be the ECR terminal. As Bosanquet, then chairman of the ECR, explained: 'We shall be bringing, as it were, Great Yarmouth, one of the most ancient and long flourishing of our sea ports, to London, renewing her youth, filling her harbour once more with that foreign commerce for which she is, by her relative position to the northern ports of Europe, so admirably adapted.' As mentioned elsewhere Yarmouth was one of the ports harmed by the greater ease of access to London brought by steam navigation, and the initial failure of the ECR followed by the subsequent preference of that company for the more modern facilities at Lowestoft left its future in the balance; in 1850 the town was described as squalid and overcrowded and was doing little more than hold its own.

The potential, however, especially in fishing, was evident. A 1¾ mile street-tramway extension was made to the fish market as early as 1847 and thereafter, as at Lowestoft, the GER did everything in its power to further the industry, and with equal success. By 1892 private investment in the herring trade alone amounted to £500,000 and by 1902 upwards of 50,000 lasts (each of 132,000 herrings) were being landed annually for processing and despatch by rail to London, Manchester, Birmingham and other centres. General harbour trade had meanwhile held up far better than might have been expected a few years earlier. In 1899 there were 317 arrivals from abroad (totalling 77,149 tons) and 839 coastal (101,451 tons); laden departures were 214 (35,245 tons) and 386 (47,669 tons) respectively. In 1903 imports were valued at £267,169 and despite some continuing water competition, the railways, connected to the quays by tramways, carried the bulk of the traffic inland. In 1987 the port handled 995,107 tonnes of Ro/Ro cargo, 111,940 of agricultural produce, 312,846 of ferti-

lisers and minerals, and 215,434 of petroleum products, but the
railway plays no part, the Quay lines having closed on 1
January 1976, and freight facilities at Vauxhall on 4 March
1985. In 1914 1,000 fishing boats were registered, but the
industry has virtually gone, replaced by servicing of North Sea
gas and oil rigs.

The railways' greatest boon to Yarmouth was in ensuring its
elevation to the leading rank of British holiday resorts, so that
some 800,000 resident visitors are received each year. A major
contributor to this was the Eastern & Midlands (with direct
through communication to the west from North Walsham on
5 April 1883 and later part of the Midland & Great Northern
Joint system—Chapter IX), running into Beach station and
bringing traffic from the midlands and north; this was also connected, over the former Yarmouth Union, authorised in 1880 and
opened on 15 May 1882, to the quayside tramways. Not only did
this establish a lasting link between the resort and the holidaymakers of the midlands, but it stimulated the GER to greater
efforts, so that Yarmouth became the best-served town of its size
in the British Isles. Best summer times from London, 363 minutes
in 1846, 275 by 1862 and 215 by 1867, fell from the 195 of 1888 to
150 from 1904 to 1914, the latter achieved on non-stop runs
headed by 'Claud Hamilton' 4–4–0s despite slowing to walking
pace to pick up pilotmen at Beccles and St Olave's swing bridges.
The non-stop 150 minute schedules were lost in World War I but
were soon restored, briefly reduced to 147, and maintained by
the LNER, but by 1939 had been increased to 155 and were Saturdays only. After 1962 timings of 156 minutes down (then 165)
and 155 up were available via Norwich connections, additional
services compensating for the declining use of the East Suffolk
line. Throughout this century a wide range of cross-country
services has been provided by both the GER and the M&GN lines.
In July 1902 the former introduced services from Liverpool and
Manchester (daily from the latter) in conjunction with the
Great Central and from Birmingham in association with the
LNWR; before 1914 a through summer working from the West
Riding had also been established, and in its latter days some
eight additional summer Saturday trains ran each way on the
M&GN.

Summer Saturday services in 1977 included through workings with Cambridge, Sheffield, Derby, Walsall, Manchester, Leeds and Newcastle (the former weekday services to York and Birmingham no longer operated). The many of these were transferred from the M&GN after its closure in 1959, but in terms of time the results were generally beneficial, for the 1960 tables showed a 96 minute acceleration from King's Norton, 67 from Shirebrook, 56 from Chesterfield, 42 and 40 from Leicester and 42 from Derby, the list providing evidence of other through trains now modified or discontinued. To accommodate the additional traffic more easily, Vauxhall station, badly damaged by bombing in May 1943, was substantially modernised in and from 1959: between then and 1961 the area was resignalled, longer platforms provided at Vauxhall where the forecourt was remodelled to reduce the interference by rail vans working over street lines to the quays, and extra sidings were put in. During 1965 495,191 tickets were collected at Vauxhall station, numbers rising to over 9,000 on peak Saturdays as compared with 6,000 before the closure of the M&GN; after 1959 a system of Seat Ticket Regulation was enforced.

At South Town station (closed in 1970) where, in the floods of 1953, water rose 1 ft over the platform and a signalman, marooned for 21 hours, was rescued in a boat, 127,964 tickets were collected in 1965 despite its reduced status. Beach terminus closed on 2 March 1959 and was subsequently converted into an omnibus station, its siding space and yard into a car park. An earlier closure was the long curving link from just outside Beach station to the Norfolk & Suffolk's Lowestoft line. The service to the latter had never enjoyed the same success as the M&GN's Yarmouth trains and when the 800 ft five-span bridge over Breydon Water fell due for major repairs the link was broken on 21 September 1953; the bridge has since been removed.

An important facet of growth in Yarmouth (24,086 inhabitants in 1841, 48,273 in 1981 has been the postwar establishment of light industries. In the nineteenth century brewing, malting and such activities as rope, twine and net making were carried on, but now footwear, clothing, textiles, radio and television, general engineering and, above all, food and drink preparation and canning have become important; the last includes a frozen-food plant of 1946 which by 1961 was despatching 50 to 100 tons of produce daily by rail to Trowse, Norwich, Chelmsford and, in a service shared with Lowestoft, to Whitemoor. During the summer months additional trains ran to centres such as Birmingham, Bedford and Doncaster and as many as 200 containers would leave in a day, but since then the traffic has been diverted to the roads.

NORWICH

The Norwich & Brandon opened on 30 July 1845 although it was not until the Trowse swing bridge was completed on 15 December that junction could be effected with the Y&N; prior to this a temporary terminal on the west bank of the Wensum was used. This bridge, designed by Bidder and built by Peto, lasted until the weekend of 12–14 August 1905. Single track, but carrying by then 170 trains a day and requiring them to crawl at 3 mph to pick up the pilot, it had become an intolerable bottleneck. The new double track bridge, with one navigable span and power operated, sufficed until 16 February 1987, when it was replaced by a new structure, upstream from the original and approached by a track diversion of 846 metres. The technical problems of carrying overhead wires across a swing bridge necessitated single track, but with modern operational procedures this is no handicap.

Such heavy usage derived principally from the EUR's Ipswich line, joining the Cambridge route at Trowse Lower Junction, and opened formally on 7 November 1849, to goods on 3 December, and to passengers nine days later. The EUR in fact had its own independent Victoria terminal, in part an old circus building on a former pleasure ground, but on 8 September 1851, as originally authorised to the Ipswich & Bury in 1846, a link was put in between Trowse Upper and Lower Junctions, from a point north of the tall five-arch Lakenham Viaduct, where both the Cambridge line and the Yare were crossed. At first Eastern Union locomotives were barred from the ECR and were obliged to run round their trains and propel them on to the latter. When reason prevailed in 1854, Victoria became something of a white elephant, but already the civic authorities had secured the insertion of a clause in the ECR's 1854 Act ratifying the lease of the EUR that 'it shall not be lawful for the company to close or discontinue' the station. By 1866 four attempts to do so had been foiled by public opinion and it was not until 22 May 1916, passenger services having long been reduced to a handful of slow services, that the GER finally got its way after prolonged negotiations. The station remains for freight only, with coal and cement predominating, although the old buildings have gone and the approach has been single-track since 21 June 1953.

Extra traffic from Trowse Lower Junction involved a road bridge (now carrying the A146) to replace the level crossing which had been authorised to the Norfolk Railway at Trowse only for as long as the Board of Trade permitted; the ECR had no option but to comply, although it did persuade Parliament to make the EUR share the cost. Trowse was also the site of a 7 acre GER cattle station, where by 1904 over 10,000 head were handled annually, and of the rows of neat houses built by the company for its employees in the extensive works at Thorpe Junction. This latter junction was formed on 1 October 1879 when the Wensum Curve was opened to allow through coastal traffic to avoid entry into Thorpe station. The curve somewhat enhanced the status of the wayside station at Trowse, a number of expresses now calling there to give Norwich connections; temporarily closed from 22 May 1916 to 1 April 1919, and finally so from 5 September 1939, it was revived to serve as a terminal during electrification works in the Thorpe station area.

Thorpe (so named when Victoria opened) at first had two sets of rails, each with a 50 ft roof, one for passengers (with a separate third class entrance) and one for luggage. The advent of the N&B led to enlargement of both station and yard. The present station, red brick with Bath stone dressing and a zinc-covered dome, was opened on a site adjoining the old terminal, now given over to goods, on 3 May 1886, having cost £60,000 but being essential to cope with ever-increasing traffic. On 9 July 1940 it sustained serious bomb damage but was closed for only one hour; in 1942 the goods depot, with a number of additional buildings dating from 1921, was similarly struck and for two months work had to be conducted in the open. In 1945 the LNER planned expenditure of £93,000 on the locomotive depot (from 1936 to 1963 dominated by a giant coaling tower) and £256,000 on the station, but it was 1955 before one of the existing platforms was lengthened by 70 ft, a new one, number

6, added and other efforts made to alleviate the congestion caused by over 200 trains on a peak summer day. Even in postwar conditions the station collected 1,361,662 tickets during 1965.

The railway facilities of Norwich were completed by the City station, opened on 2 December 1882 as the terminal of a branch from Melton Constable; authorised to the Lynn & Fakenham it was in fact opened by the Eastern & Midlands and subsequently became part of the M&GN system (Chapter IX), offering excellent services to the north Norfolk coast, connections with the principal M&GN line expresses and its own daily service to Birmingham. Closed to passengers on 2 March 1969 the station was retained for freight (coal, glass bottles, road material and general) until 3 February 1969, although a coal depot survived until 21 September 1986. After 12 September 1960 access had been via the Themelthorpe Curve linking the County School–Wroxham line to the former Melton Constable branch (Chapter IX).

Although Norwich lacked the normal prerequisites for industrial development the railways, supplemented by coastal shipping, enabled the city to grow from 62,344 inhabitants in 1841 to 121,236 in 1951 (122,270 in 1981), the period of most rapid expansion (80,386 to 113,922) coinciding with agricultural depression between 1871 and 1901. An enlarged hinterland, further exploited by GER bus services to Loddon and Beccles, and facilities such as a siding to the old cattle market (replaced in 1960), abundance of cheap labour and a choice of national markets were the key factors exploited by enterprising individuals; it is significant that as early as August 1850 a strike of ECR locomotive men could cause serious inconvenience in the city. Many and diverse industries have developed since 1845, too numerous to discuss in detail. Boot and shoe making, becoming a factory industry after 1890, rose rapidly to prominence, employing 1,700 in 1841 but 5,300 in 1861 and 7,500 in 1901. Clothing manufacturing was firmly established in the 1850s; Colmans (1856) with a GER siding and employing 2,200 by 1901, and Caleys (1860), with 2,800 workers by 1918, laid the foundations of the food and confectionery industries, and the former firm was directly instrumental, along with the needs of agriculture and printing, in stimulating major engineering industries which by 1901 ranged from portable sheds and wire netting to steam boilers. Paper mills, tanneries, breweries, maltings, coach works, rope and brush making and an artificial manures factory were just a few amongst the many that flourished.

In every sense Norwich had become a major regional capital with a sphere of influence extending over some 2,400 square miles. This is even more true today; industries have further expanded and diversified (with footwear, food processing, engineering and chemicals the leaders), the markets remain the busiest in the eastern counties, the city is a centre for insurance and other professional services, there is a successful First Division football team and, since 1960, the University of East Anglia. Rail freight, once so prominent, has much declined but is still important with gas condensate, oil, tar, steel and bricks at its heart. Alongside Thorpe Goods there is an oil depot (on the site of the old turntable and coal hopper) and at Trowse a terminal for stone and road materials. Piped gas has destroyed the coal traffic; in fact it was the reduced demand for bunker coal that was a major reason for closure of the M&GN system.

Although the opening up of markets in the midlands and north has been a major reason for the expansion of Norwich, rapidity of communication with London has been of crucial importance. In 1846 260 minutes were required from Shoreditch (with four stops), rising to 305 by the close of 1848 but falling to 195 in the autumn of 1852; this last was not maintained, however, and by 1862 the best time was 225 minutes, improving by 1864 to 210 to Thorpe or 200 to Victoria. The accompanying table outlines the subsequent pattern prior to electrification, displaying speeds and frequency superior to those enjoyed by many much larger centres.

The importance of the traffic was acknowledged by the LNER on 27 September 1937 with the introduction of the 'East Anglian', a luxury six-coach train designed by Gresley and for which two B17s (2859 and 2870, renamed *East Anglian* and *City of London* respectively) were specially streamlined, giving timings of 135 minutes, 130 from 1938, each way. After the war the train was restored with ordinary stock on 7 October 1946 (140 minutes) and on 27 September 1948 was joined by the 'Norfolkman', giving a complementary service down in the morning and

NORWICH AND LONDON

Times shown are in minutes and apply to services running at least four days a week in the May of each year cited. In each case the first column refers to the Cambridge line, the second to that via Colchester.

Up services	1874		1883		1892		1939		1954		1976	
Frequency:	4	4	6	6	6	4	7	11	6	11‡	1	17
Average time:	299	275	244	215	244	247	210	185	203	166	187	135
Fastest time:	235	235	215	185	215	185*	190	130	194	130	187	112

Down services												
Frequency:	4	4	6	7	6	6	6	8	8	12	2	18
Average time:	289	287	244	207	241	212	202	169	218	169	220	136
Fastest time:	240	230	213	185	211	180	181	130	194	120†	180	115

The quickest pre-1914 service was the 9.50 am summer express to Cromer, making its first stop at Trowse and detaching a Norwich portion to give 146 minutes into Thorpe.

 * 160 on Mondays only.   † 'The Broadsman'.
 ‡ Does not include the 11.35 pm which stood for 54 minutes at Haughley.

up in the afternoon, but unlike its partner being extended to Cromer and Sheringham in summer. From the 1951 summer both, with eight vehicles, were down to 130 minutes, and then from 15 September 1958 to 120 in each direction at which approximate level they remained until 17 June 1962, when the whole Norwich service was remodelled and their names disappeared. The recast timetable with an hourly frequency was based on alternating 120 and 150 minute up, 145 down expresses, the former timing representing the level first attained by the down 'Broadsman' (introduced in 1950) in the autumn of 1952. From 6 April 1964 a massive publicity campaign, based on the investigations of Research Projects Ltd and involving TV, house to house distribution of literature and a revised fare structure (30s day return, 40s overnight and 50s monthly— each increased by 10s in 1965 but concurrently with the removal of almost all restrictions on use) led to a 25 per cent passenger increase. The trend continued so that under InterCity the route stood second only to the East Coast Main Line in profitability. Quite apart from reduced operating costs, electrification from Ipswich thus made sound economic sense. On 9 April 1987 a staff special was the first electric train into Norwich, public services commencing on 11 May. Twenty down and nineteen up daily London services are offered in 1990, on an hourly basis through the day and with standard timings of 110 minutes. The best times were those of the reinstated 'East Anglian', namely 95 minutes down and 100 up.

Symbolic of the transformation enjoyed by Norwich and its railways is the £10 million, 12 acre rolling stock maintenance depot opened on 27 October 1982 at Crown Point in the triangle created by the River Wensum and the Yarmouth and main lines, the Wensum Curve being absorbed into the complex.

CHAPTER IX

North-east Norfolk

THE EAST NORFOLK LINES

For many years the holiday potential of the Norfolk Broads remained unappreciated, and they were left as isolated haunts of natural beauty, useful as inland waterways plied by Norfolk wherries, and supplemented by the 9 mile North Walsham & Dilham canal of 1826. Cromer, with 1,367 inhabitants in 1851, and Sheringham with 1,289, were no more than fishing villages and the GER was too poor to contemplate development north of Norwich and Yarmouth, where population was so scattered and the likely returns so poor, although it did offer 'substantial help' to any independent concern prepared to build towards Aylsham, North Walsham and Cromer.

The company that accepted the challenge was the East Norfolk, incorporated in 1864 for a line from Whitlingham Junction to North Walsham. The GER had offered to work it for 50 per cent of the receipts, a gesture described at a Norwich meeting of November 1863 'as conferring the means of accomplishing public works of the greatest benefit . . . which otherwise must have been indefinitely postponed'. Strong pleas of unfair competition from the Yarmouth Haven & Pier Commissioners and the North Walsham & Dilham Canal were disregarded both in and out of Parliament. Work began in 1865, but money was short and the death of Simpson, the contractor, halted it.* Resumption came in 1870 with the Lucas Brothers working to the plans of E. Wilson, but in 1872 extension of time had to be sought. This was coupled with authorisation for an extension to Cromer which alone could justify the line, for in 1851 North Walsham

---

* Simpson's estate became the subject of an administration action and his assets, including a block of East Norfolk shares, were temporarily frozen so that calls could not be met. The author is indebted to B. D. J. Walsh for the information in this footnote.

itself was a small market town of no more than 2,911 inhabitants. The decision, however, was not popular in Cromer which had become a refuge for those who sought peace and quiet and for whom the 22 miles distance from a railway and freedom from the 'curse' of excursionists were particular recommendations.

North Walsham was reached by single track on 20 October 1874, Gunton on 29 July 1876 and Cromer on 26 March 1877, the GER working the extension on the same terms as agreed for the original before absorbing the whole under an Act of 1881. Between 1896 and 1900 the track between Whitlingham and North Walsham was doubled, but that to the north remains single to this day and the Wroxham–North Walsham section reverted to single from 15 January 1967. By 1883 there were seven daily trains, offering cheap facilities from Norwich, 1s 6d day return or 1s after noon, but as regards connections being what a contemporary guide described as 'probably the slowest and most inconvenient . . . that could possibly be devised'. The arrival of the Eastern & Midlands at Cromer on 16 June 1887 with the possibility of reaching the area from King's Cross led to considerable improvements, and by 1892, when there were nine daily winter services and twelve in summer, the former London time of 310 minutes had been considerably reduced to between 210 and 247 minutes. The Tivetshall and Halifax Junction water-troughs, installed in 1896 and 1897 respectively, made possible a more sustained effort to develop traffic to the Cromer area. Exploited first by a Sunday evening up train running non-stop between Norwich and Liverpool Street during August 1896, there followed on 1 July 1897 the daily summer-only 'Cromer Express', non-stop in each direction between London and North Walsham, giving an overall Cromer timing of 175 minutes both ways. From 1 May 1899 a three-car restaurant set was attached and in 1907 the train was renamed the 'Norfolk Coast Express', given a twelve-coach corridor set and made to include portions for Mundesley and Sheringham. Until its end in 1914 this train was the pride of the GER. In the same years, from 1907, a second service, also using the Wensum Curve but detaching a Norwich portion at Trowse and one for Sheringham at Cromer Junction, was also giving a fast summer-weekday service in a time of 180 minutes. After the 1914 war 183 minutes was the best GER time to Cromer. Under the LNER a 170 minute journey was possible on summer Saturdays from 1934 to 1939, but in the spring of the latter year, with five daily through workings, the best up times were 195 minutes, 199 down, the best on Saturdays, 173 and 187 minutes respectively.

After 1945 services were rebuilt to a high level; in the 1958 summer, for example, there were four daily down through workings from London, three extending to Sheringham, including the 'Norfolkman' and 'Broadsman', with a best time, involving reversal at Norwich, of 194 minutes, a slowest of 215. On Saturdays there were four extras, the slowest being 241 minutes. However, even summer traffic was declining and despite their popularity as resorts Cromer and Sheringham both remained under 5,000 in population. Elsewhere, North Walsham, once the junction for five lines (see below), population only 5,014 in 1961 but 7,944 in 1981, has a canning industry and modern housing and industrial estates, together with a rail served oil condensate terminal. Wroxham, 1,101 in 1961, site of a rail linked grain depot, has risen since the 1880s as a boating centre for the Broads, and 30,614 tickets were collected there in 1965, but traffic in general was becoming increasingly sparse and the former agricultural significance, which had brought, for example, four cattle trains, two of which were from Aylsham, each Saturday in the early 1890s, had by now passed away. It was only a matter of time before drastic economies were made. From 5 January 1959 only the 'Broadsman' was left as a through weekday London working and in June 1962 this disappeared also. Through summer Saturday London workings were one only by 1968 and have now ceased, as earlier did those to Leicester and Derby. Twelve daily dmu services (conductor guards since 2 January 1967) survived, in 1989, however, one extending to Birmingham.

The branch from Wroxham to Aylsham and County School on the Dereham to Wells line (Chapter X) was also an East Norfolk enterprise, designed to provide a strategic link between east and west Norfolk and to prevent any independent promotion from Norwich to Aylsham, a market town on the old Cromer turnpike resentful of its exclusion from the original East Norfolk route. It was built in leisurely fashion from Wroxham, opening to Buxton Lamas on 8 July 1879, Aylsham on 1 January 1880, Cawston on 1 September 1880, Reepham on 2 May 1881 and County School on 1 May 1882. Within a year (5 April 1883) the Eastern & Midlands had opened through Aylsham, so vitiating the value of the branch which was in any case too circuitous for reaching Norwich; Aylsham, with 2,674 inhabitants in 1881, was in fact slightly smaller in 1961 with only 2,635. GER services fell from nine down and seven up in 1882 to six each way by 1892; in 1939, when most trains ran between Norwich and Dereham, there were six down and five up services. Hopelessly uneconomic, passenger facilities were withdrawn on 15 September 1952. Freight traffic has always been primarily agricultural, with cattle, and subsequently beet, from Cawston and Reepham often being very heavy, while in World War II RAF Coltishall was partly served by the branch, but present survival (except for the Reepham to Foulsham section, closed completely on 15 September 1952 and the Foulsham to County School stub which survived until 31 October 1964) derives from the 518 yd Themelthorpe Curve opened on 12 September 1960 from near Reepham to Whitwell on the former M&GN branch to Norwich City. Initially, the route, worked as a light railway, served City station but this was closed on 3 February 1969 leaving freight traffic, principally coal, steel, petroleum and aggregates only to Lenwade. The curve reduced the distance from Norwich Thorpe to Norwich City to 40 miles; until then a 64 mile journey from Whitlingham via Cromer and Holt was necessary even though the two points in Norwich were only 1 mile apart; it closed on 2 January 1982.

THE MIDLAND & GREAT NORTHERN JOINT RAILWAY

The Midland & Great Northern Joint Railway system extended from Peterborough (GNR and Midland) and Little Bytham (MR) in the west to Yarmouth (Beach), Norwich (City) and Cromer (Beach) in the east, constituting a second route from London (King's Cross) into Norfolk, which stimulated without harming the GER, and from the midlands and north, a more serious proposition to the home company. The M&GN was formed on 1 July 1893 to take over the Eastern & Midlands. This latter company had been in existence since 1 January 1883 when the Lynn & Fakenham, the Yarmouth & North Norfolk and the Yarmouth Union had amalgamated. On 1 July 1883 it had

gone on to absorb the Midland & Eastern, which in turn had
been constituted on 23 July 1866 from a group of lines west of
King's Lynn, the Norwich & Spalding, the Spalding & Bourn
[sic] and the Lynn & Sutton Bridge; a further element was the
Peterborough, Wisbech & Sutton Bridge, which had remained
outside the M&E but which came into the E&M in 1883.

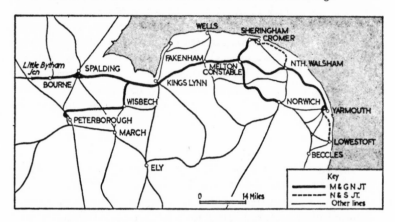

As will be seen, both the Midland Railway and the Great
Northern had strong interests in these various companies and,
after years of dispute, the formation of the M&GN represented a
sensible and mutually beneficial compromise. The two partners
had equal representation and agreed spheres of responsibility in
the working until from 1 October 1936 operation was permanently undertaken by the LNER; until then it had possessed its
own independent stock. In all there were 182 miles 32 chains of
route, of which 109 miles 18 chains were single-track, a cause of
serious operational difficulties partly ameliorated from the 1890s
by the fixing of tablet catchers to the locomotives.

Although briefly departing from the strict area approach the
M&GN must be seen as a whole. Lack of space precludes record of
the many changes in traffic, but this may be broadly described
as locally sparse (prior to closure of most of the system on
2 March 1959 there were 140 daily trains averaging 40 to 50
passengers each), supplemented by heavy peak-period summer
workings from the midlands and north; the predominance of
midland holidaymakers in Yarmouth and the Cromer district
derives largely from the habit established by the M&GN. In later

years places such as Derby, Shirebrook, Nottingham, Chester-field and Birmingham were served, the latter being linked with Norwich (City) by a daily train until 14 September 1957. Prior to 1914 there were two regular Midland services to Cromer, Lowestoft and Yarmouth from Birmingham, Nottingham and Leicester, one of which conveyed a through carriage from Man-chester (Central), while the GNR ran a summer restaurant-car express from the West Riding with Nottingham, Sheffield and Manchester portions, as well as three daily King's Cross trains (one in winter). Goods traffic was once fairly substantial and, in the mid-1930s, included each October to December, fish trains from Yarmouth (as well as fish-workers' specials from Scotland), cattle workings (this was cattle-fattening country), the move-ment of grain, beet, manufactured goods from and coal to Nor-wich, enormous quantities of fruit and produce from the Fens and much general merchandise.

However, by 1959, while eighty freights a day were still pro-vided, revenue was seriously down and traffic could for the most part be accommodated on former GER lines. Overall, closure would immediately save £640,000 a year and a further £500,000 was required by 1963 for essential engineering works; £270,000, for example, on the Ouse bridge between Clenchwharton and South Lynn. Apart from Wisbech and Lynn no intermediate place on the system had a population above even 5,000, and in view of the proximity of ex-GER routes throughout—it was no-where more than 13 miles from another railway—closure was decreed for 2 March 1959, except for certain stretches noted in the following sections.

The heart of the eastern section, with 18 miles of double track from Raynham Park to Corpusty, was Melton Constable, 'the Crewe of north Norfolk', where the town grew around the M&GN's locomotive and wagon works and surrounding villages found a major source of employment; twelve engines were built between 1897 and 1909 but the principal work was in repairs and overhauls. The LNER closed the locomotive section on 1 January 1937, but wagon and carriage maintenance was re-tained. On summer Saturdays this was a very busy junction and as late as 1953 justified the installation of a 70 ft Ransome & Rapier vacuum-operated turntable, transferred from Grantham to replace the 47 ft one of 1884 built in the town. A curious feature of the station was the private waiting room of a local nobleman; sited at ground level and opposite the main platform, it effectively prevented the provision of an up relief line.

Melton Constable was reached by the Lynn & Fakenham (Chapter X) on 19 January 1882, as part of the extensions from Fakenham to Norwich, Holt and Blakeney authorised in 1880 and now opened as far as Guestwick on the Norwich line; continuation to Lenwade was effected on 1 July 1882 and to Norwich (City) itself on 2 December. With regular connections to the midlands and (from 1887) Cromer, the line quickly proved itself and, as seen, spurred the GER to new efforts; a regular 80 minute evening express from Cromer to Norwich was a particularly popular train in early days. Only in the 1950s did housing development along the branch become evident and then it was too late to avert closure on 2 March 1959. Freight working continued throughout until the opening of the Themelthorpe Curve, after which (on 12 September 1960) the section north of it was closed and by 1962, dismantled. Apart from Norwich City (closed on 3 February 1969) the main traffic derived from a Lenwade firm specialising in prefabricated housing sections and concrete girders. Extra sidings were put in there for traffic arising from a 55 week contract signed in April 1964 (involving 45,000 tons), and in 1966 came a five year £300,000 agreement to run five trains a week to London. This ended, the curve and the line to Lenwade closed on 2 January 1982.

On 5 April 1883 the Eastern & Midlands opened a line from Melton Constable to North Walsham, there effecting an end-on junction with the Yarmouth & North Norfolk and thus completing the Peterborough/Midland Railway to Yarmouth link. Meanwhile, the Yarmouth Union, authorised in 1880 and opened on 15 May 1882, had provided a line to the quays and the GER in Yarmouth. The Y&NN originated in 1876 as the locally promoted Great Yarmouth & Stalham Light Railway, opening to Ormesby on 7 August 1877 and Hemsby on 16 May 1878; powers for the North Walsham extension having been obtained in 1878, the company was retitled. Martham was reached on 15 July 1878, Catfield on 17 January 1880, Stalham on 3 July 1880 and North Walsham on 13 June 1881. Little need be added to what has already been said of the M&GN in general as regards the Melton Constable to Yarmouth section, probably the most uneconomic on the whole system (in fact closure was discussed in 1954); except for a tiny portion at North Walsham (below) it closed entirely on 2 March 1959. As seen, North Walsham and Aylsham long remained small and undeveloped, and although Potter Heigham, where besides the main station there was a wooden platform halt beside the river, and Stalham became centres for the Broads, and Hemsby, Caister and Scratby of holiday camps and caravan sites, traffic remained totally inadequate and concentrated in the summer months; on 5 July 1937 halts for summer use were opened at Newtown, Caister Camp, California and Scratby. From June 1934 to September 1939, and from 1948 to 1958 as the 'Holiday Camps Express', a Liverpool Street service operated on summer Saturdays via Ely (before the war the up train usually travelled via Colchester), the Wensum Curve and North Walsham for Caister-on-Sea.

The branch between Melton Constable, Sheringham and Cromer opened to Holt, as authorised in 1880, on 1 October 1884, continuing to Cromer under a further Act of 1882 on 16 June 1887; in effect it was a continuation of the Norwich branch, for services between Cromer and the west required reversal in Melton Constable station. None the less, Cromer was reached from Peterborough by King's Cross services at an average of 40 mph by the best trains, even with six calls and twelve delays for picking up staffs; but the best GNR London trains required 3 hours 40 minutes or more. Apart from services mentioned elsewhere there was until September 1939 a daily summer train from Melton Constable to Yarmouth (Beach) via Cromer and Mundesley, and from July 1937 to September 1939, and October 1942 to September 1957, through carriages from Melton Constable to Liverpool Street via Cromer. These two services recalled the busy days of 1912 when the direct Melton Constable–Yarmouth line was blocked in two places by flood damage from 26 August to 11 September and all services were diverted via Cromer. For the sake of the scattered villages highly dependent on the railway, passenger services between Sheringham and Melton Constable survived until 6 April 1964, freight until 28 December when the line closed completely; in 1965 Central Norfolk Enterprises purchased the Sheringham to Weybourne section for £17,000 and (as the North Norfolk Railway) is restoring the line. Weybourne, where deep water exists, was a big disappointment to the M&GN as it never developed as hoped and the hotel built there in anticipation was demolished in the 1940s. Some compensation was found, however, in the artillery firing range established at Holt from 1936, which provided fairly extensive military traffic. Sheringham grew from 1,289 inhabitants in 1851 to 3,376 in 1911 (from 2,359 in one decade), and to 5,510 in 1981; besides the holiday industry, fishing, especially lobsters and crabs, flourishes; 46,554 tickets were collected at the station in 1965, but on 2 January 1967 the buildings were abandoned and the diesel multiple-unit service terminates at a temporary platform just short of the station. After such threatening economies it is surprising that the line still (1990) survives. Freight facilities between the town and Cromer were withdrawn on 28 December 1964. The GER gained running powers to Sheringham from 23 July 1906 and right until 1962 daily through coaches to London were provided; one through summer-Saturday working survived in the 1968 season.

Cromer, like Sheringham, retains its fresh charm and importance for fishing, but has become a well-equipped resort, its population growing from 4,073 in 1901 to 6,192 in 1981; in 1965 93,159 tickets were collected at the surviving station (for details of facilities at Cromer see below). Deeply indebted to the railways as it was Cromer might have gained yet more if the loop line from it to North Walsham via Mundesley had succeeded in creating, as was intended, a new holiday industry along the north-east coast of Norfolk; indeed plans existed for an entirely new resort between Mundesley and Overstrand, but these were frustrated by the refusal of the principal landowner to sell his property. The loop began as a North Walsham to Mundesley branch built by the M&GN and opened to goods on 20 June 1898 and passengers on 1 July.

In the same year, however, the M&GN and the GER, anxious to avoid wasteful competition in opening up the Norfolk coast, formed the Norfolk & Suffolk Joint Committee to which, in 1898, was authorised the continuation of the branch to Cromer. After delays through the bankruptcy of the contractor this extension opened on 3 August 1906 although freight facilities were not offered until the following March. Generous provision of services and the size of the stations (that at Mundesley with three through platforms and a bay) indicated the hopes entertained for the area. A number of the very wealthy were encouraged to buy estates near the line and reputedly some of the richest people in the world made use of it, but of popular development there was no sign, even though devices such as through King's Cross (winter 1906–7) and Liverpool Street (summer 1907) workings were employed. By the winter of 1922–3, services had been reduced to six each way between North Walsham and Cromer and one additional train between North Walsham and Mundesley. From that year vigorous attempts were made at economy, including for a few years concentration on the LNER station at North Walsham and the conversion of the Mundesley to Roughton Road Junction portion to one section. On the other hand efforts were made to encourage traffic. Halts were opened at Cromer Links (14 May 1923) and Sidestrand (25 May 1936); from 1926 to 1939 there was a daily Cromer (Beach)–Yarmouth (Beach) service, from 1927 a thrice-weekly summer excursion from Yarmouth that became four times weekly in 1932 and then daily, except Saturdays, in the summers of 1933 to 1939.

Local settlement was still lacking after the war when bus competition hastened the demise of the branch; on 17 April 1953 the section north of Mundesley closed completely after withdrawal of passenger services on 6 April. A push-and-pull auto-train worked the remainder until the introduction of diesel multiple-units (some with through Norwich workings) in 1956, but these also ceased on 5 October 1964, being unable, except in the summer when many trippers used the line, to attract the twenty-five passengers per train necessary to make the service viable; the six camping coaches at Mundesley were insufficient to redress the balance. Freight facilities were withdrawn on 28 December 1964.

JUNCTIONS AT CROMER AND NORTH WALSHAM

The East Norfolk's Cromer terminal, opened on 26 March 1877 and named High from 27 September 1948, comprised two platforms and a bay. Situated on a lofty escarpment overlooking the town it was inconveniently sited, a fact duly appreciated by the King's Cross authorities and the Eastern & Midlands, whose

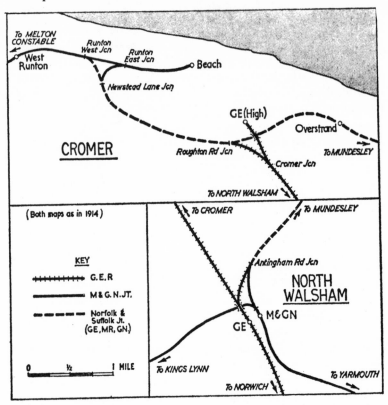

station, with a single platform and a bay, opened on 16 June 1887; named Beach, it occupied a much more central position. Physical connection between the two was established on 23 July 1906 by the openings from Roughton Road Junction to Runton West by the Norfolk & Suffolk Joint Committee, Newstead Lane to Runton East by the M&GN, and the spur to the former from Cromer Junction to Roughton Road by the GER as authorised in 1903. In this way the GER gained access to Sheringham, and Mundesley trains, commencing on 3 August, were able to use the M&GN station. A key point was Cromer Junction where down Sheringham portions were frequently detached, up portions for attachment being backed over the 50 chains to the GER station.

The modern scene is much simplified. The Mundesley to

Roughton Road section closed completely on 17 April 1953, and on 20 September 1954 High station, then with sixteen trains each way on a summer Saturday, was closed to passengers, services being diverted to Beach, then with fifteen each way on peak days, where platform faces had been extended, signalling modernised, twelve track circuits and a new turntable installed in preparation during 1954. Subsequently Newstead Lane to Runton West was closed and in 1960 lifted, so involving all Sheringham trains in reversal at Beach; on 7 March 1960 Cromer High and the approach from Cromer Junction, hitherto retained for freight, were finally abandoned. The double-line section between Cromer Junction and Roughton Road Junction was singled on 5 June 1961, that between Newstead Lane Junction and Runton East Junction in the early summer of 1963. On 20 May 1985 a single platform Halt was opened at Roughton Road to serve the outlying parts of Cromer; this resulted from a project of the Manpower Services Commission with financial aid from the North Norfolk District Council.

At North Walsham extensive closures have been coupled with one interesting addition. On 8 April 1958 the little-used spur from Antingham Road Junction to Town station (so named on 27 September 1948), formerly used by Mundesley branch trains, was closed because of the unsafe condition of an underline bridge. The freight traffic so disrupted, substantial only in the beet season, could be diverted via Melton Constable and Cromer, but more difficult was the problem of the 'Holiday Camps Express' to Caister, which hitherto had run up the Mundesley branch off the ex-GER line from Whitlingham and then reversed; the solution was a new connection opened on 4 May 1958 south of the Main station where the former GER and M&GN lines ran parallel for several hundred yards. The Caister train used this line from June to September in what was its last year of operation, but the new spur continued, as the ex-GER yard was too small and the M&GN was still needed—it was also used by demolition trains on the Yarmouth (Beach line) carrying materials for sorting at Cromer High. After this, however, the yard and spur ceased to be viable and were closed down finally on 16 October 1960.

CHAPTER X

King's Lynn and West Norfolk

KING'S LYNN

In 1841 King's Lynn, with a population of 16,039, was the 'emporium' of western Norfolk and the eastern Fens, as well as the port, through the Great Ouse and its tributaries, for parts of seven counties in an area extending to Bedford, Northampton, Cambridge, Peterborough, Bury St Edmunds and Thetford. However, monopoly had bred complacency leading to chronic neglect of the harbour and of its approaches, where on average thirty vessels a year grounded, and to the perpetuation of a system of excessively high tolls. Reform was precluded by concentration of power in a small, wealthy and tightly-knit merchant coterie.

An energetic challenge from Wisbech was already causing disquiet amongst the thoughtful when in 1844 authorisation of the ECR's lines to Brandon and Peterborough, promising to complete continuous rail communication from Yarmouth to the London & Birmingham at Blisworth, threatened at one blow to sever Lynn from half its markets, destroy the northern coal staple of the harbour (in 1845, an unusually good year, 302,463 tons of coal were imported, 41,935 tons of other goods) and generally lead trade past the town. The ECR would promise no more than a branch through rival Wisbech and the Corporation proved incapable of a solution, but J. C. Williams, a local solicitor concerned to make a personal fortune, rose to the occasion, his efforts producing the Lynn & Ely (with branches to the harbour and Wisbech), the Lynn & Dereham and the Ely & Huntingdon. All were incorporated in 1845, and in 1847 amalgamated, as intended from the outset, to form the East Anglian Railways.

The three lines soon ran into grave financial difficulties to the satisfaction of the ECR which, delighted at construction without cost to itself, awaited the opportunity for assuming a cheap lease. But in 1846 and 1847 it asked too much, and although the EAR failed to obtain extensions to Norwich, March and Spalding that might have saved the future, it determined to struggle on. Three years of actual operation produced a working profit of £8,000 on a capital debt of £1,250,000 and during 1850 and the early part of 1851 the EAR was officially bankrupt with Sheriff's

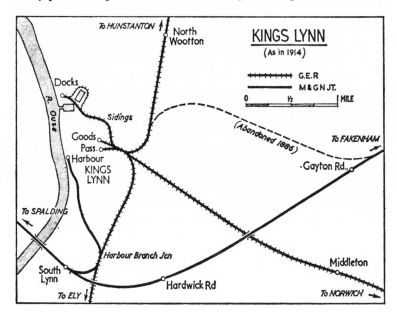

men riding on every train. In May 1851, however, the Great Northern, intending access by running powers over the ECR from Peterborough to Wisbech, agreed to work the company for 60 per cent of the receipts from 10 July, but the ECR blocked the Wisbech junction, a course of action upheld by the courts in that without Parliamentary sanction the lease was illegal, undercut EAR rates and refused through bookings. The already small revenue was reduced to an even more alarming level, and within months the GNR and EAR had thankfully accepted a renewed ECR offer to assume the lease. This became operative on 1 January 1852 and lasted until both companies were absorbed into the GER in 1862 despite violent storms over preferential rates at Lowestoft, shortage of trucks, working expenses and kindred matters.

Other lines followed, the Lynn & Hunstanton opening on 3 October 1862, the Lynn & Sutton Bridge on 1 November 1864 and the first section of the Lynn & Fakenham on 16 August 1879. The last two companies, after becoming parts of the Midland & Eastern (1866) and the Eastern & Midlands (1883) respectively, were merged into the Midland & Great Northern, of which from 1895 to 1936 Lynn was the control centre, in 1893. Initially the Lynn & Fakenham, unable to afford a terminal of its own, had used the GER station, leaving Lynn from Gaywood Junction on the Hunstanton branch, but on 1 January 1886 the opening of the South Lynn to Bawsey link permitted through running between it and the Sutton Bridge line without reversal in Lynn; the Gaywood to Bawsey section, with West Lynn station, was closed and subsequently lifted. King's Lynn station (just Lynn until 1911) was originally a mean wooden structure until rebuilt in March 1871 as a joint venture of the GER, GNR and Midland, the latter having access over the Peterborough, Wisbech & Sutton Bridge opened on 1 August 1866; it was substantially improved in 1938 by the LNER, which had worked the M&GN from 1 October 1936, and it became the basis of the present station. Other facilities in Lynn included the harbour branch, opened on 27 October 1846, completed in May 1848, but of little use until extended to the quays over a swing bridge on the Nar in 1856, and the docks branch, opened on 10 June 1870 to serve the Alexandra Dock of 7 July 1869 and subsequently the Bentinck Dock of 18 October 1883; the latter branch was the property of the independent dock company but was worked by the GER which continued to share it with the M&GN.

This system meant several things to Lynn which nevertheless at first, through 'railways at a distance', lost both trade and population, the latter rising to 19,148 in 1851 but falling to 15,981, less than in 1841, by 1861. But the railways had already opened a 'breach in the town walls', letting in 'a new race of bustling individuals' who completed the rout of the former 'gentlemanly merchants', in the words of the correspondence columns in the contemporary local press. An early result was the Norfolk Estuary Cut of 1853 giving a direct and safe approach from the sea; then came the docks. Market status, although restricted, was maintained, and alongside a preserved nucleus of former activities, new industries were attracted. Two large engineering firms were established between 1848 and 1860, in 1872 a chemical fertiliser plant, in 1893 a large roller-bearings firm, and by 1901, when population had reached 20,228, these and the traditional brewing, milling and malting (premises near the station had been served by a street tramway since a very early date) were all flourishing. The GN&GE Joint line had destroyed the former coal traffic of the port but general trade had greatly expanded, and by the end of 1917 the docks company (originally supported by Peterborough, Wisbech & Sutton Bridge and Lynn & Sutton Bridge subscriptions) had a capital of £415,499. By 1981 Lynn's population was 33,340, ten per cent up on that of 1971. Modern industrial estates have supplemented beet refining (1927), fruit and vegetable canning (1930s) and a major soup and canning factory of 1958. In 1963, the docks, benefitting from the congestion at larger ports, handled 541,124 tons, but in 1986 over a million. Of the former 477,744 were imports of which a quarter were forwarded by rail. This important link remains in 1990 with fertilisers and (since 1986) steel coil and coke being the principal commodities. The oil sidings were closed in 1985. Company trains run in association with British Industrial Sand and the beet refinery, while a chemical works, a grain depot and the soup factory are served by the town's daily Speedlink service. Such growth and commuter settlement have removed the threat to the town's future as a railhead, so much so that on 14 August 1989 electrification work on the Cambridge line was begun. Estimated costs are £20.1m. Commuter traffic is expected to rise ten-fold after completion in October 1991 when King's Cross will be the London terminal. Since May 1990, because of the works, through London workings have been suspended.

SOUTH AND WEST OF LYNN

The Lynn & Ely, hoping for a 9 per cent return on its £300,000 capital, was crippled by the insistence of the commissioners for the Little and Great Ouse on bridge clearance adequate for navigation. The bridges were expensive, but even more so the embankments involved, each necessitating 18 ft sand and gravel foundations in the marshy Fenland soil. Opened to Downham Market on 27 October 1846 and Denver Road Gate in January 1847, the line did not reach Ely North Junction (Ely station was the ECR's) until 26 October 1847. By this line Lynn was brought gradually nearer London, from 220 minutes in 1862 to 200 by 1874, 163 (155 up) by 1883 and 150 in 1888; in 1977–8 down expresses required 127 (the former 'Fenman') to 144 minutes. The best timing of all had been 126 minutes up in 1914. Services to Ely were three daily in 1854 and 1874 although by the latter year there was an additional train on Tuesdays, Lynn's principal market day. By 1892 the total was five, as in earlier years mostly between Ely and Dereham, with three goods, one local and one each to London and Cambridge, and cattle specials to Tufnell Park as required. In October 1914 passenger services had risen to eight daily; in 1939 were seven; and in 1989 ten, the latter a mixture of London expresses and diesel multiple-unit services (first introduced to the line on 3 November 1958). Of the intermediate stations Littleport, Downham Market (townships of local agricultural signifi- cance) and Magdalen Road survive—the latter closed on 9 September 1968 but reopened through local initiative and hard work on 5 May 1975. For the rest there was nothing but villages. Denver, without passenger facilities from 1 February 1870 to 1 July 1885 and thereafter used only by Stoke Ferry branch trains, closed to passengers on 22 September 1930, Hilgay (where on 1 September 1939 four died in a derailment caused by an express hitting a lorry on a crossing) and Stow Bardolph on 4 November 1963: all three were closed to freight on 13 July 1964. Ouse Bridge closed as an economy measure as long ago as 1 January 1864.

The Wisbech branch from Magdalen Road (named Watling- ton until 1 June 1875) was built with Ely & Huntingdon funds when in 1846 Hudson insisted that its construction must be a condition of any lease of the EAR lines by the ECR; thus, if the L&E was forced to close, the ECR would still have access to Lynn from its March–Wisbech line, whilst the E&H would of necessity remain incomplete, a desirable outcome that would prevent the Great Northern using the EAR's lines to enter Norfolk if the ECR negotiations broke down—as they did. An earlier reason for the branch was Williams's hope that with the Lynn & Dereham and the group of companies that in 1846 formed the Ambergate, Nottingham & Boston & Eastern Junction it would constitute part of a grand east-to-west trunk route extending from Yarmouth to Manchester. The failure of the western company to construct, except between Nottingham and Grantham, and of the L&E and L&D to gain extensions to Spalding and Norwich respectively, effectively ended a dream that financial difficulties had in any case rendered impractical.

The branch was built by Simpson & Bennett at a cost of £170,000, a sum over twice the estimate of £80,000 because, as on the main line, the river and drainage commissioners demanded unreasonable clearance by bridges, and despite the erection of temporary structures, replaced a few years later at even more cost. It was opened over bare fen on 1 February 1848 (to passengers and freight), at once losing money at an appalling rate. Built for strategic purposes it missed the principal villages of the area, and until chalk was brought from the Swaffham cutting on the Dereham line to improve the approach roads some of the stations were inaccessible in winter. As late as 1859 train after train travelled empty, although receipts from tolls on the Lynn–Wisbech turnpike did fall from £2,686 in 1845 to £1,756 in 1860. Not until the recovery of Lynn harbour brought regular traffic to and from Peterborough, later Whitemoor, did the branch begin to justify itself, and even then, from 1866, its traffic was divided with the Peterborough, Wisbech & Sutton Bridge (Chapter XI). Services were four daily in 1854, three in 1874, eight down and seven up in 1883 (when Smeeth Road and Middle Drove were still conditional stops; Magdalen Gate had closed on 1 August 1866) and ten each way in 1939. Destinations served by through services were also varied from time to time and thus included March, Liverpool Street, Peterborough, Cambridge (via St Ives) and Ely (via March) on the one hand and Dereham, Yarmouth (Vauxhall) and Hunstanton on the other. With its isolated position it was only a matter of time before the line closed, especially as Lynn–Whitemoor freight could readily be diverted by way of Ely. Diesel multiple-units were introduced on 3 November 1958, local freight ceased on 19 April 1965, and conductor guards were employed from 5 June 1967 but these economies were not enough. Revenue remained at only £7,300 against costs of £30,500 a year and

EAST ANGLIAN RAILWAYS.

TIME AND FARE TABLE.

ON AND AFTER THE TWENTY-SEVENTH OF OCTOBER, 1846.

NOTICE.—Three minutes before the time fixed for the departure of each Train the Booking Offices will be closed, after which no person can be admitted.

Lynn and Ely Line.

LYNN to DOWNHAM.	Week Days.					Sundays.		Fares.		
	1	2	3	4	5	1	2	1st class	2nd class	3rd class
STATIONS.	a. m.	a. m.	a. m.	p. m.	p. m.	a. m.	p. m.			
	h. m.	h. m.	h. m.	h. m.	h. m.	h. m.	h. m.	s. d.	s. d.	s. d.
LYNN	7 15	10 15	11 50	5 0	6 40	9 0	8 0			
Saint Germans ..	7 28	10 28	12 3	5 12	6 53	9 13	8 13	0 10	0 8	0 5
Wallington	7 36	10 36	12 11	5 21	7 1	9 21	8 21	1 0	0 9	0 6
Stow	7 43	10 43	12 18	5 28	7 8	9 28	8 28	1 5	1 2	0 9
DOWNHAM	7 50	10 50	12 25	5 35	7 15	9 35	8 35	2 0	1 6	0 11

DOWNHAM to Lynn.	Week Days.					Sundays.		Fares.		
	1	2	3	4	5	1	2	1st class	2nd class	3rd class
STATIONS.	a. m.	a. m.	p. m.	p. m.	p. m.	a. m.	p. m.			
	h. m.	h. m.	h. m.	h. m.	h. m.	h. m.	h. m.	s. d.	s. d.	s. d.
DOWNHAM	8 5	11 0	12 30	3 50	7 30	9 45	8 45			
Stow	8 12	11 7	12 43	3 57	7 37	9 52	8 52	1 0	0 9	0 3
Wallington	8 19	11 14	12 45	4 4	7 44	9 59	8 59	1 5	1 0	0 6
Saint Germans	8 27	11 28	12 57	4 12	7 56	10. 7	9 7	1 8	1 2	0 9
LYNN 40	8 40	11 35	1 10	4 25	8 0	10 20	9 20	2 0	1 6	0 11

Lynn and Dereham Line.

LYNN to NARBOROUGH.	Week Days.				Sunday.			Fares.		
	1	2	3	4	1	2	3	1st class	2nd class	3rd class
STATIONS.	a. m.	a. m.	p. m.	p. m.	a. m.	p. m.	p. m.			
	h. m.	h. m.	h. m.	h. m.	h. m.	h. m.	h. m.	s. d.	s. d.	s. d.
LYNN	8 50	11 45	4 45	8 30	9 45	8 0	6 45			
Middleton	9 0	11 56	4 56	8 40	9 55	8 10	6 55	0 5	0 4	0 4
East Winch	9 7	12 3	5 3	8 47	10 2	8 17	7 2	0 8	0 6	0 4
Pentney and Bilney	9 14	12 10	5 10	8 54	10 9	8 24	7 9	0 11	0 9	0 7
NARBOROUGH	9 20	12 16	5 16	9 0	10 15	8 30	7 15	1 5	1 0	0 9

NARBOROUGH to LYNN.	Week Days.				Sundays.			Fares.		
	1	2	3	4	1	2	3	1st class	2nd class	3rd class
STATIONS.	a. m.	p. m.	p. m.	p. m.	a. m.	p. m.	p. m.			
	h. m.	h. m.	h. m.	h. m.	h. m.	h. m.	h. m.	s. d.	s. d.	s. d.
NARBOROUGH...........	9 30	12 30	5 30	9 30	9 45	8 0	6 45			
Pentney and Bilney.........	9 36	12 36	5 36	9 36	9 51	8 6	6 51	0 5	0 4	0 3
East Winch	9 43	12 43	5 43	9 43	9 58	8 13	6 58	0 8	0 6	0 5
Middleton	9 50	12 50	5 50	9 50	10 5	8 20	7 5	1 0	0 9	0 6
LYNN	10 0	1 0	6 0	10 0	10 15	8 30	7 15	1 5	1 1	0 9

Third Class Carriages will accompany every Train.
The Company will not be answerable for any Luggage unless Booked and Paid for; and, for better security, Passengers are recommended to take small packages inside the Carriages. Passengers are particularly requested to have their addresses written on all their Luggage in full. Children under ten years of age Half-price; Children in arms, unable to walk, pass free.

N.B. The Servants of the Company are prohibited from demanding or receiving any Gratuity from Passengers, who, it is hoped, will assist the Directors in enforcing this regulation. Immediate dismissal follows the discovery of any Servant of the Company receiving any gratuity. Smoking in the Carriages and at the Stations is forbidden, under a Penalty, by Act of Parliament.

Three Time and Fare Tables on a sheet may be had gratuitously, on application to Messrs. THEW & SON, Booksellers, High Street, Lynn.

The opening timetable of the Lynn & Ely and the Lynn & Dereham while both were still incomplete. The title East Anglian Railways is used although the official amalgamation did not come until 1847. The press was a common medium for such tables in early days

essential expenditure of £130,000 on the bridges and other works was looming. Closure came on 9 September 1968.

The 7 mile 1 furlong branch from Denver to Stoke Ferry was essentially a farmers' line, built by the Downham & Stoke Ferry (1879) with a share capital of £60,000, opened under GER operation on 1 August 1882 and absorbed by it on 1 January 1898. Throughout its history up to six daily trains were provided to Downham Market with some extending to Lynn. By 1900 Stoke Ferry was a minor malting centre but passenger facilities were withdrawn on 22 September 1930, although freight continued. From Abbey & West Dereham an 18 mile standard-guage light railway was opened in 1906 to Wissington (later to Southery and Feltwell Fens) to develop the estate of A. J. Keeble, its prime mover, and assist Fenland drainage works. Local produce was the mainstay of traffic but the line's status was greatly enhanced from 1924 with the opening of the sugar beet factory at Wissington. Expiration of a lease to the British Sugar Corporation led to temporary closure from March to July 1941 before, reconditioned by the LNER, it was reopened under the Ministry of Agriculture. The BSC maintained the services as a haulage contractor to 30 June 1957 when, local growers having declined to take it over, the line closed north of Wissington. The Stoke Ferry branch closed beyond Abbey & West Dereham on 19 April 1965 and completely in January 1982.

Immediately south of Lynn station the L&E was joined by the Lynn & Sutton Bridge, promoted in 1860 by Waring, a railway contractor, as the Mid-Eastern & Great Northern Junction Railway. The intention was to join the Norwich & Spalding (Chapter XI) at Sutton Bridge to Lynn with a spur at the latter to the Dereham line over which running powers would be obtained to Swaffham, the starting point for a further branch to Thetford and Bury St Edmunds. The EAR welcomed the proposals as likely to raise its value in the impending GER amalgamation, but on incorporation in 1861 the new company was restricted to the Sutton Bridge and Lynn section and a capital of £100,000. The EAR was empowered to subscribe £50,000 but found this beyond its means, and this, plus the representations of Lynn which feared the future GER monopoly, left the company free to agree with the Great Northern which operated it from its completion on 1 November 1864. It then passed to the Midland

& Eastern and finally to the Midland & Great Northern.

Doubled throughout, and with two lines continuing to Grimston Road, this was probably the busiest section on the Midland & Great Northern system, for it had double junctions at each end, to Peterborough and Bourne in the west, to King's Lynn and Yarmouth in the east, and was used by all through services including those from Lynn to Peterborough, Spalding and Nottingham; a push-and-pull link connected Lynn and South Lynn. The latter, opened to goods from the start but to passengers only with the completion of the Lynn avoiding line to Bawsey on 1 January 1886, became a busy junction and in 1938 £42,000 was spent on enlargement and modernisation of its facilities to reduce shunting operations at the overcrowded Melton Constable. A large beet factory was established there in the 1920s and locally the line became of great importance to fruit growers, some of the stations requiring a complete daily train in season during the 1930s; even so closure came on 2 March 1959 except for the section from Lynn to South Lynn which in 1990 still served the beet factory. Earlier, in August 1960, with the demolition of Lynn's MPD its steam engines had moved to South Lynn.

EAST AND NORTH OF LYNN

The Lynn & Dereham, incorporated in 1845 with a £270,000 capital, was designed to preserve the rich central Norfolk area from Norwich merchants and, in Williams's mind, form part of an east-to-west trunk route in association with the L&E's Wisbech branch; with the latter in mind works were provided for double track. The line opened to Narborough (Chapter I) on 27 October 1846, to Swaffham on 10 August 1847, to Sporle, a temporary station closed in October 1850, on 26 October 1847 and throughout on 11 September 1848. The cost was £24,000 per mile, the result of inflated land prices, the difficult chalk cutting at Swaffham, the foolish policy, common to the EAR constituents, of bulk buying of iron when prices were high, and the bankruptcy of a contractor so that the company had to complete the work itself. Despite its initial pretensions the L&D led a placid existence with three or four daily trains in early days (when the timetables treated it as an extension of the Ely line), rising to eight in 1897 and nine in 1914, but between the wars falling to seven and then six—the level obtaining in September 1955 when diesel multiple-units were introduced to give as many as twelve services a day. A handful of through workings had included various services between Yarmouth and Peterborough, one such from 1900 to 1914 conveying through carriages for Doncaster, which were attached to a train from Liverpool Street at March. From 1916 to the coal strike in 1921 there was a Yarmouth–York service which, on resumption after settlement of the strike, was cut back to Doncaster and continued thus until September 1939. In lineal descent from this rather poorly patronised passenger and parcels link, a Yarmouth–Whitemoor (March) parcels train was introduced in January 1949, being diverted to Spalding in the following month. In September 1956 its originating point was changed to Lowestoft and in March 1959 its terminal again became Whitemoor. The train, which had no return working, was finally withdrawn from this line in November 1960.

By September 1961 passenger services had been reduced to nine daily, a level still maintained in 1967 when seven were running to and from Norwich, a substantial increase deriving from the new pattern of operation that followed the withdrawal of passenger services between Dereham and Wells-next-the-Sea on 5 October 1964. Another economy effected was the gradual withdrawal of freight facilities from the intermediate stations, a process completed by 18 April 1966, to leave freight working only between Lynn and the sand quarries adjacent to the line at Middleton Towers; in 1990 this still continues. In addition, passing loops were then removed between Swaffham and Dereham and, on 15 August 1966, all stations became unmanned halts, with booking facilities on the trains. It had been hoped that this last move might still save the line, but despite the 700 to 900 daily users, revenue of £22,000 was heavily exceeded by expenses of £46,400 and on 9 September 1968 the branch was closed. The past value of the branch to agriculture, especially livestock farmers, had been considerable, culminating in the carriage of sugar-beet after the 1920s, but the very richness of the land had prevented other developments, apart from RAF bases such as Marham. Swaffham, the former social centre of the Breckland and junction for the Thetford line (Chapter VII), experienced a temporary boost but then lost steadily to Lynn as a market; only in the present century have fruit and vegetable canning and some agricultural engineering become established, and in fact the 1961 population was only 3,202 as compared with 3,358 in 1841. In 1971 it was 4,280.

Despite its purpose of excluding Norwich the EAR was beaten to East Dereham by the Norfolk Railway's Wymondham branch, authorised in 1845 in face of strong opposition from Direct Norwich & Dereham and Wells to Thetford promotions, and opened to freight on 7 December 1846 and for passengers on 15 February 1847. In 1846 extension to Wells and a branch to Blakeney were sanctioned, but railway schemes in association failed to materialise and construction was confined to the Dereham to Fakenham section, completed on 20 March 1849. The gap to Wells, a small harbour and fishing town with its own shipyard, was filled by the Wells & Fakenham, formed in 1853 by the Earl of Leicester (whose principal seat was nearby Holkham), local landowners and a group of Norfolk Railway directors. When incorporated in 1854 with a capital of £70,000 it had already been arranged that Wells should contribute £14,000, the Earl £10,000 and the railway directors, obliged to act as private individuals as Parliament would not allow the Norfolk to subscribe, £30,000. This same caution extended also to the refusal to begin construction until it was certain that the land could be obtained on reasonable terms. This done, progress was rapid and the line opened on 1 December 1857, the occasion being marked by a public holiday. A branch to Wells harbour was added under an 1859 Act and traffic developed well with very favourable concession rates offered by the Norfolk, to the disgust of the ECR which, desirous of protecting its harbour investments elsewhere, operated the branch in a most half-hearted and unsatisfactory manner. In 1862 the W&F was vested in the GER, a prelude to more enterprising services which, by 1892, had come to include a daily through coach from Liverpool Street.

Silting and the effects of railways elsewhere caused sad decline in Wells harbour, but compensation was found in the steadily growing numbers of day trippers who came out from Norwich; as late as 1963 a really good day could bring in as many as 2,000 visitors, and the shrines at Walsingham constituted a further benefit to the line's revenue. Dairy and livestock farmers gained particularly from the branch, and even into the 1960s between 1,500 and 6,000 gallons of milk were despatched daily to London from North Elmham and as much as 12,600 when bad weather made the roads unsafe for lorries. However, agricultural traffic was falling away, Wells harbour trade was reduced to the import of potash and the export of corn (the harbour branch was lifted by 1962). Fakenham, until 1959 also served by the M&GN, had developed printing but little else and had a population of only 3,753 in 1961; Wells itself had no more than 2,491. Diesel multiple-units were introduced in September 1955 but north of Dereham the line, too dependent on summer traffic, became increasingly uneconomic and closed on 5 October 1964, a freight link to Wells surviving only a few weeks until 31 October, before being cut back to Fakenham. Closure of the coal depot left Ryburgh Mill's grain traffic until January 1983 when North Elmham, with a granary and fertiliser depot, became the terminal. This section closed on 20 January 1989.

South of Dereham the branch, with the 1884 spur to the Lynn line open to through running, prospered with the town. In 1841 (population 3,837) it already had several brewers and maltsters and two iron founderies, serving the 'Garden of Norfolk', but by 1855, it had grown to nearly 4,500 and had added a steam saw-mill, two further foundries and a greatly expanded interest in the making of agricultural implements. In that year White recorded how the town's trade had 'considerably increased' since the opening of the railways, and described the 'extensive granaries' which had been built near the station and through which 'extremely large' quantities of corn were despatched by rail. By 1911, when steam machinery was being made, population was 5,729, and by 1961 it was 7,199, with a wide range of industries including cabinet and furniture making and new departures in engineering. Regular links with Norwich increased from five down and four up daily in 1873 to ten down and nine up by 1892 (one was a London working via Forncett and another a Yarmouth to Lynn service) and twelve up and eleven down in 1967 despite the singling of the line on 13 June 1965. East Dereham (11,845 in 1981) exemplified how a railway could develop a small town well removed from a major centre, but under modern conditions it could never be viable as a terminal. Thus, passenger services to Norwich were withdrawn on 6 October 1969, coal and full freight facilities on 7 November 1983, and company traffic (building materials, grain and fertilisers, frequently not providing enough for two weekly trains) on 30 June 1989.

At Fakenham the Wells line was crossed by the M&GN, this portion being built by the Lynn & Fakenham (1876), opening from Gaywood Junction to Massingham on 16 August 1879 and Fakenham on 16 August 1880, worked on contract by three tiny ex-Cornwall Railway mineral locomotives. While being of importance to local agriculture and in later years supplying several RAF stations such as Massingham which received 571 petrol trains in World War II, it was essentially a section on a through route. Passenger services were totally abandoned on 2 March 1959, although freight service continued to South Lynn from a grain company at East Rudham and from the subsidiary sidings of the Middleton sand quarries at Gayton Road until 1 May 1968.

Hunstanton in the north-west corner of Norfolk, a pleasant and progressive resort of 3,911 inhabitants (1971), stands as a monument to the enterprise of the Lynn & Hunstanton Railway which opened its line on 3 October 1862. When the company was incorporated in 1861 Hunstanton was still a village of under 500 people, reached by two EAR-subsidised omnibus services and only just coming into favour with a few families as a watering place. Development of a deep-water fishing port at Snettisham, encouragement of local agriculture and a contribution to the revival of Lynn were incidental benefits that might be expected to accrue from the creation of a new resort. Directors of both the L&H and the EAR participated in the provision of lodging houses and the preparation of plans and guides and a limited company was formed for the development.

Because Le Strange, the principal Hunstanton landowner who had provided much of the land without charge, had persuaded his neighbours either to give their land or sell it at agricultural rates, the railway was built within its £60,000 capital so that, the GER working it for 50 per cent of the receipts, an income of £10 per mile per week would produce a 5 per cent dividend. This was in fact achieved in 1864; freight, principally corn, cattle, wool, manures and coal, had exceeded expectation

and passenger traffic, not deterred by the derailment of 3 August
1863 in which seven died and over twenty were seriously injured
(the cause was a stray bull and the accident cost the GER £10,000
in compensation and some very severe criticism of its fences),
had gained from the 1864 opening of the Lynn & Sutton Bridge
and the public interest in the area that followed the purchase of
Sandringham House by Edward Prince of Wales in 1862. By
1871 Hunstanton's population had nearly doubled and a hotel,
gas and water works and a pier had all been provided.

In 1874 the L&H merged with the West Norfolk Junction
Railway from Heacham to form the Hunstanton & West Norfolk, which was absorbed by the GER on 1 July 1890. In 1899 the
GER completed the doubling of track to Wolferton, the station
for Sandringham which at an early stage had been improved at
the Prince of Wales's expense, opened the Sandringham Arms
Hotel (now offices) at Hunstanton, and set out to develop services, especially for the day trippers who were 'brought . . .
hundreds at a time from Cambridgeshire, Lincolnshire and elsewhere' (*Murray's Guide* 1892); already the four or five daily
trains of the first years had increased to six each way in winter
and twelve in summer with London connections of 187 minutes
to Liverpool Street and 184 minutes to St Pancras. From this
basis development was continued into the 1950s. It is impossible
to specify here the many details, but highlights have included a
Sunday restaurant-car excursion from Liverpool Street for
golfers (begun in 1905) and the 1922–3 summer restaurant-car
express from St Pancras. In the 1922 summer there were fourteen daily trains each way, including four restaurant-car expresses, one with Pullman cars, between the resort and Liverpool Street, besides that to and from St Pancras, but only two
Sunday services. By 1939, the daily summer total was thirteen,
six each way being Liverpool Street workings (three with restaurant cars) plus one up service to King's Cross. Sunday trains,
however, had shown a remarkable increase to a basic total of
sixteen down and fifteen up, reflecting changing social habits
and designed to serve both Hunstanton and Heacham, which
was developing moderately in its own right, and which has since
become noted for caravan holidays—in 1959 there were 1,200
caravans in the area. Winter services, in contrast, varied little
between 1922 and 1939, with some ten trains in each direction

including two Liverpool Street restaurant-car workings. During the 1950s British Railways intensified efforts to bring traffic to the line. In the 1958 summer, for example, weekday services comprised four from Lynn, four from Cambridge, six from London (since 1949 including the 'Fenman', by then running in 191 minutes), one from Peterborough and an additional train from the M&GN on Thursdays; on Saturdays London trains were increased to nine and there were Leicester and Ely through workings, and on Sundays no less than twelve trains, deriving from a wide area of the Fens and adjacent areas, left Lynn between 10 am and noon alone.

On 3 November 1958 diesel multiple-units were introduced and thereafter through London workings were gradually whittled away; in the 1966 summer they were confined to one up on weekdays, two up and one down on summer Saturdays, but for 1967 these disappeared altogether. Local services were also then reduced in face of falling patronage, and many places formerly connected, for example on the M&GN system, were either losing railway facilities altogether or their direct access. Through Saturday workings, after being confined in 1966 to one each from Cambridge and March were withdrawn entirely. Winter traffic, inevitably low, was sustained principally by Lynn workers and shoppers from the villages. One reason for the changing pattern of services, and one that gave hope for the line's survival was that after 6 June 1966 it had been worked as a self-contained 'basic railway'. Conductor guards had been employed, through workings withdrawn and the fare structure radically simplified, even to the extent of ending return bookings, and stations were made into unmanned halts. After these initial measures all work at Hunstanton was concentrated on one platform from 12 February 1967. On 5 March of the same year, Wolferton to King's Lynn was made into a single section (on a one-engine-in-steam basis) and on 2 April, the King's Lynn–Wolferton portion having been singled, the whole branch was converted into a single section, a key token system being employed from 21 May. All signal boxes between Lynn and Hunstanton were closed and level crossing gates replaced by automatic barriers. It was hoped that costs of £100,000 a year would fall to £35,000 and revenue of £40,000 thus cover costs even without additional traffic but losses persisted and the branch closed entirely on 5 May 1969.

The Hunstanton line figured prominently in the railway dramas of the 1953 floods. On the evening of 31 January the 7.27 pm from Hunstanton was engulfed before it could reach Heacham; it was struck on the smoke box by a floating bungalow and, the vacuum brake having been damaged and the fire extinguished, stood for six hours while water rose to seat level. Eventually, making temporary repairs to the brakes and using the floor boards from the tender to restart the fire, the driver was able to raise sufficient steam to crawl back to Hunstanton. The line remained blocked between Snettisham and Heacham until 11 February, and between the latter and Hunstanton, where the wreckage of bungalows had been swept on to the line and part of the track washed away, until 23 February.

From Heacham the West Norfolk Junction Railway, incorporated in 1864, opened to Wells on 17 August 1866, although on 13 January the Prince and Princess of Wales had been carried to Holkham when visiting the Earl of Leicester. From the start the GER worked the line, in early days providing through services from Lynn that made a double journey between Heacham and Hunstanton, before absorbing it, as the Hunstanton & West Norfolk (see above), on 1 July 1890. The line rescued north-west Norfolk from isolation and saved it from the worst effects of depression, but without stimulating any economic development of note. It closed to passengers on 2 June 1952; the Holkham to Wells section was severely damaged in the 1953 floods and was abandoned (actually east of Burnham Market) although partially restored to aid work on local marsh drainage, but by 1955 track had been removed from near Holkham to Wells, ending all hope of restoration with diesel multiple-units. A daily goods service between Heacham and Burnham Market lasted until 28 December 1964.

CHAPTER XI

Peterborough and the Southern Fens

LINES TO MARCH

Although the principal centres for the southern Fenlands are King's Lynn and Peterborough, the latter evolving from a small rural market into a thriving industrial city within the Railway Age, the lesser towns, notably March, Wisbech and Spalding, attracted a disproportionate concentration of railway enterprise. This was perhaps inevitable, for, although sparsely populated and given almost exclusively to agriculture, the Fenlands assumed immense strategic significance in the efforts of the Eastern Counties and Great Eastern to reach the north and of the Great Northern and Midland to break into Norfolk. Lines proliferated, their construction eased by the level nature of the land which bears witness to the sea and marsh from which, over several centuries, it has been, and is being, reclaimed. Agriculture, in the inland districts already blessed with a black peat soil which is probably the richest in the kingdom, benefited enormously; it became still more varied with corn, vegetables (especially potatoes), fruit, sugar-beet, horticultural produce and livestock all becoming of major importance.

Central to the railway pattern was the ECR's line from Ely to Peterborough, diverted through March to meet the Midland's intended Swinton extension of 1845 (Chapter V). Peto built this line ten months within contract time despite numerous slips on the marshy soil; freight was carried from 9 December 1846 and passengers from 14 January 1847. Substantial through freight traffic quickly developed in association with the London & North Western's Blisworth–Peterborough line, and this was progressively swollen by the branches to March from Wisbech (1847), St Ives (1848) and Spalding (1867), the last built by the GNR and with the line from St Ives subsequently becoming part

of the GN&GE Joint system, as well as by general construction
east of Ely; high levels were maintained despite competition
from the Peterborough, Wisbech & Sutton Bridge opened in
1866. By 1892 some forty daily freights entered the line at Ely
alone, rather more than half of which continued to Peterborough. Passenger services took rather longer to develop, and
local traffic has never amounted to very much. Five to seven
trains a day sufficed in the 1870s over the whole, and Stonea
(closed on 7 November 1966 when earning only £140 a year but
costing £850), Black Bank (closed to passengers on 17 June 1963
and to freight on 19 April 1965) and Chettisham (closed to
passengers on 13 June 1960 and to freight on 13 July 1964)
remained conditional stops into the next decade. Besides March,
only Whittlesea, in 1990 with a fertiliser depot but formerly
providing important brick traffic (107,531 tons in 1965), and
Manea survive today although as far back as the mid 1960s the
latter's annual costs of £1,900 exceeded revenue by £550.

Since 3 November 1958 diesel multiple-units have worked the
local services, as ever well patronised by through travellers to
and from Peterborough and March or Ely, in a pattern that has
already included through links with Cambridge, Ipswich, Harwich, King's Lynn, Norwich and, since 18 June 1962, Birmingham. This perpetuates a long history of such services. They have
varied considerably, but in 1883, for example, comprised eight
down and nine up between Peterborough and Lynn, some by
March and Wisbech, others by Ely, while there was also a daily
train to and from Yarmouth and one from Ipswich; from the
1880s until World War II, and again from December 1939 to
November 1960, Liverpool Street was also served once or twice
daily. In a wider context the GER's Doncaster and York trains,
the 'North Country Continental', and a large number of services
between the midlands, the north, the Norfolk coast, Norwich,
Harwich and Clacton, many of which have been described in
earlier chapters (see also the Postscript), have used this line as a
whole or the section between March and Ely.

The one dead-end branch from this line was that for freight
only from Three Horse Shoes Junction to Benwick (747 inhabitants in 1901), completed on 2 August 1898 after an earlier
opening to Burnt House on 1 September 1897. Well supplied
with collection points this represented a typical and successful

GER attempt to help the farmer in depression, and played a major role in promoting local recovery. Services continued until 13 July 1964.

The Wisbech, St Ives & Cambridge Junction of 1846 was, in the words of an ECR report, 'one of the very few railways originating with landowners in an agricultural district'. It aimed to carry the cattle and corn of St Ives markets to the harbour at Wisbech, and, after opening north of March on 3 May 1847 and to its south on 1 February 1848, in fact conveyed most of the grain, valued at £33,820, sent to the harbour during 1848. Absorbed by the ECR prior to completion the southern section was quickly integrated in the company's through workings to Peterborough, and its strategic importance for freight was further enhanced by its inclusion in the GN&GE Joint line established in 1882. Serving only villages, local services, operated by diesel multiple-units from 3 November 1958 and generally working through to Cambridge, Peterborough or King's Lynn, ceased on 6 March 1967 north of St Ives. The Wisbech section remains open for freight (in 1975 8,000 tonnes were despatched and 45,000 received), in 1989 carrying principally grain; the harbour branch closed on 28 December 1964. March to Wisbech passenger services were withdrawn on 9 September 1968. Coldham, the one intermediate station lost its freight facilities on 19 April 1965 and passenger status on 7 March 1966; by then it was costing £550 to collect an annual revenue of £15.

The St Ives section threw off a branch to Ramsey, a small market town stranded between the GNR and GER main lines, in what proved an interesting microcosm of inter-company rivalries. After the rejection in Parliament of an 1847 ECR proposal for a branch, local feeling turned in favour of a link with the GNR. The outcome was the 5½ mile Ramsey Railway from Holme, authorised in 1861 and opened on 22 July 1863; this was of necessity worked by the GNR although the GER interest constituted a majority in the £30,000 capital. In 1875, fearful that the GNR might somehow use the line as the basis for an extension towards Ely, the GER had the branch vested in itself and gave successful backing to the Ramsey & Somersham incorporated in that year. Doubly safeguarded, the GER passed the original line to the GNR on lease and made little effort to forward the Somersham branch, which in fact did not open until 16 September

1889 and on 1 January 1897 was transferred to the GN&GE Joint Committee; the authorised link between the two Ramsey terminals was never implemented. Despite its two branches Ramsey remained small, with only 5,697 inhabitants in 1961. Under the LNER two lines clearly constituted an unjustifiable luxury and that from Somersham lost its passenger facilities on 22 September 1930; freight services ceased beyond Warboys on 17 September 1956 (except for a few private sidings that remained open until the following August) and on the surviving stub on 13 July 1964. The Holme passenger service was withdrawn on 6 October 1947, but freight, principally grain, seed, potatoes, coal and general, remained to Ramsey North until July 1973. Earlier, St Mary's, an unstaffed Public Delivery Siding after 2 May 1960 had closed in February 1972. Meanwhile Holme had lost its main line passenger services on 6 April 1959.

The GNR's March to Spalding line, opened on 1 April 1867, was more the product of railway politics than of local need. The desire of the ECR and then the GER to buttress dividends by participation in northern coal traffic had never flagged and the breakdown of the 1851–2 truce through GNR interest in the Hertford line (Chapter V) and in those from Spalding towards King's Lynn (below) precipitated new efforts. In 1863 the GER entered a Spalding–March bill, also seeking running powers to Doncaster, which immediately provoked a GNR promotion to link the two places. The latter was successful although the Lords insisted on GER running powers to Spalding. Ill-content, the GER then backed a Great Eastern Northern Junction project from Long Stanton to Askern, near Doncaster, and promised 50 per cent of the capital, but this was rejected by Parliament in both 1864 and 1865; meanwhile in 1864 the GNR had obtained powers to extend from Gainsborough to Doncaster, a line completed on 15 July 1867. Thrice worsted, the GER then turned to the possibilities of co-operation, and in 1866 actually arranged to assume a share in the lines to Doncaster by contributing half the cost of the March–Spalding and Gainsborough–Doncaster constructions, with running powers to Wakefield and exchange facilities at Lincoln for Lancashire traffic as additional benefits. At the GNR's suggestion a Spalding–Lincoln bill was prepared, but the whole concept collapsed when an internal upheaval and inquiry amongst GER proprietors revealed that £1,500,000 was already needed to put the existing system in good order.

Revived negotiations in 1867 broke down when the GNR refused to betray the allied Manchester, Sheffield & Lincolnshire by allowing the GER Lincoln exchange facilities with the Lancashire & Yorkshire. They failed again in 1876, the GER proposing total amalgamation for 1884, over stock fusion, the GNR offering £50 of its own for each £100 of the GER's, the latter insisting on £55. In 1877 the GER entered a Lincoln–Spalding bill. The GNR's duplicate measure, prepared in haste, in fact failed at Standing Orders, but it also had a March–Shepreth proposal ready, and this had not advanced far when the GER, recognising both the willingness of the GNR to fight and its own inferior position, gave way and proposed a resumption of amalgamation talks. This time a 50 per cent stock adjustment and an earlier fusion date, in 1883, were agreed, but rupture came over the GER's insistence on a guaranteed dividend of 6 per cent for ten years although the GNR's level had currently fallen to 5½ per cent, and also over the amount that the GER should spend on renewals prior to amalgamation.

The GER turned again to a joint-ownership agreement, but this in turn foundered when the GNR, while offering facilities at Doncaster, insisted on running powers to Cambridge, Newmarket, Norwich and Yarmouth, and the immediate joint ownership of all lines from Doncaster to Shepreth. Attempting to break the deadlock while securing its position, the GNR, although financially hard pressed and unable to undertake a March to Shepreth line, entered an 1878 bill for a Spalding–Lincoln extension. For its part the GER revived the 1864 project as the Great Eastern Northern Extension, backing it with alluring prospects of cut rates, 5s a ton off certain Yorkshire manufactured goods and a charge of ¼d per ton mile on block loads of coal exceeding 400 tons. Once again, however, the GNR was successful, although Parliament added the rider that the GER ought to have access to the north. It was a timely comment. Both companies were coming to see the folly of such competition and of duplicating lines. The GNR accordingly dropped its demands for running powers to Norwich and Yarmouth, and proposed a joint line, with Huntingdon rather than Shepreth as the southern point. The GER agreed, and the outcome was the authorisation on 3 July 1879 of the GN&GE Joint Committee, to be composed of five directors from each company; the elements of the joint line were Huntingdon to St Ives (EAR, 1847), St Ives —more strictly, Needingworth Junction—to March (ECR, 1848), March to Spalding (GNR, 1867), a new Spalding to Lincoln line, as authorised in 1878 and opened to Ruskington on 6 March 1882 and through to Lincoln on 1 August 1882, and thence GNR lines via Gainsborough to a point on the main line just south of Doncaster.

Previous sections have emphasised the significance of the March to Spalding line as a through route, especially for northern coal, but as the latter declined and improved operation on the GNR main line increased capacity, it made economic sense to transfer both freight and passenger services to it. Thus, total closure occurred between March and Spalding on 30 October 1982, since when the track has been lifted. Locally the line had generated much farm traffic but little else and starting with Murrow West on 6 July 1953 (goods on 1 September 1947) and concluding with Postland and Cowbit (both once noted for vegetable traffic) on 11 September 1961, local passenger services had long since gone. At Murrow, where the line was crossed on the level by the M&GN, the latter's closure in 1959 was followed by the laying of a spur to link Whitemoor Yard with the Eye Green and Dogsthorpe brickworks and Wisbech Harbour (North) but this lasted only until 20 July 1966.

The GN&GE line had confirmed the significance of March as an interchange for both passengers and freight. To 1925 there were extensive sidings but in four wastefully scattered yards; this, the developing beet traffic and the heavy coal flow led the LNER, in 1925, to initiate a £285,000 scheme for a fully mechanised, gravity worked up-yard with the first rail retarders in Britain. Completed in 1929, it was followed in 1933 by a similarly reconstructed down yard. Wagon transit time was cut from twenty-four to twelve hours and the scope of Whitemoor was extended to servicing the whole of the eastern counties and London. One August day in 1942 the up hump handled fifty-nine trains (3,814 wagons) and by 1953 with radio telephony (1949) and other modern equipment overall yard capacity had become 7,000 wagons a day. In 1977 the yards, by now reduced to 68 acres and mainly concerned with movement between the East Anglia the Midlands and the North still handled 1,500 wagons a day, but the decline and eventual loss of the Spalding line, diversion of traffic to the GN and the reduced coal flow made Whitemoor an anachronism. Closure came on 7 May 1984, other than for Speedlink interchange traffic; a prison now occupies a large area of the former yards.

March station has similarly declined with loss of junction status and the transfer of its once considerable parcels and mail (up to 5,000 bags a day) to Peterborough. In 1963 it became one of the four main diesel maintenance depots on the former GER lines, but this also is scheduled to close. The town grew with the railway which once employed 2,000. The 1901 population was 7,565 (a new Corn Exchange opened in 1900 and the market revived) and some engineering had been established; the 1971 population was 14,475 but that of 1981 14,285.

WISBECH, SUTTON BRIDGE AND SPALDING

Wisbech, 'Queen of the Fens', 8,530 in 1841, expended large sums on its harbour and approaches to oust Lynn as the foremost Fenland port. Some Baltic timber was indeed diverted and in 1847 the harbour handled 167,443 tons, but assured superiority inevitably rested on rail communication. The Wisbech, St. Ives & Cambridge Junction opened to its South Brink station on 3 May 1847, the East Anglian to its own wooden structure, later rebuilt and used by the GER, on 1 February 1848. The neglect of the GNR to obtain running powers over the connection between the two lines was the factor that enabled the ECR to ruin the former's attempt to take the EAR on lease in 1851. Unfortunately for Wisbech the London route was too indirect, the Lynn & Ely line did not close as might have been hoped, and ECR services, likened in slowness to Wisbech church clock which had long been out of repair, left much to be desired. In 1862 a further £60,000 was spent on new wharfs, but harbour traffic, like that of Lynn, was suffering badly from the effects of railways elsewhere—in 1855 it amounted to only 88,082 tons—and the town's population had actually fallen, from 10,178 to 9,218, between 1851 and 1861. GNR plans to build 5 acres of docks and those of the ECR for installations of 13 acres had come to nothing.

New hope came, however, with the Peterborough, Wisbech & Sutton Bridge (Wisbeach in the Act), incorporated in 1863, opened for goods on 1 June 1866 and for passengers on 1 August. The new line was worked by the Midland Railway for 50 per cent of the receipts, although deriving from the GNR stronghold of Peterborough in the south-west and meeting the GNR-controlled Norwich & Spalding and Lynn & Sutton Bridge in the north. The Norwich & Spalding, incorporated in 1853 as the Spalding & Holbeach and the work of pure speculators such as Cobbold and Bruff of Ipswich, had commenced passenger services to Holbeach on 15 November 1858, extending to Sutton Bridge, with four daily trains, on 1 July 1862. The pretentious title derived from plans to build a branch to Wisbech, obtain running powers over the EAR lines to East Dereham, and extend from there to Norwich, either by a new line or by running powers over the Norfolk Railway via Wymondham. Wisbech, however, sacrificing its best chance for new midland and northern markets, had shortsightedly opposed the branch that would cross the river to the seaward side of the town, and Lynn had pressed for a direct line from Sutton Bridge, so that the project had emerged from Parliament in a severely restricted form. There was also a somewhat sinister connotation, for one of those deeply involved was Waddington, the ejected ECR chairman, who was seeking revenge on his old company by providing the East Anglian and the Norfolk with an independent outlet that would inevitably raise the values of their stocks in the 1862 fusion.

Before returning to Wisbech the overall pattern must be sketched. The GNR worked both the Norwich & Spalding and the Lynn & Sutton Bridge (Chapter X) and also a Spalding & Bourn [sic] incorporated in 1862 and completed on 1 August 1866; hopes of an east-to-west trunk route had caused the three to resist total absorption. In 1866 the trio combined as the Midland & Eastern, jointly worked by the Midland, allowed in by the GNR to avert the possibility of a Bourne–Saxby construction, and the GNR with a £15,000 annual guarantee; the new company had running powers over the Peterborough, Wisbech & Sutton Bridge. The latter company subsequently complained with some bitterness that the Midland, which worked it, was starving the line of traffic to ensure that the guarantee to the M&E was met, but in fact the Midland was using the GER via March more than either the Wisbech or Spalding lines for cross-

Midland Railway.

OPENING OF THE LINE BETWEEN
PETERBORO', WISBEACH,
SUTTON BRIDGE, AND LYNN.
WORKING TIME-TABLE
Of Passenger, Goods, and Mineral Trains.
AUGUST 1st, 1866, AND UNTIL FURTHER NOTICE.

PETERBORO' AND LYNN.

Distance	STATIONS.		1 Goods and Coal	2 Pass.	3 Pass.	4 Goods and Coal	5 Pass. & Goods	6 Pass.	7	8	9	10	11	12	13	14
Miles			a.m.	a.m.	a.m.	p.m.	p.m.	p.m.								
..	PETEROBRO' G.E.	dep.	6 15	8 50	11 40	12 30	..	6 50	..	..	..	..	.	..	..	..
½	Peterboro', G. N. Station		..	8 53	11 43	..	..	6 53	..	..	..	..	..	..	..	..
	Peterboro' Crescent	....	6 20	..	..	12 45	..	..	..	..	..	..	..	..	..	..
	Wisbeach Junction {	arr.	6 20	..	..	12 45	..	..	..	..	..	..	..	..	..	..
..	Peterboro'	dep.	..	..	..	..	..	..	..	..	..	..	..	..	..	..
6	Eye............ {	arr.	6 37	..	..	12 53	..	..	..	..	..	..	..	..	..	..
		dep.	6 43	9 6	11 56	1 8	..	7 6	..	..	..	..	..	..	..	..
9¼	Thorney .... {	arr.	6 54	..	..	1 19	..	..	..	..	..	..	..	..	..	..
		dep.	7 2	9 15	12 5	1 29	..	7 15	..	..	..	..	..	..	..	..
11¼	Wryde		7 ..	9 21	12 11	1 4.	..	7 21	..	..	..	..	..	..	..	..
15½	Murrow		7 ..	9 29	12 19	1 59	..	7 29	..	..	..	..	..	..	..	..
18½	Wisbeach, St. Mary		7 3.	..	..	2 16	..	..	..	..	..	..	..	..	..	..
20½	Wisbeach, Passenger		7 4.	9 37	12 27	..	..	7 37	..	..	..	..	..	..	..	..
21	Wisbeach, Goods.. {	arr.	7 41	..	..	2 24	..	..	..	..	..	..	..	..	..	..
		dep.	7 51	9 45	12 33	2 42	..	7 43	..	..	..	..	..	..	..	..
23½	Ferry		7 5.	9 50	12 4.	2 51	..	7 51	..	..	..	..	..	..	..	..
26½	Tydd, St. Mary		8 7	9 56	12 46	3 6	..	7 56	..	..	..	..	..	..	..	..
28½	Sutton Bridge .... {	arr.	8 15	10 3	12 53	3 15	..	8 3	..	..	..	..	..	..	..	..
		dep.	..	10 5	12 5.	..	4 35	8 5	..	..	..	..	..	..	..	..
31	Walpole................		..	10 10	1 0	..	4 44	8 10	..	..	..	..	..	..	..	..

The first full timetable of the Peterborough–Sutton Bridge line, although freight had been carried since 1 June. The extension to Walpole reflects the Midland Railway's share in the operation of the Midland & Eastern. Note the relegation of Crescent station to goods only and the old spelling of Wisbech

country traffic, one reason being the awkwardness of the junctions at Sutton Bridge and King's Lynn. On 1 July 1883, however, the PW&SB was absorbed with the M&E into the Eastern & Midlands, passing thence into the Midland & Great Northern on 1 July 1893, although Midland locomotives continued to work it until 31 December 1894. The Bourne–Little Bytham–Saxby line opened to passengers on 1 May 1894 (freight had commenced on 5 June 1893), passing into M&GN hands as far as Little Bytham Junction and permitting cross-country working without reference to Peterborough.

These western lines of the M&GN, continuous double track existing only for the 9 miles between Twenty and Little Bytham, always retained a peculiar charm of their own, epitomised by the frequently isolated but homely flower-bedecked stations; basic local services were mainly those between King's Lynn or Yarmouth and Peterborough, and Lynn and Spalding, with Norfolk coast expresses working over both lines. Careful planning allowed good speeds despite the predominance of single track, and as early as 1898 one daily up Cromer–King's Cross train took only 57 minutes over the 36½ miles from South Lynn to Peterborough, with one intermediate stop at Wisbech. Probably the fastest train ever on M&GN metals was a one-coach special bearing the 1936 election results from Peterborough to Lynn in 46 minutes. But above all, these lines are to be remembered for the aid they gave to agriculture, and particularly in enabling farmers to specialise in perishable produce; by 1900, for example, there were 5,000 acres of fruit, flowers and general horticultural crops within 7 miles of Wisbech alone. In 1896 the M&GN carried 4,400 tons of fruit (soft varieties followed by plums and apples) out of Wisbech between June and September, and in 1898 3,980 tons by goods train, 230 by passenger services; similar totals were achieved by the GER, averaging 60 tons a day over the season. By the 1930s further growth had occurred and at the peak of the season small stations like Sutton Bridge, Murrow (East), Long Sutton, Gedney and Holbeach were each despatching trains of up to sixty vans daily for centres such as London, Manchester, Liverpool, Birmingham, Cardiff, Leeds, Sheffield and Edinburgh. And this was not all. Pea traffic coincided with the soft fruit, potatoes were carried the whole year, shortly after Christmas the movement of flowers began and continued for four months, steam-heated vacuum stock for their carriage being provided between Lynn and Bourne by the 1930s, in the early spring large quantities of cabbage and broccoli were conveyed, and later in the year came plums, apples and pears, and sugar-beet.

Only after World War II did these heavy traffics begin to flag, and the two lines generally exhibit the disabilities common to the M&GN system as a whole. Withdrawal of passenger services on 2 March 1959 was complete west of Lynn, but freight spurs were left from Spalding to Bourne (made single track and operated as a siding by 1961), and to Sutton Bridge. At Murrow, on the former PW&SB, connection was established with the March–Spalding line to permit working from the brick works at Eye Green and Dogsthorpe, two places long linked by aerial railway alongside the Peterborough line, which in the year prior to cessation of service on 20 July 1966 forwarded 31,075 tons. The connection also gave access to the M&GN's Wisbech Harbour branch, which, unlike the GER's, directly served the quaysides. This had brought substantial traffic to the M&GN but closed on 20 September 1964, the Murrow–Wisbech section outliving it only until 28 December of the same year.

Sutton Bridge station, rebuilt in 1898, fell into a sad state of disrepair, and Cross Keys Swing Bridge, also rebuilt in 1898, has been converted to road use. A section of a golf course occupies part of the site of an even more dismal disappointment of hopes. Having contemplated docks at Sutton Bridge in 1846 and 1847 but being defeated by the Boston, Stamford & Birmingham, authorised to Wisbech in 1846 and Sutton Bridge in 1847 but reaching neither, the GNR revived its efforts in 1875 when it became the largest shareholder in a new dock company. Begun in 1878, the dock was opened on 14 May 1881, but on 15 May the entrance lock was found to be leaking; it was then ascertained that the whole construction stood on treacherous sand, and when in June the concave west slope gave way the engineers recommended against reconstruction. The only ship to use the dock was an arrival with Norwegian timber on the opening day, leaving with coal on the next.

All this was to the benefit of Wisbech, which, shed of its grand illusions, had, with the help of agricultural development in the area, settled to steady recovery as a market centre and minor port; it was well equipped with internal rail facilities, for besides the two harbour branches the M&GN had a street tramway to the old market and the GER offered similar facilities to various wharfs and warehouses. In 1903 imports, principally timber, corn, wool, iron and seeds, were valued at £136,595, exports at £1,286; above all the harbour had clung to the leading position established in the timber trade during earlier years, in 1896, for example, handling 66,323 tons as compared with 58,408 at Yarmouth and 50,033 at Lynn. By 1900 planing and saw-mills had developed alongside other forms of timber working (such as

weather proofing), and brewing, malting, oil cake, jam manufacturing (1892) and agricultural-implement making were also
important. Today, the harbour has some 80,000 tons a year
passing through it and the town, with canning (the former GER
harbour line served a factory) and other relatively new industries,
had grown to 17,332 inhabitants in 1981. In November 1965 a
consortium of local growers signed a five-year contract with
British Rail for the despatch of fruit and flowers, and generally
freight levels remain reasonable; but Wisbech, as described
above, has now lost its passenger services.

A further important feeder was the 7¾ mile standard-gauge
Wisbech & Upwell Tramway, authorised in 1882 and built by
the GER from its station yard to Outwell, alongside the Wisbech–
Outwell canal of 1794 and public roads, on 20 August 1883 and
extended to Upwell on 8 September 1884 at a cost of just under
£2,300 a mile. Passengers were carried until 2 January 1928.
Coaches, one of which later featured in the comedy film *The
Titfield Thunderbolt*, others being transferred to the Kelvedon
line (Chapter II), were provided with gangways and end-steps
as the stations lacked platforms—trains, once eight daily,
stopped anywhere on the route. The main purpose of the line,
however, was agricultural. In 1888 up to 500 tons of produce
and supplies were being carried in good weeks, and in 1910
14,549 tons overall; indeed, the branch was long cited as an
example of what light railways could achieve. However, road
competition bit deeply by the 1930s, services being restricted by
the 8 mph speed limit imposed because of proximity to public
roads (the old tram locomotives had noiseless blasts and enclosed motion to avoid frightening horses, as well as fenders and
warning bells), and by 1937 there were only three trains a day.
By 1962 only one remained, except in the fruit season, and
withdrawal of services from intermediate points began on
5 November 1962 until the whole line was finally closed on
23 May 1966. Working in the latter years was by diesel mechani-
cal locomotives, fitted with skirts over the motion and cow-
catchers.

Spalding, with 16,951 inhabitants in 1971, has long been an
important market centre. The Syston to Peterborough branch
(below) destroyed the former river trade with Stamford, but
growth as a junction sustained the town, the GNR, GN&GE Joint

and the M&GN, for the western division of which Spalding was
the headquarters until 1 January 1895, all passing through it.
The pattern of local lines was completed on 5 June 1893 by construction of the short link from Cuckoo Junction to Welland
Bank which permitted through M&GN working without entry
into the station and reversal; this was little used after 1955 when
signs of subsidence became apparent and was closed on 15 September 1958.

PETERBOROUGH

Although only a small market centre and river port of 6,959
inhabitants in 1841 the cathedral city of Peterborough had sufficient potential as a railhead and point of entry into the eastern
counties to attract a London˙ & Birmingham Railway branch
from Blisworth and Northampton. Authorised in 1843 this
opened to passengers on 2 June 1845 and to goods on 15 December. Proposals made by the L&B to the ECR, which in 1844 had
been empowered to construct from Ely, for a joint station having
been rebuffed, use was made of the ECR's existing premises
(named East in 1923), as yet an isolated outpost in that the Ely
line was not completed for goods traffic until 10 December 1846
and for passengers until 14 January 1847.

Meanwhile, traffic on the L&B branch had so expanded that
the track into Peterborough was doubled in September 1846.
On 2 October of that year, still in advance of the ECR, the
Midland Railway, crossing the Nene by a timber bridge that
was not replaced by the present steel structure until 1932, also
opened into the station from a temporary terminal at Stamford.
This represented part of the 48 mile Syston–Peterborough line,
authorised in 1845 in fulfilment of Hudson's promise to provide
the ECR with a new outlet in return for sacrificing its own
independent northern plans (Chapter V) and as a means of
strangling future GNR traffic. The branch had opened from
Syston to Melton Mowbray on 1 September 1846, but difficulties with landowners delayed completion of the middle section
until 20 March 1848 (passenger services began on 1 May); in
the meantime the isolated southern portion had been worked
first by the London & North Western, of which the London &
Birmingham had become a part, and then, with a Stamford–Ely
service, by the ECR.

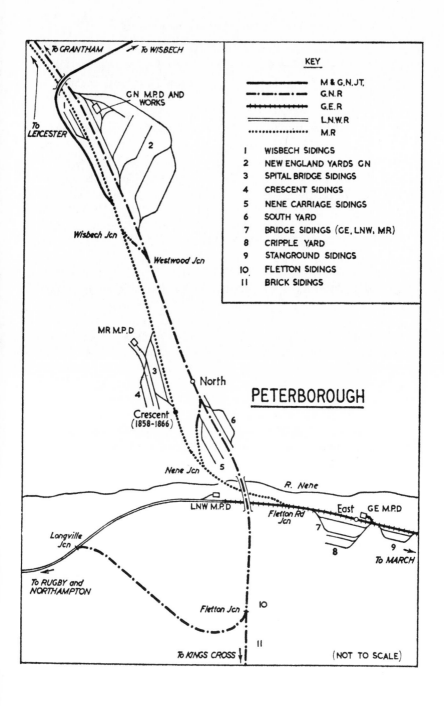

The Great Northern, delayed in the Peterborough area by the need to obtain deviation powers to share bridges, culverts and works as far as Helpston with the Midland, a condition imposed in the Lords to minimise interference with private property, entered the city from Lincoln on 17 October 1848, running off the 'loop' line at Werrington Junction over a temporary spur to the Midland line and continuing into the ECR station. The almost inevitable disputes over tolls followed with the ECR. However, on 7 August 1850 the Maiden Lane to Werrington Junction line was completed, the spur (eventually to be relaid in 1959) was lifted and the GNR opened its own station (North from 1923) ¾ mile from the town centre; the continuation north from Werrington Junction to Retford was completed for freight on 15 July 1852 and for passengers on 1 August.

Within a very few years Peterborough had entered fully into its continuing role as a major interchange point for both passengers and freight; in 1863 coal traffic alone amounted to 110,000 tons on the Midland and 182,000 on the GNR. Working quickly became cramped and unnecessarily expensive as each company sought to provide a full range of facilities. There were, for example, seven separate yards, staging between which became an increasingly massive and complex matter, and four locomotive depots, the GNR's at New England, the GER's from 1846 to 1939, the Midland's at Spital Bridge from 1871 to 1960 and that of the LNWR which, after sharing the inadequate GER facilities, opened its own on the opposite bank of the Nene in 1880, this remaining in use until 1932. Between 1 February 1858 and 1 August 1866 the Midland added further to the duplications by providing its own station at Crescent, alongside the GNR's, as a calling point for trains to and from the GER terminal, but this was closed with the commencement of passenger services on the Peterborough, Wisbech & Sutton Bridge; the new trains, as well as those of the Midland in general, were permitted to call at the GNR station, where an additional platform had been provided. Even so, the PW&SB services continued to the GER station, enlarged by an island but still having only two main platform lines, until 30 September 1904.

By 1904 Peterborough was growing considerably, the GNR's direct contributions including a locomotive-repair works (1852), which expanded to employ 1,500 men, a rope and covers works and a sheet stores, as well as the housing, accompanied by churches and schools, provided for its employees, and a first-rate hotel. But additional to this, industrial growth had been noticeable in the area since the 1870s, particularly in engineering and in brick making at Yaxley, Fletton and Whittlesea. This, and alleviation of congestion, explained the last major construction in the district, the 1¾ mile loop from Fletton Junction to the LNWR at Longville Junction. Authorised in 1873 this opened on 2 July 1883. The line attracted further industrial expansion, including a beet refinery in the 1920s, and until 1 April 1916 carried the GNR's Peterborough–Leicester (Belgrave Road) passenger service. The LNWR junction was closed in December 1929, the former running lines of the branch in effect becoming sidings, but, after a temporary link through the British Sugar Corporation sidings in the war, was permanently reopened in December 1947 for the use of brick trains from Yaxley, two a day by 1953. By then brick traffic had long been of enormous dimensions. In 1946, to take just one example, 25,000,000 bricks, in twenty monthly trains of fifty wagons each over a five-month period, were forwarded to Scotland under one contract alone; such heavy block loads to London and other centres have been regular features of operation since long before 1923, and in 1967 there were five a week to the north-east. In the twelve months to 27 September 1965 Fletton handled 35,153 wagons, and overall in 1965 Fletton and Yaxley together forwarded 379,042 tons, principally in bricks and beet pulp. A later development was the carrying of fly-ash into the area from power stations in the Trent Valley to fill in disused clay pits and permit land reclamation. By 1967 a 1½ mile merry-go-round line had been opened around the site and it was estimated that when fully developed the traffic would amount to 1¾ million tons a year.

By 1981 the energy of the Peterborough New Town Development Corporation had created a splendid modern city of 114,108 (in 1987, 130,000). The old industries continue to flourish but alongside a host of newcomers in modern industrial estates. During 1965 local traffic comprised 13,217 tons of sundries inwards, 10,018 tons in wagon loads and 3,486 in smalls outwards. In the same year passenger-ticket issues and collections, taking no account of the thousands who changed trains in the city, totalled 202,406 (plus 370 season) and 432,152 respectively at North, 34,620 and 127,091 at East, the discrepancies at each station indicating the extent to which Peterborough had attracted workers, shoppers and pleasure seekers from a wide surrounding area. Mail traffic (subsequently to increase with the decline of March) was also heavy, North Station handling 4,000 bags a day or more at the busy Christmas period.

All this is a striking reflection of what the railways have achieved, but above all Peterborough has been notable for transit traffic, the King's Cross Division in the city handling 89,658 tons as late as 1965, despite increasing through workings and diversions to Whitemoor. In the year ending 27 September 1965 this section handled 98,337 wagons with the low average Terminal Wagon Time of only 1·41 days. This was a remarkable achievement, for as has been implied the practical difficulties of operation in the area have always been acute, and much of the railway history concerns attempts to expedite traffic. Particular problems have ever been the dog-leg curves through North station, probably the result of deviation towards the Midland, restricting through running to 20 mph, and also access to the New England yards which, from the slow, involves blockage of both fast lines. The extent of the handicaps may be better appreciated by noting that by 1910 there were a thousand movements a day through the GNR station, and by 1922 the New England yards were annually handling 10,000,000 tons of coal, over 60,000 livestock and substantial quantities of bricks and general merchandise. Movement in connection with the GNR locomotive depot, where 200 engines were allocated by 1922 (although the number has now been dramatically reduced), added to the congestion. The Midland was operating three yards on the down side of the main line as well as its own locomotive depot, and the link between the two stations required a special service. The GER station, where there were further yards and a very heavy freight flow in and out of the eastern counties, was even more cramped than its neighbour. Inter-yard staging was a constant complication.

As early as 1898 the Corporation had been prepared to contribute £10,000 to a new GNR station, but neither the plans of that year nor those of 1908 were implemented, although the

Crescent road bridge, in April 1913 replacing an excessively inconvenient level crossing just to the south of the GNR station, had a span clearly designed to accommodate a realigned main line. In 1920 the GNR river basin was filled in to make way for the Nene carriage sidings and on 2 November 1924 widening to quadruple track, involving a second viaduct over the Nene and the western approaches to East station, was completed between Fletton Junction and the Crescent. On 20 September 1934 a new road bridge replaced another highly troublesome level crossing just to the west of East station. From the early 1930s the development of Whitemoor contributed to relieving pressure, although by no means solving the problems of Peterborough. In 1945 the LNER proposed a rebuilt central station and the closure of East, and in 1959, when electrification of the main line was envisaged, a comprehensive £5½ million scheme was promulgated for the whole area, under which North station was to be enlarged and completely remodelled to give through running at 85 mph instead of 20; again East was to be closed. In the end, influenced by projected growth of the city to 175,000, and prospects of electrification a new station was provided, involving new down platforms, the first of which was brought into use on 25 June 1972, track realignment to permit through running at 100 mph and resignalling. This was to be the final scheme but in 1976 the Victorian buildings on the up side (excluded from the plan because the Development Corporation was unable to offer financial help) were found to be unsafe and had to be demolished. Temporary wooden buildings were provided. Eventually the newer station was completed in September 1980. Meanwhile, on 2 December 1972 the new power box had opened to control the 56 miles of main line from Sandy to Stoke Tunnel. North Station remains an extremely busy centre, for as well as the main line traffic and the increased stopping services to King's Cross there is also the much developed cross country traffic between the eastern counties and the Midlands and North (see Postscript), first developed when from 7 May 1973 the 'North Country Continental' was diverted from its traditional Lincoln route.

Meanwhile considerable rationalisation has been achieved in other ways. On 12 April 1953 the three former Midland Railway yards were closed, and the LNWR's combined with the GER's

Peterborough Bridge sidings; sorting for the west was transferred to Whitemoor, from where a whole new set of provincial services was provided. In this way £100,000 a year was saved, mainly by the drastic reduction of unproductive shunting. On 14 June 1965, as a consequence of the declining call for domestic coal, diversion to Whitemoor and more through workings, a large section of the New England yards was closed, leaving the new depot of 1960 as a Resididual Tranship Depot for Sundries and container handling facilities. The next closure was the West-wood Yard in April 1966, followed by that of West Yard on 1 August, both under the National Freight Train Plan which envisaged New England dealing with 950 wagons a week, as opposed to the previous 2,200.

On 6 June 1966 passenger facilities, as had long been threat-ened, were withdrawn from the East station with the ending of services on the Rugby line (closed completely except for iron ore traffic to Kingscliffe which lasted to November 1972) and of local passenger trains to Leicester; Northampton services had already ceased on 4 May 1964. Through workings to Leicester and Birmingham are now routed through North station. East station became a parcels centre, dealing with some 15,000 a day, and the base for the East Anglian British Rail Universal Trolley Equip-ment (BRUTE) service introduced on 11 July 1966, in which one eleven-vehicle train made two daily round trips between Liver-pool Street and Peterborough—once each way via Cambridge, once each way via Bury St Edmunds and Ipswich. The through single line at Peterborough East was then filled in and the platform level raised to facilitate trolley operation, but subse-quently the parcels work was transferred to the new parcels terminal constructed on the site of the former New England Motive Power Depot and East station closed completely in September 1972.

CHAPTER XII

Postscript: 1990

When this book was first published in 1968 it seemed that the railway system of the eastern counties had had its day. For 120 years crucial in shaping the economic and demographic patterns of the region and breaking down its isolation, it was now to be finally overwhelmed by road competition and left with only a very minor role. The Beeching Plan of 1966 had seemingly confirmed this view, and already a massive programme of closures, extending even to some sections of main line (vide Yarmouth to Beccles), was under way. This negative phase, other than for continuing rationalisation and closures in the freight area, ended in 1970, although question marks remained over a number of rather surprising survivors, Mark's Tey to Sudbury and the rest of the East Suffolk line amongst them. Government subsidies were high; in 1973 £733,000 on services linking the eastern counties with the Midlands and North was the largest single item but a dozen others were listed, some like those from Norwich to Yarmouth and Lowestoft, once so busy, giving grounds for the most pessimistic view of the future. In 1976 newspapers carried accounts of the Serpell Report and its proposals for a further round of massive cuts; east of the King's Cross to Peterborough line and outside Essex there would be nothing left north of Cambridge and Norwich would be reduced to just the Ipswich line. Political considerations and a rather more positive attitude by management and government towards railway investment resulted in the shelving of these ideas, and with the progress made in suburban electrification and the spread of London commuters beyond Essex in mind, it became possible to conclude in the 1978 edition of this book that 'there has been the re-establishment of reasonable stability and even the appearance of some elements of growth'.

That stability was to be shaken in the deep recession of 1980 and 1981. From 5 January 1981 services were reduced and later in the year British Rail Eastern Region called for a national debate on rural services and the 'yawning gulf' between costs and actual revenue. The Eastern Region had thirty-four loss makers of which twelve were in the eastern counties: Manning-tree to Harwich, those from Cambridge to Ely and Norwich; Ipswich, Peterborough and Doncaster; from Norwich to Peter-borough, Yarmouth, Lowestoft and Sheringham; from Ipswich to Felixstowe and Lowestoft and that from Peterborough to Spalding. The situation was exacerbated by the run-down state of the fleet of elderly diesel multiple-units then employed; despite cuts in their numbers, maintenance had cost £11¼m in 1979 and £14m in 1980, was estimated at £17m for the current year and was likely to be £20m in 1982. There were currently 180 speed restrictions because of the deterioration of track, many essential renewals having already been deferred for up to eighteen months. The £13m spent in 1980 had done no more than preserve the status quo, and withdrawal of services on grounds of safety was becoming a real possibility. In that the Region had, through rationalisation and innovations such as the 'basic railway' concept and 'Pay trains', done everything possible to effect economy, government help was an urgent necessity. The only bright spots were the extension of com-muters and some upward trend in general passenger traffic brought about by vigorous publicity.

The reference to commuters was in fact recognition of the clue to the profound changes that for perhaps a decade had been building up in the eastern counties but which, then, were only just becoming fully apparent, prior to a striking acceler-ation. Between 1981 and 1987 the counties of Norfolk, Suffolk and Cambridgeshire (their individual populations in these years increasing 4.9, 5.5 and 8.6 per cent respectively) together constituted the fastest growing region in the Kingdom, with another 12 per cent overall growth anticipated by 2001. The birth rate, at 12.1 per 1000, was, however, the lowest in Britain, emphasising that this was increased by migration. With it came prosperity, in regional terms East Anglia being the third high-est in the proportion of households where the principal earner was of professional rank. More significant still, against a national average of 320 per 1000 of the population, the East

Anglian figure of cars owned was 370; 19 per cent of households had a second car. In terms of the local economy the region's contribution (£12.2 billion) to the Gross National Product had risen, increased from 3.1 per cent in 1978 to 3.5 by 1987. On the ground these trends manifested themselves in extensive house building and rising prices, a proliferation of industrial estates and modern shopping complexes, together with intensive road development. It has also meant a new pattern of settlement, the commuters (whether for London or a local centre) buying houses in a huge range of villages and small towns, prepared to drive often quite substantial distances to a station. The desire for a country based life could thus still be satisfied, for despite the fundamental changes the East Anglia region, with only 160 inhabitants to the square kilometre, is still the most sparsely populated in England.

Many factors combined to bring about the changes. Expansion of London's finance industry and the ideal situation of Liverpool Street in relation to its heart, the City, was a major cause. High house prices in London and preservation of the Green Belt inhibiting suburban growth was important, as the high cost of season tickets could be set against the even higher costs of mortgages in the capital. Within the region, microchip technology underlay many of the new industrial activities, being of particular consequence in the Cambridge area and Hertfordshire. North Sea oil and gas have brought many workers into the region and an important new element into the economies of Yarmouth and Lowestoft. The proximity of the area to the other Common Market countries has brought some in and certainly enhanced the importance of Harwich; Felixstowe has come from obscurity to major national ranking as a port (for container traffic it is the foremost), and in Essex, the development of Stansted as London's third airport is another magnet to settlement. At several places, notably Peterborough in recent years, deliberate planning in the New Town context has resulted in successful and considerable growth. Road improvement has both followed and stimulated change. Chelmsford, Colchester and Ipswich have each acquired splendid new by-passes to end notorious bottlenecks, and most significantly there is the opening of the M11 to Cambridge and its link with the A604. When the initial relatively low house prices of the region are taken into account (although they have now risen substantially) it is easy to see how the situation first developed. From the railway viewpoint there is great potential in off-peak and general traffic, but that generated by the commuters must be the most significant. As the eastern counties revolution got under way the railways, diminished as they were, provided a crucial sustaining force. Then came the new opportunities which allowed them to assume a positive and expanding role, which nothing but national economic collapse or excessive pricing should hinder. The positive response has centred around electrification.

In the years after 1923, electrification within the old GER territory was first mooted in 1935, the government seeking to alleviate depression and unemployment by guaranteeing loans to stimulate such works. The LNER put forward the Shenfield line, but war intervened and it was 1949 and in different circumstances before this became reality. In December 1956 the system was extended to Southend and to Chelmsford. Meanwhile, in 1955 BR's Modernisation Plan, backed by government funds and intended to cover a fifteen year span, had envisaged three major projects, namely Euston to Birmingham, Liverpool and Manchester; King's Cross to Leeds and possibly York; and Chelmsford to Ipswich, Felixstowe, Clacton and Harwich. In 1957, however, the two latter were deferred until after 1964, although now consideration was being given to the lines beyond Ipswich, and the desirability of including the Bishop's Stortford to Cambridge line was stressed. In the event the general economic situation determined that only the West Coast scheme, now extended from Weaver Junction to Glasgow, was implemented. Although this was disappointing, the Colchester/Clacton/Walton project had already been sanctioned and was duly completed in 1959. As indicated in the area chapter, this was a pilot scheme for the 25kVac system (in place of 1500DC used so far); proving successful, this was adopted in the early 1960s as the BR standard for all regions, other than the Southern. However, so as not to cause undue disruption to the Chelmsford and Southend lines these were converted to 6.25kV as an intermediate stage in November 1960 and March 1961 respectively, this coinciding with the suburban electrification from Liverpool Street to Enfield, Chingford and Bishop's Stortford completed in November 1960.

Here matters rested. In June 1962 the Chelmsford to Colchester gap was filled (at the same time as the London Tilbury & Southend); in May 1969 the Lea Valley (Clapton Junction to Cheshunt) was converted and in October (with government assistance) the Braintree branch; all these were logical completions rather than new schemes, primarily to be justified by the reduced operating costs that would result. Indeed, when in 1964/5 the projected extension beyond Colchester was reconsidered, it was again deferred because of the poor returns anticipated and the high capital costs, these including much premature track renewal. Revived interest in the early 1970s for extension to Ipswich with push and pull units working from there to Norwich came to nothing because of the high cost of trailers. Then in 1973 came the first oil crisis and permanently increased fuel costs, leading, eventually to a new set of perspectives. Thus, in 1978 the two schemes, Anglia East (Colchester to Harwich and Norwich) and Anglia West (Bishop's Stortford and Royston to Cambridge) were approved at an estimated £71m. It was anticipated that costs could be kept down because the Advanced Passenger Train would be available to release locomotives from the Euston line. The APT was of course a failure, and this coupled with recession, delayed final approval until September 1982. Anglia East was approved in entirety but the government insisted on the dropping of the Royston section from the West scheme on the grounds of non-viability. BR wanted to pursue the West scheme first because of the threat to its markets from the M11, and the advanced state of resignalling and track improvement at Cambridge, but the government insisted on Anglia East. Only 70 per cent of the estimated traffic would make it viable, there was a good off-peak potential, and much of the resignalling work was either done or due. The Wickford–Southminster line was added; apart from its own potential its conversion (with that of the Romford–Upminster line) would allow withdrawal of dmu facilities from Stratford, a significant saving in itself. As described elsewhere this was completed in 1987. Meanwhile, in January 1984 approval had been given for the reinstatement of the Royston branch although the electric multiple-unit maintenance depot at Cambridge (so far a stumbling block in terms of cost) was deleted, the superior availability of the new 315 fleet having produced spare capacity at Ilford. Before the completion of Anglia West in 1987 the line to Stansted airport had been added.

Electrification was all important, but it had to be backed up by a great deal more. This has happened. Train services have been given distinctive names and liveries, stations have been smartened, even to the extent of the return of hanging flower baskets and certainly a great deal more access to travel information. The cascade system has at last brought much better rolling stock into the eastern counties and generally there is an improved cleanliness. Very important has been the provision of extensive, tarmac car parks at numerous stations such as Audley End, Manningtree and even North Fambridge and Woodham Ferrers on the Southminster branch. The public may be confused by the multiplicity of authorities and titles (Network Southeast, InterCity Eastern Region, Great Northern and Anglia Region), but it certainly enjoys the undoubted benefits that have been produced. Many thoughtful packages have been drawn up to attract custom; one such, very much for the first class passenger, and entitled the 'Electric Executive' appeared in May 1987. A return fare from Norwich to London at £47.20 included an airline style ticket, seat reservations, 24 hours free parking, a £2 Travellers Fare voucher, two Central Zone Underground tickets and a 15 per cent discount on car hire; breakfast could be had for an additional £8. Competition must be considered real. London traffic conditions deter the majority but there was, for example as started in 1987, a daily coach from Norwich to Oxford Street and Victoria, offering refreshments and air-conditioning, for only £6 return.

Smart timings, frequent services at regular intervals and careful integration of stopping services and expresses along the main lines, to give maximum benefits, have brought most East Anglians within two hours of London; but, this is once a station has been reached. The closures of the 1960s left many wide gaps. Haverhill, 12 miles from Cambridge on the former Long Melford line, lost its own station in 1967; in 1961 its population was 5,445 but by 1971 12,421; in 1981 it was 17,146 and would have benefitted greatly today from a rail-link with Cambridge, as indeed would British Rail. A welcome sign of the times is the

activity of local councils and pressure groups to get lines reinstated, stations reopened (successfully at Melton, not so at, for
example, Bramford and Haughley) or stations provided for the
first time. Springfield, on the outskirts of Chelmsford, is an
instance of the latter, the Essex County Council pressing for
some years, but the cost has been variously estimated at
£500,000 to £1m and timetables on an already heavily used line
would inevitably be disrupted and no decision has been
reached.

One major improvement has been the introduction of a
comprehensive service between the eastern counties and the
provinces. On a typical weekday at the close of 1989 there were,
operated by Sprinter Units, to Birmingham six trains from
Cambridge, six from Norwich, two from Ipswich, and one each
from Sheringham, Lowestoft and Harwich. The other main
axis is to Liverpool via Manchester. Norwich has five services
to these (one substituting Blackpool for Liverpool), Cambridge
three to Manchester (continuing, one each, to Barrow, Blackpool and Liverpool), Ipswich two (one to Barrow), Harwich
three (one terminating at Manchester) and Colchester and
Yarmouth one each. No other development illustrates the new
spirit of the railway and the modern status of the eastern
counties better than this.

Freight traffic has undergone equally fundamental changes.
The great loss was that of coal, movement becoming concentrated on a dozen or so centres, although of these Dereham,
Melton, Leiston and Norwich (Victoria) have now closed. The
cement works at Barrington and Claydon are the only recipi-
ents of direct delivery. Agricultural produce has been diverted
to the roads other than for grain handled at ten central depots;
the fertiliser depots as at Braintree, Whittlesea, Great Chesterford and, formerly, Dereham are the main rail contacts with
this industry; service to the beet refineries has shrunk to the
delivery of limestone from Derbyshire to just two of them,
Cantley and South Lynn. On the other hand Freightliner traffic, concentrated on Felixstowe and Parkeston, is a substantial
new source of revenue with room for more expansion. Oil
depots at Cambridge, Stansted and Norwich look to the railways, and from North Walsham to Parkeston is the movement
of gas condensate piped to the former along the old Mundesley

branch from Bacton. Amidst a variety of company trains, road materials are brought into the region and sand taken out. Speedlink serves a wide range of customers, some with their own private sidings; just one example is that of T. P. Dibdin of Welwyn Garden City which in 1983 was granted from government funds £822,000 towards a warehouse and distribution centre in the former goods yard, to be served by Speedlink. All this is encouraging, but perspective has to be kept. In 1987 East Anglia contributed only 2.3m tonnes of the 143.7m put on the railways of the Kingdom, and in the region itself that year 76m tonnes were despatched by road.

Mention should be made of three railway preservation schemes which constitute major tourist attractions. The North Norfolk Railway, formed in 1970, has the former GER/BR station at Sheringham as its base. In 1976 it reopened the former M&GN line as far as Weybourne, extending to Kelling Camp Halt in August 1983 and Holt in 1987, the line's centenary year. In Essex the Colne Valley Railway was constituted in 1973; its base is Castle Hedingham where the town's station was dismantled and re-erected on its present site by the society; there is one mile of track but plans exist for extensions. Biggest of all is the Nene Valley Railway with its headquarters at Wansford station near Peterborough and extending six miles to Orton Mere. Help was received from the Peterborough Development Corporation and the first trains ran in the spring of 1977. The line is unusual in having clearances sufficient to operate mainland European locomotives, giving the line an international flavour with ten countries represented amongst the locomotives and rolling stock.

A newcomer of somewhat different character is the Bure Valley Railway, a £2½m 15in gauge line opened on 10 July 1990 between Wroxham and Aylsham along nine miles of the former BR trackbed. Eight daily services are being offered to late October, powered by the company's own diesel and two locomotives leased from the Romney, Hythe & Dymchurch Light Railway.

Bibliography and Acknowledgments

Space precludes anything like a complete bibliography, but the following shows the particularly valuable sources used in the compilation of this work.

PRIMARY SOURCES

Company materials have included public and working time-tables, leaflets, reports, contracts, surveyors' and general maps, rule books and much else concerning various lines to be found in museums, libraries, County Record Offices and private collections. Many prospectuses have been read, these often throwing considerable light on the general economic background to a line. A number of pamphlets are still extant to shed light on major issues although care must always be taken to correct bias —of several extensively used *A Word or Two about 'EU'* (anon, 1860) was of perhaps the most value. Railway guides consulted include those to the Ely and Peterborough line (undated but probably 1848), the ECR (1851) and the GER (1864). Enormously detailed coverage of company affairs in general and meetings in particular was given in *Herapath's Railway Journal* (1835–1903) and the *Railway Times* (1837–1914) amongst others, and also in local newspapers of which the most valuable used has been the *Lynn News & Advertiser*. C. Mackie's *Norfolk Annals* provided many extremely useful nineteenth-century extracts from the *Norfolk Chronicle*. *Bradshaw's Railway Manual*, from 1850 on, was a major source of reference, giving year by year concise summaries of each company's affairs. Company Acts studied have included the GER's of 1862 as well as many smaller ones, and *Hansard* has yielded a number of details. Various Parliamentary Reports and Returns have been used of which that on *Schemes for Extending Railway Communication in the Counties of Norfolk and*

Suffolk (Board of Trade, 1845), that of the Select Committee of the Lords on the *London & York Subscription Contracts* (1845) and the *Admiralty Preliminary Inquiry into the Norfolk Estuary Bill* (1849) are just three of direct application. Similar documents and reports of the Poor Law authorities have provided social background. The *Census* tables and reports have been of fundamental importance. For local information the directories and guides of White (particularly for *Norfolk* 1845, 1854, and 1864, *Suffolk* 1855, *Essex* 1862), Murray (*Eastern Counties* 1892) and Kelly (for example, *Hertfordshire* 1926) are the principal examples of a wide category of material extensively used, and supplemented by books such as *English Agriculture in 1850–51* by J. Caird (1852), *The Port of King's Lynn* by W. Armes (1852) and *Rural England* by H. R. Haggard (1902).

SECONDARY SOURCES

Company histories consulted have been *The Great Eastern Railway* (4th edition, 1967) and *The London & North Eastern Railway* (1966), both by C. J. Allen and published by Ian Allan Ltd, as was also *The Great Northern Railway* (1958) by O. S. Nock. *The History of the Great Northern Railway* by C. H. Grinling was also a valuable source—written in 1898 this was republished by Allen & Unwin in 1966 with additional chapters by H. V. Borley and C. Hamilton Ellis to bring the story to 1923. Valuable chapters on both the GNR and GER are found in *Our Home Railways* (1910) by W. J. Gordon, and many references in *A History of the English Railway* (two volumes, 1851) by J. Francis, *Our Iron Roads* (1888 edition) by F. S. Williams and *The Railways of England* (1889) by Sir W. Acworth. There is a very helpful section devoted specifically to Suffolk in *The Railways of Britain* (1961) by Professor J. Simmons, and, in dealing with both the GER and GNR, *A Regional History of the Railways of Great Britain: Volume 3, Greater London* (1963) by H. P. White complements this present work. Histories of individual lines or companies to which reference has been made are *The First Railway in Norfolk* (second edition, 1947) by G. Dow, *The Eastern Union Railway, 1846–1862* (1946) by H. F. Hilton, *The Story of the Colne Valley* (1951) by R. A. Whitehead and F. D. Simpson, *The Southwold Railway* (1950, but in 1965 republished in a revised edition by Ian Allan Ltd) by

A. R. Taylor and E. S. Tonks, *Memories of the Southwold Railway* (1964) by A. Barrett Jenkins, *The Mistley, Thorpe & Walton Railway* (1846) by T. B. Peacock, and the Oakwood Press publications, *The Mid-Suffolk Light Railway* (1963) by N. A. Comfort and *Railways to Cambridge* by Canon R. B. Fellows. Certain books used have sections on particular lines, notably *Light Railways: Their Rise and Decline* (1964) by W. J. K. Davies and H. A. Vallance's *Branch Lines* (1965). H. G. Lewin's *Early British Railways, 1801–1844* (1925) and *The Railway Mania & Its Aftermath, 1845–1852* (1936) have as ever proved indispensable. *Red for Danger* (1955) by L. T. C. Rolt is invaluable for accident material and H. Grieve's *The Great Tide* (1959) is extremely helpful on the effects of the 1953 floods on railways in the eastern counties. N. Crump's *By Rail to Victory* (1948) has been a major source for the World War II period. *Titled Trains of Great Britain* (third edition, 1953) by C. J. Allen has given many valuable leads. Volumes of the *Universal Directory of Railway Officials and Railway Year Book* have been consulted for their statistical information, and of course, the two *Beeching Reports* now major landmarks in railway history, have been studied. *The Heads of Information* (BR) have been very useful in connection with proposed closures.

One cannot be other than deeply indebted to *Trains Illustrated*, its successor *Modern Railways*, the *Railway World* and the *Railway Magazine*, so thorough are their historical articles and coverage of current events. Of especial value in the latter periodical have been the several articles of B. D. J. Walsh and, one particular source, *The Railways of Peterborough* by C. R. Clinker and R. A. Dane in the April 1959 issue. Invaluable reference on closure dates is Volume II (1900–64) of C. R. Clinker's *Register of Closed Passenger Stations and Goods Depots in England, Scotland and Wales*, published privately.

For regional material a wide variety of works has been used, supplemented by extensive personal travel through the region. Of fundamental value have been the *Victoria County Histories*, particularly for *Essex* and *Cambridgeshire*, the *Land Utilisation Surveys*, of *Norfolk* by J. E. Mosby in 1938 and of *Essex* by N. V. Scarfe in 1942, the *Suffolk Planning Survey of 1946*, the British Association for the Advancement of Science's publications, the *Cambridge Region* (1938, edited by H. C. Darby and 1965, edited by J. A. Steers) and *Norwich and Its Region* (1961), *Great Britain: Geographical Essays* (1962) edited by J. Mitchell, *Field Studies in the British Isles* (1964) edited by J. A. Steers, *The Major Seaports of the United Kingdom* (1963) by J. Bird, and *Industry in the Country Towns of Norfolk and Suffolk* (1951) by T. Eastwood. Older works consulted include *The History of Cambridgeshire* (1897) by E. Conybeare and H. R. Barker's *West Suffolk Illustrated* (1907) and *East Suffolk Illustrated* (1908-9). Amongst purely historical books to which reference was made were L. M. Springall's *Labouring Life in Norfolk Villages, 1834-1914* (1934) and two very useful publications by the Essex Record Office, *English History from Essex Sources, 1750-1900* (1952) edited by A. F. J. Brown, and *Victorian Essex*. Individual town studies are numerous. Amongst those read have been *The History of Brightlingsea* by E. P. Dickin, *Old and New Halstead* by W. J. Evans, *The Story of Southwold* by M. J. Beecher and *Ipswich Through the Ages* by L. J. Redstone; outstandingly comprehensive works used were *A History of the Borough of King's Lynn* (1907) by R. J. Hillen and *History of Wisbech and Neighbourhood, 1848-1898* (1898) by F. J. Gardiner. Many guides have proved rewarding sources, particularly *The Port of King's Lynn* (anon, and undated but for the late 1950s) and that to *Felixstowe Docks* for 1967. Of all such works consulted the most generally fruitful have been the *Little Guides* (Methuen) in their revised forms, *Norfolk* (9th edition, 1949) by E. T. Long, *Suffolk* (6th edition, 1957) by P. G. M. Dickinson, *Essex* (7th edition, 1952) by C. H. Warren and, above all, *Hertfordshire* (5th edition, 1957) by W. B. Johnson. Finally, a number of useful leads and details have derived from periodicals such as the *East Anglian Magazine*, *Essex Countryside* and *Essex Review*.

My indebtedness to individuals is great, and pleasure in acknowledging this is marred only by the necessity of having to include so many in a very sincere but general 'thank you'. But individual mention must be made of Mr J. Hibbs, formerly of Eastern Region Headquarters, British Rail, who has made so many valuable suggestions and provided me with so much information, and of Mr C. V. Barret, Movements Assistant at the Norwich Division's Headquarters, who was more than generous both with his time and with information based on a working lifetime's experience of railways. Mr C. Hankins, the Manager of the Norwich Division, not only allowed me access to material but accorded me a long and valuable interview for which I am extremely grateful. My warm thanks are also extended to Mr M. B. Thomas, the Eastern Region's Public Relations & Publicity Officer, the Assistant PRO, Mr Munn and all their staff, to Mr P. R. Gillett, the PRO of the Liverpool Street Division, the staff of the Photographic Department at Liverpool Street, Mr Cox of Great Northern House and to all the other railwaymen I have met who were so generous in their help and interest. Outside the railway service I would like to mention Mr J. Hunter, Curator of the Saffron Walden Museum, for his very helpful interest, Mr A. Germany, the librarian, and his staff at the Alfreton Public Library, Derbyshire, who went to endless trouble to obtain many of the works listed above, and three students at the Saffron Walden College of Education, Miss M. Johnson, Miss C. Pike and Miss M. Jack, whose own researches in aspects of regional history provided me with a number of interesting details and worthwhile leads as well as much interesting discussion. I must also thank many individuals who have so generously offered help with the photographs; acknowledgment of those used appears at the front.

In the closing stages I became indebted to Mr B. D. J. Walsh, who not only went through the manuscript with infinite care but also freely placed his encyclopaedic knowledge of the region's railways at my disposal, thus providing many illuminating details. I am also sincerely grateful to Mr A. Patmore of the Department of Geography at Liverpool University for his many helpful criticisms in editing the work, and to Mr Victor Welch for drawing the large folding map inside the back cover. Last but certainly not least I am indebted to my wife Barbara for her constant encouragement, critical suggestions and help, particularly in drawing the maps, and to my mother who has done the typing, assisted in checking the manuscript and who generally made many helpful comments.

In the preparation of the second edition I gladly acknowledge my renewed indebtedness to British Rail (Eastern Region) and to various correspondents who kindly took the trouble to draw my attention to a number of ambiguities and minor errors of detail in the original edition. Lack of space precludes names and I trust that all will again accept my sincere thanks.

Additional Bibliography

Since this book was first written many works have been published on the Region's railways, of which just a few are given here.

Ian C. Allen	East Anglian Album	Oxford Publishing Company	1976
G. Body	PSL Field Guide: Railways of the Eastern Region	Guild Publishing	1986
I. Cowley	Anglia East: The Transformation of a Railway	David & Charles	1987
G. Freeman Allan	The Eastern Since 1948	Ian Allan	1979
C. Hawkins & G. Reeve	Great Eastern Railway Engine Sheds (2 vols)	Wild Swan	1986/87
R. S. Joby	Forgotten Railways: East Anglia	David & Charles (2nd edition)	1985
R. S. Joby	Regional Railway Handbooks: East Anglia	David & Charles	1987
H. Moffat	East Anglia's First Railways	Lavenham Press	1987
J. Rhodes	The Midland & Great Northern Joint	Ian Allan	1980
P. Swingler	Railway History in Pictures: East Anglia	David & Charles	1982
A. J. Wrottesley	The Midland & Great Northern Joint Railway	David & Charles (2nd edition)	1981

Regional Trends published by Her Majesty's Stationery Office remains as ever an essential source and starting point for general economic background.

Index

Heavy type denotes principal treatment of a subject. Abbreviations used are brn = branch, elec = electrification, xtn = extension, jnc = junction, rly = railway, tfc = traffic

Abbey & West Dereham, 213
Abbot's Ripton, 134, 137
Aberdeen; Rly Race to, 133
Accidents: Abbot's Ripton, 134; Arlesey, 134; Brentwood, 30; Hatfield, 133; Hilgay, 210; Hunstanton brn, 219; Littlebury, 114; on Norwich & Brandon, 172; Romford, 30; (near) Royston, 151; Soham, 148–9; Thorpe, 178–9; Tottenham, 30; Welwyn, 134; Welwyn North Tunnel, 133; Witham, 48.
Acle, 178, 179
Acrow (Engineers), company's halt, 123
Addenbrooke's Hospital (Cambridge), 142
Admiral de Ruyter; The, 80
Advanced Passenger Train, 245
Agriculture, **13–4, 19–23,** 37, 39, **46–47,** 82, **100–1,** 153, 156, **158, 222, 231.** *See also* individual lines and Traffic, Leading.
Aldeburgh, 25, **96–7;** brn 52, 91, 92, **96–7**
Aldeby, 183
Alexandra Dock, Lynn, 208
Alresford, 68, 69
Ambergate, Nottingham, Boston & Eastern Junction Railway, 211
Amsinck, Major, 112
Anglia East (Elec project), 162, 165, 245; Anglia West, 165, 245, 246
Antingham Road Junction, 205
Antwerp, Services to, 75, 76
Antwerp Continental; The, 79
Ardleigh, 74
Arlesey (& Henlow), 134, 137
Ashwellthorpe, 175
Askern, 225

Attimore Hall, 127
Attleborough, 70, 173, 177
Audley End (Wenden), 114, 116, 119, 120, 121, 161, 162; Mansion 114; Tunnel, 114
Automatic Warning System, 134
Aylsham, 109, 194, 196, 197, 201

Bacton, 248
Baldock, 152
Ballard, Stephen, 132
Baltic timber, 228, 232
Bank Holidays, 23, 179
BAOR, 80
Barford Power Station, 137
Barham, 101
Barkway, 105
Barnes (architect), 70
Barnham, 170
Barnwell Jnc, 149
Baron's Lane Halt, 55
Barrington, 152, 247
Barrow, 168, 247
Bartlow, 73, 121, 160
'Basic' rlys, 92, 145, 173, 220, 242
Basildon, 16
Bawsey, 208, 214
Bawtry, 112
Baxter, Robert, 112
Bealings, 92
Beccles, 25, 85, **87–8,** 91, 92, 93, 103, 175; GER omnibuses to, 190; Swing Bridge, 86, 186; to Yarmouth, 91, 183, 241
Bedford, 132, 133, 139, 152, 188, 206; to Cambridge, 135, 150, 151; to Hitchin, 132, 135; St Johns, 153
Bedford & Cambridge Rly, 151

Bedford & London & Birmingham Rly, 154
Beeching Report, 34, 50, 51, 56, 153, 174, 241
Benjamin Britten, The, 80
Bentinck Dock, Lynn, 208
Bentley, 74
Benwick, 223
Berney Arms, 177
Bidder, G. P., 110, 188
Biggleswade, 137
Bignold, Samuel, 99
Birdbrook, 162, 166
Birmingham; Services to, 11, 66, 77, 79, 155, 168, 173, 184, 185, 186, 187, 188, 190, 199, 223, 231, 244, 246, 247
Birmingham & Derby Junction Rly, 110-1
Bishopsgate, 46, 148
Bishop's Stortford, 28, 50, 105, 109, 110, 114, 115, 117, **118-9**, 120, 122; Elec to, 141, 244, 245
Bishop's Stortford, Dunmow & Braintree Rly, 120
Black Bank, 223
Blackbridge Sidings, 136
Blackpool, 168, 247
Blackwater, River, 49, 50
Blakeney, 200, 216
Bletchley, 153, 154
Blisworth, 206, 222, 234
Bluntisham, 156
Blythe, River, 87; Swing Bridge, 98
Bocking, 50; see also Braintree
Boreham House, 44
Bosanquet, Henry (ECR chairman), 39, 185
Boston, 111, 112, 131, 227
Boston, Stamford & Birmingham Rly, 232
Bourne, 214, 227, 228, 229
Bradfield, 81
Bradshaw, 43
Bradwell, 56, 57
Braintree (& Bocking), **50**, 66, 120; Witham brn, 46, **50-1**, 162, 245, 247; Bishop's Stortford line, 50
Braithwaite, John, 37, 39, 40, 145
Bramford, 84, 100, 247
Brampton, 93
Brandon, 28, 110, 114, 139, 171, 172, **173**, 174, 177, 206
Brantham, 70, 74
Brassey, Thomas, 131
Braughing, 131
Braybrooke, Lord, 114
Breckland, 20, 173, 215
Brentwood, 30, 41, 44
Brewster, Mr, 162
Bremerhaven, 76
Breydon, Jnc, 178; Breydon Water Bridge, 187

Brightlingsea, **68**
Britannia, The, 80, 168
British Rail (Railways), 16, 26, 34, 46, 52, 66, 92, 135, 137, 220, 233, 242, 244, 246
British Sugar Corporation, 213, 237
Broad Gauge, 40, 42, 109, 110; Hertford brn, 131
Broad Street, 129, 135
Broads, 19, 177, 179, 184, 194, 196, 201
Broadsman, The, 100, 192, 196
Broxbourne (& Hoddesdon), 109, 114, 118, **119**, 120; Hertford brn, 109, 123, 124, 127, 130
Bruce, Henry, 113
Bruff, Peter, 62, 70, 98, 229
Brundall, 178; Gardens Halt, 179
Brunel I. K., 112
BRUTE, 240
Buckenham, 178
Bungay, 102, 103, 104
Buntingford, 130
Bure, River, 177; Bure Valley Railway, 248
Bures, 160
Burnham Market, 221
Burnham-on-Crouch, 56
Burnt Fen, 173; see also Shippea Hill
Burnt House, 223
Burnt Mill, 119
Burston, 101
Burwell, 149
Bury St. Edmunds, 25, 158, 161, 167, **170**; lines and services to, 28, 42, 55 (omnibuses), 66, 91, 98, 139, 145, 147, 148, 159, 160, **167-71**, 213, 240
Bury St Edmunds & Thetford Rly, **169**
Buxton Lamas, 196

Cadwell, 135
Caird, James, 46
Caister, 201, 205; Camp Halt, 201
Calais, 75
Caleys, 191
California Halt, 201
Cam, River, 105, 140, 153
Cambridge, 23, 24, 34, **139-45**, 148, 152, 158, 161; lines & services to, 28, 60, 66, 105, 106, 108, 110, 112, 114-5, 116-18, 119, 135, 138, 150, 151, 152, 155, 160, 162, 165, 168, 172, 173, 179, 186, 188, 210, 211, 219, 220, 223, 224, 226, 240, 241, 242, 243, 244, 245, 247; Buffet Car Expresses, 152
Cambridge & Lincoln Railway, 112
Cambridge & York Rly, 111
Cambridge Transverse Rly, 139
Camping Coaches, 203
Campsea Ashe, 95
Cantley, 23, 179
Cardiff, 231

Carlton Colville 181; *see also* Oulton Broad
Castle Hedingham, 248
Catfield, 200
Cathedrals Route, 116
Cattawade Bridge, 70, 74
Cawston, 196, 197
Central Norfolk Enterprises, 201–2
Chappel, 159, 160, 162; Viaduct, 159
Chaste Petition, 113
Chelmer Navigation, 47, 51
Chelmsford, 24, 30, 44, 45, 46, **47–8**, 59, 188, 243, 244, 245, 247
Cheshunt, 245
Chesterfield, 187, 199
Chesterton Jnc, 153, 155
Chingford, 244
Chippenham Curve, 167
Clacton-on-Sea (& Holland-on-Sea), 26, 59, 60, **61**, 62; elec to, 34, 46; lines & services to, **63–8**, 94, 148, 155, 160, 166, 168, 223, 244; Supper Train, 64
Clacton Belle, The, 64
Clacton-on-Sea Rly, 63
Clapton Jnc, 245
Clare, 21, 159, 160, 162
Claydon, 100, 247
Clenchwharton, 199
Coastal Shipping, 14, 19, 25, 37, 39, 51, 59, 62, 84, 96, 176, 180, 183, 185, 191, 206, 217
Cobbold, J. C., 69, 73, 83, 87, 98, 229
Colchester, 19, 24, 27, 48, **58–61**, 62, 67, 68, 73, 158, 160, 243; elec to, 45–6, 66–7, 244–5; lines to, 58–61, 67–8, 82, 139; main line, 28, **37–48**, 69–70, 73–4; North Station, 19, 60–1; Norwich route, 37, 86, 99, 192, 201; services to, 42–6, 63, 66, 69, 82, 158, 247
Colchester, Stour Valley, Sudbury & Halstead Rly, 59, **159–61**, 162
Coldham Common, 142
Coldham (Wisbech brn) 224
Cold Norton, 55, 56
Cole Green, 127
Colmans, Norwich, 190
Colne, 166
Colne, River, 59, 60, 62, 69
Colne Valley Rly, 16, 60, 159, 160, **161–7**, 248
Coltishall, 197
Committee X, 112
Commuters, 26, 47–8, 51, 56, 60, 61, 62, 63, 66, 67, 74, 101, 118, 119, 123, 135, 136, 153, 162, 180, 241, 242, 243; *see also* individual lines and stations
Conington South, 134
Continental Express, The, 79
Cooper (GER Inspector), 178, 179
Cooper, Sir Richard, 62
Cornwall Mineral Railway, 216

Corpusty, 199
Corton, 183
Cottenham, 153
County School, 109, 191, 196, 197
Cowbit, 227
Cowbridge, 123, 127
Cranbourne, Lord, 32
Cratfield, 102
Cressing, 50
Cromer, 26, 109, 191, 194, 195, 197, 198, 201, **202**; services & lines to, 109, 195–6, 199, 200, 201, 203, 231; Stations and juncs, **203–5**
Cromer Express, The, 48, 73, 195
Cromford (Derbyshire), 105
Cross Keys Swing Bridge, 232
Croucher, Mr, 113
Crown Point (Norwich), 184
Cubitt, Lewis, 58; William, 111, 131
Cuckoo Jnc, 234
Cuffley, 129
Cundy, Nicholas, 105

Dalhousie's Board (Five Kings), 112
Darsham, 93
Day Continental, The, 79
Debenham, 102
Denison, E., 111, 113, 127
Denver, 210, 213; Road Gate, 210
Derby, 29, 111, 186, 187, 196, 198
Dimes & Boyman (Solicitors), 39
Direct Northern, The, 112, 113
Direct Norwich & Dereham, 216
Diss, 28, 100
Ditchingham, 103
Dogsthorpe, 227, 232
Doncaster, 26, 115, 117, 118, 134, 155, 188, 215, 225, 226, 227, 242; services from Liverpool Street, 116, 223
Dover, 75, 76
Doves Hole, 157
Dovercourt, 34, 80
Downham Market, 210, 213
Downham & Stoke Ferry Rly, 213
Dullingham, 147, 168
Dunkirk, 76
Dunmow, Great, 25, 105, 120
Dunstable brn, 136, 149
Dunston, 99

Earith Bridge, 156
Earl's Colne, 148, 166
Earsham, 103
East Anglian, The, 99–100, 193
East Anglian Rly (1840–41), 109
East Anglian Railways (1847), 137, 146, 206–209, 213, 218 (omnibuses), 229; & ECR, 146, 154, 180, **206–8**, 210, 226; & GNR, 154–5, 207, 210, 228; to East Dereham, **214**, 216; to Ely, 210; to Hun-

tingdon, 137, 154, 227; to Wisbech, 210, 211, 228; *see also* Lynn & Ely Rly, Lynn & Dereham Rly and Ely & Huntingdon Rly

East Dereham, 14, 25, 28, 124, 169, 173, 197, 210, 217; line to Lynn, 11, 167, 211, 213, **214–16**, 229; to Wells and Wymondham, 196, 197, 215, 216–7, 247

East Essex Enterprise, The, 59

East Essex Rly, 63

East Norfolk Rly, 194–5, 203

East Rudham, 218

East Suffolk Rly, 86–7, 95, 97, 179, 186, 241

East Suffolk Travellers Association, 92

East Winch, 13

Easterling, The, 92

Eastern Belle, The, 69, 96

Eastern Counties Rly, 106, 113, 121, 123, 137, 168, 176, 185, 206, 224, 227, 229; character & operation, 20–1, **27–32**, 102–3, 114, 115, 151, 167, 171–2, 184; Brandon & Peterborough Xtn, 28, 110, 114–5, 171, 234, 236; Cambridge line, 27–88, 106, 114–5, 139, 142, 145, 153, 156; Colchester line & brns, **37–41, 42–4**, 47, 50, 59, 61, 69, 75, 82–3; northern xtn, 29, 106, 111, 113–4, 139, 206, 222, 225, 227; & CVR, 159; and EAR, 146, 154, 180, **206–8**, 210, 228; and ESR, 86, 87; & EUR, 19, 30, 42, 59, 69, 70, 73, 75, 83, 86, **98–9**, 162, 188, 189; and GNR, 29, 30, 112–4, 117, 124, 127, 130, 149–50, 155, 207, 223, 224, 228, 236; and MR, 29, 117; and Newmarket, **145–7**, 167; and Norfolk, 42, 73, 86, 145, 146, 171, 172, 178, 180, 184, 188, 216; and N & E, 28, 40, 42, 105, 106, 109, 110, 114–5; and Waveney Valley Railway, 102–3; shipping, 75

Easton Lodge, 120

Eastern & Midlands Rly, 109, 186, 191, 195, 196, 197, 198, 200, 203, 208, 230

Eastern Union Rly, 119, 37, 42, 102; to Colchester, 58, **69–70, 73**, 74–5, 82–3, 86, 114; leases & xtns, 59, 159, 167; Norwich xtn, 42, 70, **98–9**, 175, 188; Woodbridge xtn, 86, 87; omnibuses, 99; shipping, 75, 99; and ECR, 19, 30, 42, 58–9, 69, 70, 73, 75, 83, 86, 98–9, 162, 188, 189

Eastern Union & Hadleigh Junction Rly, **74**

Eccles Road, 173

Edinburgh, 80, 167

Egg & Poultry Demonstration Train, 21

Electric Executive, The, 246

Electrification, **192–3**, 241, **244–46**; to Braintree, 51; to Broxbourne, 130; to Cambridge, 118, 141; to Chelmsford, 45, 47–8; to Clacton and Walton, 34, 46, **66–7**; to Colchester, 45–6, 66, 73; to Ely and King's Lynn, 157; to Harwich, 80; Hertford Loop, 129; to Ipswich, 85; King's Cross suburban, 34, 135; Liverpool Street suburban, 34, 45, 70, 116–7, 118; to Norwich, 100; to Peterborough, 134–35, 239; to Royston, 152; to Southminster, **56–7**

Ellingham, 103

Elmswell, 168

Elsenham, 70, 121

Elsenham & Thaxted Light Railway, **120–21**

Ely, 25, 28, 91, 116, 141, 145, 148, 149, 153, 154, 155–6, **156–7**, 167, 171, 172, 201, 208, 210, 214, 220, 222, 223, 224, 234, 244; West Curve, 156

Ely & Bedford Rly, 154, 206, 210

Ely & Bury St Edmunds Rly, 167

Ely, Haddenham & Sutton Rly, 155

Ely & Huntingdon Rly, 123, 137, 138, 154

Ely & Newmarket Rly, 148

Ely & St. Ives Rly, 155

Enfield, 244; brn, 129

Epping, 120

Esbjerg, 78

Esbjerg Continental, The, 79 (*see also* Scandinavian, The)

Essex Coast Express, The, 45, 66

Euston Square Confederacy, 132

Everard, William, 25

Eye, 37, 82; brn, **101**

Eye Green (M & GN), 227, 232

Fakenham, 200, 216, 217, 218

Fane, Cecil, 147

Farmers' Lines, 73

Farquhar, Mr (Solicitor), 112

Fawley, 135

Felixstowe, 26, 77, 78, 83, 93, 168, 242, 243, 244, 247; brn, 52, **93–95**; lines & services to, 84, 91, 94; Docks, 94, **95**

Felixstowe Railway & Pier Company, 93–94

Felstead, 120

Fen Drayton, 154

Fenman, The, 116, 168

Fens Line, 111

Finningham, 99

Finsbury Park, 129

Fisons, 84

Fitzwilliam, Earl, 112

Fleet Jnc, 181, 183

Fletton, 239

Flushing, 78; Flushing Continental, The, 79

Ford Gate, 166 (See Earl's Colne)

Fordham, 149

Forncett, 175

Foulsham, 197
Foxton, 152
Framlingham, 86, **95**; brn. **95**
Fred Olsen Line, 78
Freightliner, 77, 85, 95
Frinton, 62, 64
Fulbourn, 147

Gainsborough, 225, 227
Galton, Capt, 87
Garret, Mr, 96; Engineers, 96
Gayton Road, 216
Gaywood Junction, 208, 216
Gedney, 231
Geldeston, 103
General Steam Navigation Co, 78
Gibbs, Joseph, 105, 109, 111
Gibson (Banker), 121
Gimbert, Driver, 142
Gipping, River, 82, 84, 100
Gladstone, W. H., 40; 'Gladstone's Act',
  154
Glasgow, 77, 79, 167, 244
Glemsford, 161
Godmanchester, 137, 153, 155
Gooch, Sir Daniel, 165
Gorleston, 92, 183
Gothenburg, 78
Grantham, 199, 211
Great Bentley, 64, 67
Great Central Railway, 32
Great Chesterford, 88, 119, 145, 146, 147,
  247
Great Eastern Railway, **32-3**, 48, 63, 74,
  83, 88, 98, 112, 115, 119, 138, 142, 145,
  148, 152, 162, 165, 175, 176, 184, 187,
  188, 189, 190, 205, 213, 228, 232; Act
  (1862) & Formation, 32, 87, 107, 165,
  204, 207, 213, 216, 229; xtns & leases,
  32, 49, 55, 60, 62, 63, 68, 93, 94, 101,
  103, 120, 121, 130, 148, 149, 153, 159,
  160, 162, 168, 169, 170, 194, 198, 216,
  219, 224; hotels, 32, 34, 78, 94, 219;
  operation & services, 32, 42, **44-5**, 47,
  52, 56, 63, 64, 65, 80, 81, 92, 93, 94, 95,
  96, 99, 101, 115, 117, 118, 120, 128, 131,
  153, 157, 160, 166, 178-9, 184, 185, 186,
  188, 189, 195, 197, 200, 219, 221, 228,
  231, 232, 236, 238, 239; omnibuses, 32,
  47, 55, 60, 83, 97, 170, 183, 190; Shipping Services, 25-6, 32, **75-7**, 80, 81,
  94; 'New Essex' Lines, 16, 56-7; northern xtn (see also GN & GE), 26, 115, 117,
  223, 224, **225-7**; and CVR, 162, 165;
  and ESR, 52, 87, 88; and GCR, 32; and
  GNR, 26, 32, 115, 116, 151, 152, 181,
  208, 224-5, 225-7; and M & GNR, 32,
  181, 186, 197, 199, 200, 202, 203, 204,
  208; and N & S Jnt. Committee, 32, 181,
  202, 204; and agriculture, 21, 22, 46,
  153, 224, 225, 226, 229, 231; at Cambridge, 139, 142, 143, 151
Great Eastern Train ferries Ltd, 76
Great Exhibition, 132
Great Northern Rly (1836), 40, 105-6,
  109-11
Great Northern Railway, 36; Act & Formation, **110-14**; main line, 115, 116,
  118, 123-4, 129, **131-4**, 145, 150 (omnibuses), 224, 233, 236-7, 239; xnts, leases
  & operation, 123-4, 127, 131-4, 150,
  225-7, 226, 228, 229, 232, 237; to Cambridge, 139, 141, 145, **150-2**; and EAR,
  154-5, 207, 210, 228; and ECR, 20, 30,
  112-4, 117, 124, 127, 130, 149-50, 155,
  207, 223, 224, 228, 236; and GER, 26,
  32, 115, 116, 151, 152, 181, 208, 224-5,
  225-7; and MR, 131, 198, 208, 229, 236;
  and M & GNR, 198, 199, 201, 222. See
  also GN & GE Jnt. Rly
Great Northern & Great Eastern Jnt. Rly,
  26, 32, 115, 117, 138, 153, 155, 209, 224,
  225-7
Great Waldingfield, 158
Great Waltham, 47
Great Western Railway, 40, 44, 152
Grimston Road, 213-4
Grissell & Peto, 114, 171, 176-7
Guestwick, 200
Gunton, 195

Haddenham, 156
Haddiscoe, 181, 182
Hadham, 131
Hadleigh, 25, 74; brn, 60, **74**
Halesworth, 23, 85, **88**, 91, 92, 93, 97, 98,
  101, 102
Halesworth, Beccles & Haddiscoe Rly,
  85-6
Halifax Junction, 83; troughs, 77, 195
Halstead, 160, 161, 166, 167
Hamburg, 76, 78
Handley, James, 105
Hardwicke, Earl of, 105
Harleston, 102, 103
Harling Road, 173
Harlow, 16, 109, 118, **119**; Mill, 119
Harston, 153
Harwich, 25-6, 34, 37, 49, 58, **75-81**, 93,
  139, 148, 162, 168, 243; brn, 60, **80-1**,
  84, 244; services to, **79-80**, 84, 95, 148,
  168, 223, 242, 247; shipping, **75-9**;
  Train Ferry, 65, 76-7
Hotel, at Harwich, 34
Hatfield, 129, 133, 135, **136**
Hatfield Hyde, 127
Hatfield Peverel, **48**, 162
Haughley, 86, 98, 101, 102, 192, 247
Haverhill, 55, 66, 121, 159, 160, **161**, 162,
  165, 166, 167, 246

Heacham, 219, 221
Hedingham, 162
Helpston, 236
Hemsby, 200, 201
Herringfleet, 181
Hertford, 75, 109, 115, 120, **121, 123–4, 127, 129**, 130, 136; Loop, **129–30**
Hertford, Luton & Dunstable Rly, 124
Hertford & Welwyn Jnc Rly, 123, 127
Hertingfordbury, 127
Hethersett, 162
Heybridge, 51–2
High Peak Railway, 105
High Speed Trains, 60, 133, 135
Hilgay, 201
Histon, 153
Hitchin, 130, 132, **135**, 142, 151
Hoddesdon, 119
Holiday Camps Express, The, 201, 205
Holbeach, 229, 231
Holkham, 216, 221
Holme, 134, 137, 224, 225
Holme Hale (Norfolk), 174
Holt, 197, 198, 201, 248
Holwell Pit, 127
Holywell-cum-Needingworth, 155
Hook Continental, The, 79
Hook of Holland, 76, 78, 80
Hopton, 183
Hornor, Mr, 162
Horn's Mill Viaduct, 129
Hornsey, 135
Hotels, 19, 32, 58, 62, 78, 93, 97, 124, 219
Hudson, George, 28, 111, 112, 113, 139, 146, 150, 154, 210, 234
Hudson (of Castleacre), 20
Hull, 139
Hunstanton, 26, 224; brn, 208, **218–21**; services to, 115, 116, 154, 156, 172, 211, 218, **219–20**
Hunstanton & West Norfolk Rly, 219, 221
Huntingdon, 130, 134, 135, **137–8**, 154, 155, 166, 226, 227, 247

Ilford, 88, 245
Industries, 13, 16, 19, 23, 24, 60, 243; Fishing, 19, 37; see also individual towns and railways
Ingatestone, 44, **48**
Inworth, 49
Ipswich, 14, 25, 27, 32, 57, 59, 62, 79, 94, 95, 148, 158, 160, 227, 229, 240, 241, 242, 243, 244, 245; population & growth, 13, 24, **82–85**; to Bury St. Edmunds & Cambridge, 42, 83, 145, 147, 159, 223; to Colchester and London, 42, 45, **69–70, 73–4**, 83; to Felixstowe, 93–5; to Lowestoft and Yarmouth, **85–88, 91–2**, 182; to Norwich, 27, 28, 31, 57, 98–100, 175, 188; ship- ping and docks, 82, 84, 85; stations at, 83
Ipswich & Bury St. Edmunds Rly, 42, 83, 98, 159, 167, 188
Ipswich, Norwich & Yarmouth Rly, 87
Isleham, 88
Islington, 106

Jackson, Mr., 101, 159
James, William, 105
Jockey Club, 146

Keeble, A. J., 213
Kelling Camp Halt, 248
Kelvedon, 41, 47, 48, 49; brn, **49–50**
Kelvedon, Tiptree & Tollesbury Pier Light Rly, 16, **49–50**, 233
Kennett, 168
Kentford, 167
Kenton, 101, 102
Kerrison, Sir Edward, 40
Kessingland, 98
Kettering, 138, 154, 155
Kettering, Thrapstone & Huntingdon Rly, 138
Kingscliffe, 240
King's Cross, 58, 112, 116, 129, 130, 132, 133, 141, 150, 152, 195, 197, 201, 203, 219, 231, 238
King's Lynn, 14, 16, 25, 139, 180, 198, 199, **206–9**, 211, 215, 218, 222, 224, 228, 229, 230, 231, 232; lines to, 11, 12, 28, 105, 116, 117, 124, 139, 148, 154, 156, 167, 169, 172, **214–16**; rivalry with Ipswich, 25, 83, 167; rivalry with Norwich, 25, 214; services to, 116, 124, 154, 172, 210, 211, 212, 213, 215, 217, 219, 220, 221, 223, 224, 231
King's Norton, 187
Kirby Cross, 62, 64
Kirkley, 181
Knebworth, 131, 136
Kristiansand, 78

Labouchere, Mr, 40–1
Lake Lothing, 185
Lakenham, 98; Viaduct, 188
Lancashire, Derbyshire & East Coast Rly, 117
Langford & Ulting, 55
Langley Junction, 129
Lark, River, 148, 167
Lavenham, 25, 74, 159, **168–9**
Laxfield, 55, 101, 102
Le Strange, Mr, 216
Lea Valley, 105, 106, 118, 123, 245; Lea Valley Enterprise, The, 118; River, 105, 106, 118, 123
Leeds, 47, 186, 231, 246
Leeds & Selby Rly, 105, 113

Leicester, 66, 67, 168, 186, 187, 196, 199, 220, 237, 240, 247
Leicester, Earl of, 216, 221
Leiston, 86, 96, 97
Lenwade, 200
Letchworth Garden City, 152
Lincoln, 28, 105, 110, 112, 116, 117, 139, 155, 225, 227, 236, 240
Little Bytham, 197, 230, 231
Littlebury, 114; tunnel, 114, 118
Littleport, 210
Liverpool, 39, 77, 79, 80, 168, 173, 184, 185, 231, 244, 245, 247; & Manchester Rly, 176; 'Leviathans', 39
Liverpool Street, 45, 46, 64, 66, 91, 96, 115, 116, 118, 127, 131, 141, 162, 165, 175, 195, 201, 203, 211, 215, 216, 219, 223, 220, 240, 245, 246
Locke, Joseph, 70, 98, 111, 149
Loddon, 191
London, 20, 21, 23, 30, 40, 47, 59, 62, 102, 109, 110, 114, 115, 117, 118, 139, 141, 158, 170, 183, 241, 243, 246; connections, Norwich, 14, 21, 27, 31, 70, 91, 99–100, 114–7, 145, 171–3, 178, 191–193; connections, regional, 20, 21, 26, 28, 46, 60, 66, 67, 73, 75, 77, 80, 91, 92, 93, 94, 105, 110, 115, 117, 133, 139, 141, 156, 158, 167, 172, 185, 195, 196, 198, 201, 210, 216, 217, 219, 220, 227, 228; Docks, 50, 115, 117; Viaduct, 40. *See also* commuters
London & Birmingham Rly, 28, 110, 111, 206, 234
London & Ipswich Rly, 82
London, Midland & Scottish Rly, 155, 198
London & North Eastern Rly, 33, 34, 44, 45, 55, 60, 76, 78, 79, 96, 98, 99, 102, 121–2, 127, 148, 149, 156, 166, 172, 186, 190, 193, 195–6, 194, 198, 199, 203, 213, 225, 227, 239, 240, 244
London & North Western Rly, 20, 118, 124, 132, 139, 151, 162, 187, 222, 234, 236, 237, 239
London, Tilbury & Southend Rly, 51, 86, 245
London & York Rly, 29, 11–114, 226; *see also* Great Northern Rly
Long Melford, 55, 159, 160, 161, 168
Long Stanton, 225
Long Sutton, 231
Longville Junction, 237, 240
Lord's Bridge, 151
Loreley, The, 80, 168
Lowestoft, 19, 24, 25, 75, 86, 87, 97, 173, 176, 181, 182, 183, **184–5**, 208; as a port, **180–81**, 183, 241, 243, 247; lines to, 84, 85–91, 183; services to, 91, 92, 93, 94, 178, 179, 181, 183, **184**, 199, 215; Railway & Harbour Company, **179–80**

Lowestoft & Beccles Railway, 86, 87, 181
Lucas Brothers, 194
Luton, Dunstable & Welwyn Junction Rly, 123–4
Lynn & Dereham Rly, 11, 124, 154, 206, 210, 211, 212, 214–5, 217, 218, 241
Lynn & Ely Railway, 124, 154, 167, 206, 209, 211, 212, 213, 214, 228
Lynn & Fakenham Rly, 191, 197, 200, 208, 218
Lynn & Sutton Bridge Rly, 198, 208, 209, 213, 219, 229
Lynn & Hunstanton Rly, 208, 218, 219, 241

Maas, River, 76
MacCalmont, Col, 147
Mackenzie & Brassey, 98
Magdalen Road, 210; Gate, 211
Maiden Lane 132, 236
Maldon, 46, 47, **50–2**, 55, **55–6**
Maldon, Witham & Braintree Rly, **50–1**
Manchester, 66, 77, 79, 80, 132, 168, 186, 199, 211, 231, 244, 245, 247
Manchester, Sheffield & Lincolnshire Rly, 132, 226
Manea, 223
Manningtree, 59, 73, 74, 75, 80, 242, 246; North Curve, 84
March, 26, 111, 113, 115, 117, 153, 155, 160, 207, 209, 210, 211, 213, 220, 222, 223, 224, 226, 227, 228, 229
Mardock, 131
Marham, 215
Market Harborough, 139
Mark's Tey, 19, 44, 47, **48**, 59, 159, 160–1, 165, 167, 168, 241
Marriotts, Messrs, 11, 12
Marsh Junction, 181
Martham, 201
Massingham, 218
Mellis, 99
Mellis & Eye Rly, 101
Melton, 92, 246, 247
Melton Constable, 26, 191, 199, 200, 201, 205, 214
Melton Mowbray, 234
Mendlesham, 102
Methwold Fen, 213
Mickley, Mr, 130
Mid-Eastern & Great Northern Junction Rly, 213
Middle Drove, 211
Middleton, 218
Middleton Towers, 215
Midland & Eastern Rly, **32, 173**, 197, 198, 208, 213, 229, 230
Midland & Great Northern Joint Rly, 183, 186, 187, 191, **197–202**, 205, 208, 217–8, 220, 221, 223, 227, 228, 230, 232;

character & tfc, 213–14, 231; closure, **26**, 173, 179, 192, 197

Midland Counties Rly, 110

Midland Rly, 29, 111, 112, 115, 117, 132, 138, 139, 145, 152, 155, 197, 198, 199, 200, 208, 222, 229, 230, 234, 236, 238, 239

Mid-Suffolk Light Rly, 55, **101–2**

Mildenhall, 88, **149**

Mile End, 41

Minram, River, 131

Mistley, 74, 80–1

Mistley, Thorpe & Walton Rly, 62

Moorgate, 129

Mountnessing, 41

Mowatt, Mr, 111

Mundesley, 127, 195, 201, 202, 203, 204, 205, 247

Munro (Contractor), 62, 63, 69

Murrow, East 231; spur, 227, 232; West 227

Nar, River, 11

Narborough (& Pentney), 11–13, 20, 214

National Freight Train Plan, 59

National Steam Car Company, 47, 166

Needham Market, 100

Needingworth Junction, 155, 227

Nene, River, 229, 234, 236, 239; Valley Rly Coy, 248

New Cut, 176

New England, 236, 238, 239

'New Essex' lines, 16, 51, 55–7

New Waterway, 76

Newcastle, 186, 244, 246

Newmarket, 28, 70, 109, 115, 127, 146, **147**, 148, 156, 167, 168, 226, 244; brn, 142

Newmarket & Chesterford Rly, 127, 141, **145–47**

Newmarket Rly, 88, 127, 141, 145–47, 150, 167

Newport, 70, 109, 110, 114, 119, 139, 165, 171

Newstead Lane Junction, 204, 207

Newton, 158

Newtown, 201

Nightall, Fireman, 148–9

Norfolk Coast Express, The, 195

Norfolk & Eastern Coal Company, 180

Norfolk Estuary Cut, 208

Norfolk, Suffolk & Essex Railroad, 82

Norfolkman, The, 193, 196

Norfolk Railway, 75, 86, 98, 145, 169, 177, 181, 216, 229; and ECR, 42, 73, 86, 146, 171–72, 189, 216; Lowestoft line, 180, 181; and Newmarket Rly, 146; *see also* Norwich & Brandon Rly and Yarmouth & Norwich Rly.

Norfolk & Suffolk Joint Committee, 32, 127, 181, 183, 187, 202, 204

North of Europe Steamship Company, 75, 180

North Country Continental, The, 79, 148, 168, 223, 239, 240

North Eastern Railway, 116

North Elmham, 217

North Fambridge, 246

North London Rly, 135

North Midland Rly, 111

North Norfolk Rly, 248

North Sea Gas & Oil, 243

North Walsham, 73, 186, 194, 195, 196, 200, 201, **202–3**, **205**, 247

North Walsham & Dilham Canal, 194

Northampton, 139, 206, 234, 240

Northern & Eastern Rly, 28, 40, 42, 105–6, **109–11**, **114**, 139, 141

Northern Railroad Company, 105

Norwich, 12, 13, 14, 21, 23, 24, 27, 32, 40, 69, 100, 110, 171, 176, 178, 179, 180, 185, **188–93**, 193, 194, 197, 216, 226, 229, 241, 242, 245, 246, 247; lines to, 11, 27, 28, 37, 39, 40, 42, 44, 70, 84, 98, 99, 105, 106, 109, 110, 139, 149, 156, 158, 171, 176–7, 178, 188, 196, 201, 207, 209, 229; rivalry with King's Lynn, 25, 214; services & traffic, 31, 45, 91, 99–100, 114–5, 116–7, 171–3, 177, 178, 179, 186, 187, 189, 191–3, 195, 196, 199, 200, 203, 215, 217; stations, (City), 190, 197, 199, 200: (Thorpe), 99, 106, 171, 178, 189, 192, 197: (Victoria), 98, 99, 188–9, 192

Norwich & Brandon Rly, 28, 69, 110, 171, 188, 189

Norwich & Lowestoft Navigation, 180

Norwich & Spalding Rly, 198, 213, 229

Nottingham, 198, 199, 211, 214

Oakington, 153

Octuple Agreement, 132

Offord (& Buckden), 134, 137

Ongar, 46

Ormesby, 200

Orwell, River, 34, 82, 83, 95; Haven, 34

Oulton Broad, 181, 183; Swing Bridge, 181

Oslo, 78

Ouse, River, 134, 154, 169, 199, 206, 209; Bridge, 210

Outwell, 142, 233

Overstrand, 202

Oxford & Cambridge Rly, 139 (1836), 149 (1846)

Parham, 95

Parker, Inspector, 178

Parkes, C. H., 77, 95

Parkeston Quay, 34, 76, **77–9**, 80, 247

Peel, Captain, 151

Perlback, H. J. & Sons, 78

Peterborough, 24, 25, 229, **234–40**; main line, 30, 110, 111, 112, 131–8; rlys and trf at, 28, 110, 111, 112, 135, 154, 197, 234–40; services & lines to, 110, 111, 112, 117, 130, 131, 133, 134, 135, 136, 145, 154, 156, 160, 173, 175, 197, 200, 201, 206, 207, 209, 214, 215, 222, 223, 224, 230, 231, 232, 233, 234, 236, 240, 241, 242, 243, 248; stations, (East), 234, 236, 238, 239, 240: (North), 236, 238–9, 240; Development Corporation, 237, 239, 248
Peterborough, Wisbech & Sutton Bridge Rly, 198, 208, 209, 211, 223, 228–30
Peto, Sir Samuel Morton, 19, 58, 86, 171, 180, 181, 222
Petre, Lord, 40
Pitsea, 86
Ponsbourne Tunnel, 129
Port of Ipswich & Suffolk Rly, 82
Postland, 227
Potten, 151
Potter Heigham, 201
Potters Bar, 134
Princes & Princess of Wales, 219, 221
Priors (Coal Merchants), 180
Pulham Market, 103
Pullman Services, 64, 79, 148, 219

Queen Victoria & Prince Albert, 133

Radical Alterations Timetable, 44–5, 55, 64, 84
Radio Electronic Token Block, 93
Ramsey, 224–5; brn, 224–5
Ramsey & Somersham Rly, **224–25**
Rastrick, J. U., 109
Rayne, 120
Raynham Park, 199
Redenhall, 103
Reedham, 176, 178, 179–80, 181
Reepham, 196, 197
Rendell, Mr., 112
Rennie, Sir John, 195, 112; George, 105
Research Projects Ltd, 193
Retford, 111, 236
Rigby, Mr, 39
River Navigations, 11, **14**, 24, 25, 74, 87, 102, 105, 106, 139–40, 153, 156; see also individual rivers
Roads, 11, 12, **14, 16**, 39, 42, 243; coach routes (1834) 38; M11 Motorway, 118, 143, 245; see also individual lines
Robson, (GER clerk), 178, 179
Roll on/Roll off, 76, 77, 85, 120, 177
Romford, 30, 41, 245
Rossington, 112
Rotterdam, 75, 76, 171
Roudham Junction, 172, 174
Roughton Road Junction, 203, 204, 205; Halt, 205

Royal Agricultural Show, 47
Royal Danish Mail, 78
Royston, 28, 141, 146, 151, 152, 245
Royston & Hitchin Rly, 146, **149–51**
Rugby, 299, 110
Rugby & Huntingdon Rly, 137, 154
Runton, East & West Junctions, 204, 205
Ruskington, 227
Ryburgh Mill, 217

Saffron Walden, 25, 50, 73, 105, 120, **122**; Rly Coy & brn, **121**, 122, **123, 128**
Sancton Wood, 141
Sandringham, Arms Hotel, 219; House, 219
Sandy, 134, 151, 152, 239, 247
Sawston, 119
Sayer, Henry, 39
Saxby, 229, 230
Saxmundham, 88, 92, 93, 96
Scandinavian, The, 79
Scratby, 201
Scotsman, The, 134
Serpell Report, 241
Shaftholme Junction, 116
Sheffield, 94, 112, 186, 199, 231
Shelford, 60, 119, 121, 130, 150, 151, 160, 161
Shenfield, 44, 45, 46, 51, 244
Shepreth, 150, 151, 226
Sheringham, 26, 173, 191, 194, 195, 196, 201, 202, 204, 205, 242, 247, 248
Shippea Hill, 149, 173
Shirebrook, 187, 198
Shoreditch, 28, 37, 41, 42, 109, 146, 191
Shotley, 83
Sible & Castle Hedingham, 16
Sibleys, 121
Sidestrand, 203
Sinclair, Robert, 44
Silver Jubilee, The, 133
Simpson, (Contractor), 194; & Bennett, 211
Sise Lane Committee, 113
Six Mile Bottom, 88, 145, 147
Sizewell Power Station, 97
Smeeth Road, 211
Snailwell Junction, 148
Snape, 84; brn, 52, 86, 95–6
Snettisham, 218, 221
Soham, 88, 148
Somerleyton, 180
Somersham, 225
South Lynn, 23, 199, 208, 214, 218, 231
South Milford, 113
Southend, 45, 51, 52, 244
Southminster, 16, **56–7**, 165, 245
Southwold, 25, **97–8**, 184
South Woodham Ferrers: see Woodham Ferrers

Spalding, 112, 131, 142, 207, 209, 214, 215, 222, 225, 229, 231, 232, **233–4**, 242
Spalding & Bourn Rly, 198
Spalding & Holbeach Rly: see Norwich & Spalding
Speedlink, 59, 85, 95, 167, 184, 200, 219, 248
Spellbrook, 109, 118
Spital Bridge, 236
Spitalfields, 118
Sporle, 214
Springfield (Chelmsford), 247
Sprinter Units, 247
St. Albans; brn. 136
St. Ives, 137–8, **153**, 154, 155–6, 211, 222, 224, 227, 241
St. Margarets, 130
St. Mary's, 225
St. Neot's, 137
St. Nicholas (ship), 78
St. Olave's Swing Bridge, 182, 184, 187
St. Osyth (Norfolk), 201
St. Pancras, 115, 116, 120, 127, 133, 148, 219
Stalham, 200, 201
Stamford, 233, 234
Standon, 131
Stansted, 70, 119, Brn to airport **119–20**, 243, 246, 247
Stanton, 55, 170
Starston, 103
Stephenson, Robert, 42, 114, 145, 176, 177; & George, 171
Stevenage, 129, **135**
Stevenson, Mr. (MR), 101
Stoke (Suffolk), 55
Stoke Ferry, 210, 213
Stoke Hill Tunnel, 37, 83, 239
Stonea, 223
Stort, River, 106
Stour, River, 59, 70, 80, 158, 159, 160; Valley, 19, 45, 168
Stow Bardolph, 210
Stow Bedon, 174
Stow St. Mary Halt, 55
Stowmarket, 25, 82, **100**, 101, 159
Stratford, 40, 42, 44, 109, 165
Subsidies, 241, 242
Sudbury, 27, 59, 159, **160–1, 161**, 162, 166, 241
Sutton, 155, 156
Sutton Bridge, 208, 213, 229, 230, 232
Swaffham, 14, 25, 169, **174–5**, 211, 213
Swainsthorpe, 100
Swansea, 77
Swing Bridge Junction, 181
Swinton, 222
Syston, 233, 234

Takeley, 120

Telegraph, 171, 172
Tempsford, 137
Tendring Hundred Rly, **59–60, 62**, 63
Thames, River, 20, 37, 75
Thaxted, 73, **120–21**
Themelthorpe Curve, 190, 197, 200
Thetford, 28, 109, 145, 146, 167, 169, 170, **173**, 206, 213, 216; to Swaffham, 174–5; Bridge, 169, 170; and Watton, 169–70, 174
Thetford & Watton Rly, 169–70, 174; Thornton, Mr., 44, 116
Thorpe Junction, 189; village, 178
Thorpe-le-Soken, 61, 63, 64, 66, 67
Thorpeness Halt, 96
Three Counties, 137
Three Horse Shoes Jnc, and brn, 223–4
Thule Shipping Line, 78
Thurston, 168
Tiptree, 49, 50
'Titfield Thunderbolt', 233
Tivetshall, 99, 102, 103, 195
Tollesbury, 16, 49; Pier, 49
Tomline, Col, 93, 94
Tor Line, 78
Tottenham, 106, 115, 118, 120
Tottenham & Hampstead Joint Rly, 115
Towgood, Mr, 119
'Town's Line', 111, 112
Traffic, Leading, **247–8**; agricultural, **20–3**, 26, 34, **46–7**, 49, 50, 51, 59, 60, 70, 84, 88, 91, 96, 97, 101, 103, 117–8, 119, 145, 148, 153, 173, 174, 196, 197, 199, 214, 218, 224, 225, 227, 231–2 (M & GN), 233, 238; beet sugar, 21, 95, 101, 103, 145, 157, 168, 170, 197, 199, 214, 215, 227, 229, 237; milk, 88, 217; bricks, stones & minerals, 48, 57, 101, 119, 154, 157, 215, 223, 237, 238; coal, 26, 50, 84, 95, 103, **117–8**, 132-3, 137, 141, 152, 167, 180, 183, 188, 192, 217, 218, 225, 226, 228; fish, 16, 60, 68, 69, 96, 97, 181, 183, 185, 199; general, 50, 52, 59, 74, **77**, 85, **95**, 117–8, 136, 137, 157, 177, 184, 185, 187, 189–90, 198–9 (M & GN), 199, 200, 209, 211, 213, 223, 225, 227–8, 237–8; see also individual lines and towns Train Ferries, 76–7
Trimley, 94, 95
Trowse, 175, 188; Hythe, 176; jncs at 98, 99, 189, 190; station, 99, 110, 190, 192, 195; Swing Bridge 171, 188
Trumpington, 105
Tudwick Road Sidings, 50
Tufnell Park, 210
Tyssen Tyrell, Sir John, 44
Twenty, 231

United Shipping Company, 78
Upminster, 245

Victoria, Queen, 133
Vignoles, Charles, 37

Waddington (ECR Chairman), 29–30, 73,
    180, 229
Wakefield, 225
Wakefield, Lincoln & Boston Rly, 111–2
Walpole, 230
Walsall, 186
Walsingham, 216
Waltham Cross, 120
Walton-on-the-Naze, 26, 34, 46, 59, **63–8**,
    244
Wansford, 248
Warboys, 225
Ward, Mr, 106
Ware, 73, 130, 150
Ware, Hadham & Buntingford Rly, 130–1
Waring (Contractor), 213
Warren Hill, station & tunnel, 148
Walker, James, 105, 106, 111
Warwick, Earl & Countess, 120
Watlington, 210; *see also* Magdalen Road
Watton, 174, 175
Watton & Swaffham Rly, 169
Watton-at-Stone, 135–6; Waveney, River,
    102, 177
Waveney Valley Rly, **102–3**
Weaver Junction, 244
Weeley, 62
Welland Bank, 234
Wells-next-the Sea, 25, 124, 172, 175, 196,
    215, **216–7**, 219
Wells & Fakenham Rly, 216
Welwyn, 123, 134, 136; Garden City, 135,
    136, 248; Jnc, 124, 127, 136; tunnels,
    131, 133; Viaduct, 129, 131, 134, 145
Wenden, 114 (*see* Audley End)
Wensum, River, 189; Curve, 190, 195,
    201; Reach, 176
Werrington, 236
West Lynn, 208
West Norfolk Junction Rly, 219, 221
West Riding, 186, 199
Westerfield, 93, 94, 101
Westmill, 131
Weybourne, 201, 202, 248
Wherries, 177, 194
White Colne, 166
Whitemoor, 26, 118, 148, 187, 209, 211,
    215, **227**, 238, 239
Whitlingham, 178, 179, 194, 195, 197, 205,
    247
Whittlesea, 237, 247
Whittlesey Mere, 131
Whittlesford, 118, 119
Whitwell, 197
Wickford, 52, 165, 245; brn to Southmin-
    ster, **56–7**
Wickham Bishops, 51, 55

Wickham Market, **88**, 95
Widford, 131
Wilkins, A. C., 49; Jam Factory, 49
Williams, J., 296, 210, 214
Wilson, E., 194
Wirksworth, 23
Wisbech 28, 154, 155, 199, 206, 207, 209,
    210, 211, 214, 222, 223, 224, 227, 228–9,
    230, 231, **232–4**
Wisbech & Outwell Canal, 233
Wisbech, St. Ives & Cambridge Jnc Rly,
    224, 228
Wisbech & Upwell Rly, 21, 49, 142, **233**
Wissington, 213
Witham, 44, 46, 47, **48**, 49, **50–52**, 55, 162
Wivenhoe, 62, 64, **68–9**
Wivenhoe & Brightlingsea Rly, 62–3
Wixoe, 162
Wolferton, 219, 220
Woodbridge, 74, 86, 87, **88, 90**, 92
Wood Green, 127
Woodham Ferrers (South) 16, 51–2, **55–6**
Woolmer Green, 134
Woosung Rly, China, 97
Worcester, 139
World War I, 44, 55, 103, 170, 175, 186,
    210; World War II, 34, 49, 60, 94, 101,
    102, 103, 123, 149, 158, 160, 166, 170,
    173, 174, 197, 216, 223, 231
Wortwell, 103
Wrabness, 80
Writtle, 47
Wretham & Hockham, 174
Wroxham, 109, 191, 195, 196
Wymondham, 172, **173**, 175, 216, 229
Wylie, Mr, 29

Yare, River, 177, 188
Yarmouth, Great, 11, 23, 24, 25, 28, 39,
    40, 41, 176, 177, 180, 183, **185–8**, 194,
    198, 200, 206, 215, 224, 232, 241, 242,
    243, 247; as a port, 37, 39, 176; lines &
    services to, 37, 79, 84, **85–93**, 106, 109,
    115, 156, 171, 173, 176–79, 181, 183,
    188, 199, 200–1, 214, 217, 223, 231
Yarmouth & Haddiscoe Rly, 86, 87, 181
Yarmouth Haven & Pier Company, 194
Yarmouth & North Norfolk Rly, 197, 200
Yarmouth & Norwich Rly, 28, 69, 171,
    176–8; *see also* Norfolk Rly
Yarmouth & Stalham Light Rly, 200
Yarmouth Union Rly, 186, 197, 200
Yaxley, 137, 237; & Farcett, 137; Halt, 101
Yeldham, 162, 167
York, 79, 93, 105, 110, 111, 116, 129, 132,
    186, 215, 223, 244
York & North Midland Rly, 111, 113

Zeebrugge, 76, 77
Zeeland Shipping Company, 78